THE FACE OF POWER

THE FACE OF POWER

Matt Guest

Copyright © 2001 by Matt Guest.

Library of Congress Number: 2001119081
ISBN #:   Softcover   1-4010-2539-0

All rights reserved. No part of this book may be reproduced or transmitted in any form or by any means, electronic or mechanical, including photocopying, recording, or by any information storage and retrieval system, without prior permission in writing from the copyright owner, except for brief excerpts within reviews. Please email requests to: administrator@thefaceofpower.com. Questions regarding this work may be addressed to: questions@thefaceofpower.com. Please note: Questions may be answered anonymously via public postings on the Question and Answer page of this website. Additional copies of this book may be located by visiting the order page at: www.thefaceofpower.com.

This book was printed in the United States of America.

FIRST EDITION

Grateful acknowledgement is made to the following for permission to reprint:

From THE COMPLETE GOSPELS: ANNOTATED SCHOLARS VERSION / Robert J. Miller, editor. Copyright © 1992, 1994. Used by permission of Polebridge Press.

From THE OTHER GOSPELS: NON-CANONICAL TEXTS. Copyright © 1982 by Ron Cameron. Used by permission of Westminster John Knox Press.

From THE OTHER GOSPELS: NON-CANONICAL TEXTS. Copyright © 1982 by Ron Cameron. Used by permission of The Lutterworth Press.

From THE YELLOW EMPEROR'S CLASSIC OF INTERNAL MEDICINE. Copyright © 1947, 1975 by Ilza Veith. Used by permission of the University of California Press.

Bibliographical Note: From TAO TE CHING by Lao Tzu / James Legge, translator. Originally published by Oxford University Press, 1891.

The author wishes to express his thanks to Mantak and Maneewan Chia for their invaluable books on sexual energy.

All of these stories are true.
Some of the names and places in this book have been changed to protect the right to privacy of those involved.

DISCLAIMER: The purpose of this book is to educate and to enhance awareness. It is sold under the condition that all parties involved in the creation and production of this work shall have neither the liability nor the responsibility for any injury caused, or alleged to be caused, directly or indirectly by anything contained herein. The assimilation and application of the material offered in this book is done so at the reader's sole discretion and responsibility. Furthermore, this book's contents should not be construed as final medical advice, especially in extreme cases. Every physical body and dreaming body is unique, and has been formed by events specific to it. To obtain recommendations appropriate to your particular physical body or dreaming body, please consult with the appropriate professional. If you choose to use this information without the approval or guidance of a professional, you must, and will, assume the responsibility and the risk.

However, nothing and no one can substitute for the awareness provided by direct knowledge and the innate wisdom of each individual's physical and dreaming bodies. It is the intention of this work to ultimately bring you into contact with this awareness, so that your awareness will ultimately supersede any limitations imposed by your perception, and lead you to fulfillment—with or without the help of others.

*To all of my teachers, Susan,
and those family members and friends
who are still with me:
This dream is a mirror for those that seek the Truth.
Watch, listen, and* know.

PROLOGUE

I am lying in the tall grass that has overgrown the strawberry patch in my grandmother's backyard. Today, it is breezy, with a slight hint of summer in the billowy white clouds that float lazily in that ominous blue sky. The cottonwood trees shimmer and whisper in my buzzing ears. I am filled with a quiet and lusty sensuality, for I am awaiting my lover who will be arriving very soon. I am filled with anticipation and excitement. My heart is on fire. I am three years old…

CONTENTS

INTRODUCTION 15
THE CRYSTAL CLEAR REFLECTION 19
THE SPACE BETWEEN THOUGHTS 47
LELA'S SHADOW 81
SEX, POWER, AND AFFECTION 116
THE LONGING 151
THE PREDILECTION TO DREAM 167
THE MANY FACES OF POWER 204
NEW UNITS OF AWARENESS 243
EPILOGUE 263

INTRODUCTION

*Those who seek should not stop seeking
until they find.
When they find, they will be disturbed.
When they are disturbed, they will marvel,
and will reign over all.*

-The Gospel of Thomas, verse 2-

If you are reading this, then you and I have begun a journey—an extraordinary adventure together. I am a man of power. I am a navigator of the Unknown.

Ever since I can remember, something has moved deep within me. I have experienced an endless string of unusual events brought about by an unseen force. This force has constantly pushed me beyond my limits, compelling me to recreate myself without rest. It is the voice that speaks of the mystery of life. It has taken me almost half of my life to recognize and manifest this power.

Because of this, I have become unrecognizable to those who knew me well. I have become a man of power. A man of power is simply a man who relinquishes his own petty agenda for the agenda of the Unknown—the agenda of the Spirit. He allows the energy of creation to flow through him in an unadulterated and unfiltered manner. He becomes a mirror of Truth for all of those who cross his path.

This book is an expression of my absolute affection for the Spirit, and my unyielding desire to express Truth as an act of sheer power and joy. The power of Truth is consuming, like a shudder—a shiver from head to toe. It is a reminder of the inevitable end of my journey here on earth. It is a surge of energy that comes from without, and attempts to find expression in the words and deeds of this time and space. My entire energetic corporeality struggles without rest to bring forth this energy in its purest sense, without obstruction, without fail. There is no greater happiness or satisfaction. To be an instrument of the Spirit is my path with heart, and an expression of my infinite gratitude.

To resonate, to vibrate with the energy of the Spirit is the fiercest joy imaginable. It is the precursor to venturing into nameless realms. It is the unification, the making whole—the blending of the dreaming body and the physical body. It is the act of making this corporeality—this energy—vibrate at the same frequency as the energy that comes from the Unknown. It is divine ecstasy and perfection, and nothing in this world, or in any other, is as consuming or purifying. All of mankind struggles to imitate that vibration in this world. Some do it through music or art, others through writing or science, still others through sex or drugs. But all of these are trivial approximations to the affection and power felt by one who gets out of the way of the power and expression of the Spirit.

I have always brought change to the people placed along my path. These people have simultaneously experienced great comfort and tremendous agitation when faced with their own reflection in the mirror of the Spirit within me. They have been shown on an energetic and physical level the natural conclusion of the path that they have chosen. Most of them do not like what they see and so they retreat, because the reflection shows them that they are not living a path with heart. This has made some of these encounters very brief and very tragic. It is unbelievably difficult to watch a human being crumble under the force of the Unknown. But I am only a messenger. I am another link to a new consciousness. I have overcome my fear.

I have had many teachers. Their collective efforts have provided me with the clarity and syntactical tools necessary to understand myself. I have learned from them how to get out of my own way. I have become aware of the obstacles that keep me from freedom and fulfillment. I have experienced the descent of the Spirit, and I now see that this path was chosen for me. Now I must recognize, accept, and become what I am, or I will be destroyed by the very power within me.

There is a force in this universe that has been left untended and untouched for, literally, thousands of years. This force was once active on a worldwide scale, but has since been practically obliterated from our awareness. This force is the energy of intention and deliberate power—the ultimate of human potential. My intention is to provide the impetus for the continued advancement of this awareness by exploring the parameters of this dream for myself and for those who have a need. I have fortified my intention and connection to the source of direct knowledge, and abolished my self-imposed limitations. Now is the time to reveal myself.

I refer to this unseen power as *the energy of deliberate intention*. The energy of deliberate intention is what ties us to this world, to ancient worlds, and to those worlds yet to be seen. It is the birthright of *every* human being. The energy of deliberate intention is the tool that I use to describe the irreducible reality of traveling to other worlds in lucid dreaming, and to describe ultra-pragmatic ways of living in order to achieve a very real and living goal called absolute freedom. This absolute freedom has always been available to us. It was once pursued on a daily basis by many ancient cultures that have since vanished off the face of the earth. Attaining absolute freedom is accomplished by readjusting the expenditure of personal energy. Humanity, however, has failed to recognize or take full advantage of this ability. We have been reduced by the world at large to mere shadows of ourselves. Because of this, I present my story as a reminder to those who are not satisfied—to those who long for a beacon.

This book contains the highlights of my life up until recently. I have written about these events in order to demonstrate that the world of non-ordinary reality is not limited to faraway places or unconventional circumstances. Non-ordinary reality can, and does, take place in our modern world. It is not necessary to rely on drugs of any kind in order to create the experience. All of the altered states that I have experienced have come naturally through various circumstances and through the energy that I received at the moment of conception. These events serve as examples, as energetic points in time. Their intention is to promote understanding–the kind of awareness that sets us free.

Nothing in this book is a rule. Nothing in this book is an absolute. Nothing in this book is dogma or should ever be construed as such. Every path that has ever been created or delineated, whether it has been preserved by a culture as a religion, philosophy, art, science, mythology or tale, is simply a description of the world at large painted to its fullest energetic extent by the one traveling that path. Any limitations are self-imposed by the author. These once genuine paths that have led an individual, or group of individuals, to freedom are intended to serve as an inspiration to those that follow–they remind us of who we really are. This one is no exception. There are no accidents. There are no victims.

THE CRYSTAL CLEAR REFLECTION

*When you know yourselves, then you will be known,
and you will understand that you are children
of the living Father.
But if you do not know yourselves,
then you live in poverty,
and you are the poverty.*

-The Gospel of Thomas, verse 3-

Court and I were sitting in his living room one evening in southern California. The ocean air blended perfectly with the smoky luminescence of the twilight. He was busily puffing away on another clove cigarette and drinking coffee. This was his method of cleansing his lymphatic system of the lead and other toxic buildup from his earlier years.

"Native Americans knew the power of tobacco," he said. "Unfortunately, modern man has turned it into something bad, both with his intention and his mass production. Tobacco and coffee help to open the lymphatic system and flush toxins from the body."

I smiled and inhaled deeply. When he and I got together there was often a presence that filled the room. It did not happen on every occasion, but it was here tonight. It would create the thickest silence and the most tangible feeling, something that I could reach out and sink my hand into. We would just sit sometimes and not even speak. Everything was complete and full already.

We had been talking about my earliest memories, the times that demonstrated the presence of the Spirit in my life before I had any conscious knowledge of its power. These were moments when the Spirit unquestioningly and deliberately made its presence known and felt. They were intended to remind me that life was indeed a mystery.

I told Court that I had chosen parents that encouraged constant creativity, and fostered the development of intelligence and common sense. They were peaceful, introspective, religious, and madly in love. We lived a simple life in a small and quiet town in California. The strange things that happened to me as a child were never interfered with because I never felt that these things were really odd or out of the ordinary. We never talked about our dreams or dreaming adventures, not because they were too personal or taboo, but because we did not consider them to be relevant to our waking world. My parents seemed to be captivated by the energy that lived in me. They watched with wonder and amusement.

Religion played a significant role in my early years, and I somehow managed to escape the dogmatic and rigid aspects of it that plagued my sister and friends. Church was the one place where I could commune with the Spirit without feeling self-conscious about it. I liked the silence and mystery that surrounded the rituals. I liked the somber mood of the music. I was able to see, in my own way, that the intention of the rituals and the music was to transport me to the proper mood in order to receive the Spirit. In addition, the stories of the Old and New Testaments that I heard on a weekly basis made many of the unusual things that happened to me seem normal. But I also did not know that being the first-born male child had increased the frequency and intensity of my experiences.

"Why do you think that King Herod killed all of the first-born males in his kingdom when he was told of the coming of

Jesus?" Court asked me. "He and other ancient rulers knew that the first-born males were the ones chosen by the Spirit to be men of power. It was their birthright. They were the greatest inheritors of their parents' life force and the only ones with enough energy to be a threat to the ones currently in power. Doesn't Genesis say that the first-born male is dedicated to God? The Spirit pursued those ancient seers until they finally surrendered. Then they became expressions of the Spirit—vehicles of the Unknown. Our ancient ancestors had a much better grip on the workings of the Unknown than we do in our scientific age. They were much closer to the Truth."

He lit another cigarette. "What is your earliest memory of the presence of the Unknown?"

My first experience occurred at the age of two, I told him. My parents took me to a beach on the central California coast. I remember how few people were there—it just seemed like the three of us. We laid out our beach towels in a small cove where the beach ended and the high rocks met the water. It was breezy and sunny with just a few clouds hanging around, and the ocean with its deafening roar and blue-black immensity overwhelmed me. I had never seen an ocean before. My dad tried to take me for a swim, but I was too scared. I was standing by my mother who was sitting on her beach blanket. I was busy studying a clamshell and the gritty sand that had invaded my mouth.

"Come on," said my dad. "You can hang onto my neck and ride piggy-back, just like we do at home. I'll wade out a little bit, and your head will never go under the water."

After much hesitation, I gave in. He slowly waded into the water with me on his back, and I watched with mounting fear as the water rose around our bodies until it came up to the tops of our shoulders. All I could see was a never-ending sea—a glassy forever that reflected something other than the well-defined security that I cherished at home. I felt his feet leave the ocean floor and he started to swim. I wasn't sure if I liked the feeling of being weightless and at the mercy of this entity called the ocean.

Then, without warning, a wave came upon us. The water lapped into my mouth and nose and I started coughing. The towering waves and tremendous energy of the ocean created so much fear in me that I had trouble hanging on. I started to let go in order to wipe the stinging salt-water out of my eyes.

"Don't let go!" my father said, somewhat startled. He grabbed my arms and swung me around against his chest. He tried carrying me in his arms for a bit. I felt much more secure now and I remember that I liked the way the water smelled on his naked skin. He finally put me back on the beach. My mom started teasing me a little.

"Don't be afraid of the water. It won't hurt you." She was trying to get me to wade in the water. "Just let it come up and touch your toes."

I was standing back from where the waves were breaking, transfixed by the constant merging of the finite earth and the infinite water. I could barely hear her words. Something in me could sense that there was another world below the surface of the water and that it was complete and independent of our own. I knew that the depths and the darkness held many mysteries and memories, and I was afraid of free-falling into those depths and being swallowed by the darkness. I liked the light of this new life too much.

As I stood on the edge of the water and watched the way that it lapped at my little feet, I relished in the purity of the salty breeze as it licked at my bare skin. I took a very cautious step toward the water, then immediately ran backwards when it came after me. But then, something took hold of me and I found myself staring at the sky. It was something that I did constantly. It was always a possession, a not-doing, a way of being that consumed me completely. Oh, how I loved that feeling! As I marveled at the peaceful power of those great white clouds, the world gently changed and I felt the most glorious bathing of energy and peace. The earth was all around me and inside of me. I was becoming one with the air and the clouds, and I allowed myself to be carried up and away by them.

What suddenly snapped me back to the moment was the feeling of concern coming from my mother as she ran over to pick me up. A larger wave had come and knocked me down on my back, and had washed over my entire body. I hadn't even noticed that I was halfway submerged in the wet sand. The change in my perspective surprised me, but not enough to break my fixation on the clouds in the sky. Actually, the change afforded me a more comfortable view of them. It felt like a baptism, a communion, as if a benign force had laid me down and caressed me with watery hands. It wouldn't have surprised me if I had actually been breathing under the water.

"Why didn't you see the wave coming?" My mother's voice was full of worry as she asked me the same question over and over. She picked me up and held me in her arms while she brushed the wet sand off of me. I knew that she was always afraid that I would not be strong enough or smart enough. At that moment, she may have even thought that I was a little bit dumb or unaware. But it made no difference. The feeling I had was crystal clear.

Court turned on the small, dim lamp by the couch. Looking around the barely lit room, I marveled at his artwork that looked so mysterious in the shadows. He had been a skateboard artist and had created the logos and designs for a famous skateboard company in the early eighties. At that time, I had been a teenager consumed with skateboarding. I remembered his work very well, even though I had not met him yet. Now, his work was focused on the Unknown and its strangely impersonal power.

"What do you remember next?" he asked me.

"Ever since I was a small boy, I've had this recurring feeling of being split-off, or not present in my body," I said. "I've been asking people for years if they knew what was happening to me."

"When did you begin feeling this way?"

"At a very early age–maybe three or four."

I told Court that I had always felt threatened in crowded public places, especially at that age. I remembered that the noise created by large crowds of people used to overwhelm me. It was too much for me to process all at once, and I would always see a darkness approaching as the noise intensified. I began to recognize this darkness, and was terrified of it every time I saw it because I knew that I would soon be leaving my body. One Saturday, I went with my family to the mall. As I walked into the mall on this particular morning, I suddenly felt consumed by fear as the split-off feeling approached. Usually, I didn't get the feeling until I was surrounded by the high-pitched sound frequencies of all of the televisions in the electronics section of the mall. But today it occurred almost immediately.

The feeling always began in my bowels like the clammy heat of fear. The back of my neck and head would go cold and scalding hot, all at the same time, while the rest of my body would turn cold and slightly numb. Colors would change hues, darken, and then swirl. My vision and hearing would feel as though they had been compressed into a narrow and suffocating tunnel. My hands and feet would feel skinny and then thick. My arms and legs would start to tingle like they were asleep, and then "pop!"– the me that I normally knew would suddenly be just outside of, and above, the back of my head. It felt like somebody took "me" and put him into the control tower of a human body and said, "OK, here is the control for moving your body forward, here's the one for making the left arm move, and over here are the buttons for forming speech." All of the sudden, my bodily movements became slightly jerky and foreign to me, and I could hear myself talking but it didn't feel like me–it felt like I was hearing somebody else speaking, almost like I was dreaming. Sometimes, I would say things that were completely out of character for me, and I could see the look of surprise in my parents' faces. At other times, hunger, fatigue, or pain would push me into this state. I remember my mother wondering what was wrong with me on more than one occasion.

This condition would usually last until after we got home. Then, about an hour or two later, I would start to feel like I was sitting naked in front of a large group of people, even if I was by myself. It was a very vulnerable and sexual feeling, but not the feeling of horror that most people might associate with sitting naked in front of others. This was like an arousal, a bursting sensation filled with energy, and was focused just below my navel. I would feel a rush as something filled my entire body and the whole room would become very alive–it suddenly felt as though I was connected to everything around me. All of my physical senses became extremely heightened: every sound, smell, color, and mood was amplified and fat with meaning. I became very happy at this point and would secretly dread the next occurrence of losing touch with this rich physicality.

Court asked me if I knew at that time what was going on. I said no.

"Your fear of crowds and of uncontrollable situations was sufficient enough to push your dreaming body out of your physical body. It remained there until you were safe at home again."

"That split-off feeling was my dreaming body moving outside of, or above, my physical body?" I asked.

"Yes. The hot and cold feeling at the back of your neck and the narrowing of your vision are the first signs that your dreaming body is leaving your physical body."

"What is my dreaming body, exactly?" I asked him.

"Your dreaming body is a duplicate of your physical body, except that it is pure energy without physical matter. It is similar to the concept of a soul, though without all of the religious implications. Your dreaming body can be driven away from your physical body by fear. It is your perception that creates this fear. You see, there are two parts to the world that you and every other human being can perceive–the *known* and the *Unknown*. The known is made up of everything that your mind can comprehend and perceive and, therefore, be afraid of. The Unknown is what's left over."

"Can't I experience fear of the Unknown?" I asked him.

"No," he replied. "There is no fear of the Unknown, only the fear of losing the known, of losing your tentative grip on your flimsy perception."

I thought for a moment. "So, is the known everything that I *perceive* or is it everything that I *am*?"

"Is there a difference? Isn't what you perceive your reality?"

"Yes, but I'm trying to differentiate between perception, and facts that are independent of my perception. There are things that exist in this world that are not dependent on me or my perception."

"That's true. But for you, or for anyone else, your perception is what determines *how* you conceive the world at large. Your perception is what takes the boundless energy of the universe and converts it into understandable bits of reality. It determines what you *are*. As you believe, so shall you be. It can be changed, however, to more accurately perceive the boundless energy of the universe, or the facts that exist independently of your perception."

"How am I, as a human being, related to the Unknown?" I asked.

"Your dreaming body is literally a microcosm, or a small container, of a finite portion of the Unknown. The manner in which you relate to your own portion of the Unknown is determined by your thoughts, beliefs, and expectations. Your perception determines your reality."

"That means that we are all capable of unimaginable things," I mumbled.

"Of course it does," he replied forcefully. "You see what you choose to see. What you *believe* is your truth, but it is not *the Truth*. Your fears make you want to cling even more to your thoughts, beliefs, and expectations. Your fears keep you from knowing yourself and, therefore, from knowing others–your fears keep you from seeing what is in front of your face. The known is your own creation. You live and die with this creation, and your world and its subsequent events are simply a reflection of it."

"What is fear then?" I asked.

"Fear is an energetic indulgence, a feeling that you get when something doesn't fit into the little world that you have created for yourself. You have a finite amount of energy that you are born with. You choose on a constant basis how to invest that energy. You can either invest that energy in the known and the linear patterning of your thoughts–the things that limit you, or you can invest it in the Unknown with its parallel worlds and unexplored possibilities."

"Physical fears, like the fear of standing in the middle of a freeway, are helpful because they protect your body from damage and destruction," he continued. "Other fears, like the fear of not being liked or admired, are indulgences that you have learned to protect your ego or self-image, and are an absolute waste of your precious energy. A self-image is nothing more than a presentation of your *self* as something other than what it really is. That is why it has to be defended at any cost. People who indulge in this kind of fear are using fear like they use any other kind of sensational stimulant–to get a rush, and distract themselves from their own boredom and self-imposed restrictions. A life of fear is no life at all."

"I understand that I invest energy in the known and my self-image by feeding my thoughts, beliefs, expectations, and fears. But how do I invest energy in the Unknown?"

"By not investing in the known," he declared.

"That doesn't make a lot of sense," I stated flatly.

Court chuckled. "It's a not-doing. By *not* investing energy in the known, your energy is available for the Unknown to utilize. It's called the Unknown because you can't even begin to understand its workings. Unhinge your energy from the concerns of the known and the Unknown will determine how to use it. Remove the filter that obstructs your link to the Unknown and the energy will guide you. You can't think about these things. If you do, then you have applied the known to the Unknown, and that is ridiculous! You have to *feel* it. That's just the way that it works. If we knew how it worked it wouldn't be a mystery, and life would be boring and unoriginal."

"So how did I develop a fear of crowds?" I asked him.

"Probably from your parents," he replied. "Most of us are afraid of losing control of the known in one form or another, and being overwhelmed by a crowd is an uncontrollable situation."

"And how did my learned fear of crowds push my dreaming body out of my physical body?" I asked.

"Fright transfers the vast majority of your available energy into your dreaming body and this enables it to move outside of, and above, your physical body as a protective response to a perceived danger. That is why you feel a sinking feeling below your navel, or coldness in the lower half of your body, and a strong heat at the back of your head. You feel split-off, or not present in your body. This sudden transfer of energy disengages energy from the known and its encumbering and sluggish thought processes. Because your dreaming body is now outside of the limitations of your physical body, it is aware of the things that the eyes and senses of your physical body are not. This is called *seeing*. Some people refer to it as spider-sense–a tingling in the top of the head. In this state, you are capable of great feats of immediate and spontaneous action. Your dreaming body now directs your physical body. You are capable of knowing the next move of your adversary before he has a chance to act. It is an ancient survival mechanism. It enables you to act without thought. It keeps you alive."

My body shook involuntarily, and I felt a memory surfacing. Court watched me intently. Then he urged me to tell him what I had just remembered.

"One Saturday night, about eleven o'clock," I said, "I stopped at a drive-up bank teller to get some cash to buy food. I was in my late twenties at the time. I had punched in my identification number and was waiting for the cash to dispense when I saw someone walking towards my car. He was Caucasian, about forty-five years old. He was dressed in nice, casual attire and had emerged from a newer Cadillac with a map in his hand."

"Excuse me, sir, excuse me," he said as he walked towards my car, pointing at his map as if he needed directions. He did not appear to be threatening in the least bit. But suddenly, the top of my head started buzzing violently. This buzzing, or sharp tingling, radiated in a fraction of a second to cover my entire body and I felt something else quickly take over. I saw my left arm fly out of the driver's window and pound the 'Cancel' button on the teller machine very rapidly. I felt my ears and senses shut off to his pleas as I slammed my car into first gear and sped out of the parking lot without retrieving my card or even looking back at him. I vaguely remember him staring at me from about five feet away as I sped off.

I drove around the block for two minutes and then came back to the drive-up teller. Another car had just pulled up to the machine, and that driver was staring blankly at my card as it stuck out of the beeping machine. I got out of my car and walked right up to the machine. I retrieved my card, got back into my car, and drove off. The man and his Cadillac had vanished without a trace.

"I had never felt such a spider-sense before," I said to Court. "My body was in a complete state of alarm and readiness, and yet it flowed so beautifully at that speed. I knew, because of the urgency of my actions and the fact that I was viewing this event from somewhere outside of my body, that this man had intended to harm me."

"You knew what he intended because your dreaming body *saw* his intention and reacted perfectly. What else did you notice?" he asked.

I looked blankly back at Court.

"What did you notice as you drove past him?" he asked me again.

There was a feeling tucked away in a corner, and I focused on it until it surfaced. "I remember that I felt his body sigh as I drove past him," I said. "I sensed that it was the release of his intention toward me as my energy rose up to dominate his. My will was stronger than his."

"Exactly. You ceased to be a victim."

Something was still not clear to me about the relationship of my dreaming body to my perception. I thought about it for a few minutes while he puffed away.

"How does my brain relate to the workings of the known?" I finally asked.

"Your brain takes your perception–what you allow yourself to know–and makes it linear. It is the device that allows you to communicate your perceptions with others through speech, writing, art, music, body language or any other form of physical communication."

"Why do I feel like I'm dreaming when my dreaming body is outside of my physical body–why do I feel disconnected from the world?"

"For two reasons," he replied. "First, your physical body is the instrument that you use to experience the physical world. It enables you to see, hear, smell, taste and feel the things around you. Once your dreaming body is outside of your physical body, it has no direct link to the physical world that you live in. You cannot directly feel your connection to the things of this world. Secondly, because your dreaming body is outside of your physical body, it is unfettered by the modes of perception that you have adopted. Now, the awareness of your dreaming body is returned to its original state–the state that it was in prior to entering this world. In this state, it sees that this world is a dream."

"A dream?" I asked.

"Yes, a dream. Your dreaming body dreams up this world. Every person that you encounter is doing the same thing. That is what makes this world so real–a shared consensus among all of us who dream the same dream. But when your dreaming body steps out of your physical body, it is able to remind you that this is only a dream. It is able to remind you of the things that bring true happiness."

He looked at me for a few minutes with an absent-minded stare. "I can see that your dreaming body is still above your physical body. There is a huge glow around your head where it is hovering. As I look at the lower half of your body, the glow gets dimmer. It's quite a sight for a seer to witness. When was the last time you came back into your physical body?"

I thought for a minute. "It's been about seventeen years, since sometime in my freshman year at college. I remember staring out the old dormitory window on a hot fall day. I was watching the eucalyptus trees blowing in a mild Santa Ana wind and wondering if I would ever come back. It was frightening because I had never been gone for more than a day or two in the past. This time I had been gone for a couple of weeks. But being outside of my body enabled me to be very detached, and I wasn't able to worry about it too much."

"Being in this state for so long has been extremely helpful for your awareness," Court said. "You've learned how to handle *seeing* in day-to-day living. It has obviously given you unbelievable experience navigating in this dream, and it has also given you much insight into others. Most people who find themselves in this situation do not have enough energy to accept and command this condition, and so wind up living in the 'victim' mode. They usually spend their time feeling sorry for themselves and indulging in apathetic passivity because they see that so many things that are considered important in our world are a farce–they lead nowhere. The one thing that does matter–the joy of fulfillment through the embodiment of the Unknown–is the one thing that nobody pays any attention to. You, however, have managed to take advantage of the situation."

"How can living like this be a good thing when it has kept me from enjoying so many moments?" I protested. "I'm always aware of my motives and other peoples' motives because I'm just far enough outside of this physical dream to be able to see their intentions before they manifest into action. I find myself realizing that everyone has a secret agenda."

He laughed. "It's like watching a movie when you've already read the script, isn't it?"

"Yes," I replied. "There's not a whole lot of newness or surprise left. It's almost clinical. When I see that fear is what drives almost every human being, I start to be affected by that hysteria. I just want to hide because I feel heavy with despair. Yet, I have to continue to function in this world. I have to make a living if I want to continue my journey."

"Sometimes the clarity that you experience in this state is more debilitating than the fear that first put you there," Court said. "Apathetic passivity is produced by the deadly combination of fear and knowledge. A persistent pursuit of the Unknown is the only way out of this trap."

He smiled and looked at me intently. "Your physical body has deteriorated unnecessarily because your dreaming body has spent so much time outside of your physical body. Being outside of your body decreases your sensitivity to the workings of your physical body. You may injure yourself too easily. It's not healthy for your physical body. It puts too much stress on it. Your physical body needs the nourishment of your dreaming body. Your dreaming body fills your physical body like water fills the container of a potted plant, and feeds it. You need to get back into your physical body."

Court stood up and walked to the front door. He flicked on the porch light and told me to follow him, but to take off my shoes first. I followed him down the steps of his front porch and into his front yard. He led me to a damp patch of dirt surrounding a banana tree.

"Stand here," he commanded. I did so, and I felt my feet take pleasure in the moist coolness of the rich earth. He stood next to me. I noticed that he was breathing deeply.

"One way to encourage your dreaming body to come back

into your physical body is to slow down and reconnect with the energy of the earth," he said. I breathed deeply, and felt my solar plexus and abdomen relax. As I continued to relax, I noticed a change in the hue of the surrounding darkness. It was almost as if someone had turned on a lamp. I perceived a glow around the trees and plants.

"That's better," Court said. "If you continue to reconnect in this manner, you will eventually find yourself back in your body."

We stood there for a few more minutes. I noticed that I was feeling warmer inside as well. Court made his way back to the front porch and into his house. I followed him, and we settled back into our chairs. We sat quietly for a while.

"I remember, Court, how my father used to wrap me on the head with his knuckles whenever I did something stupid. He would say, 'Think, think, think,' or, 'What were you thinking? Pay attention.' This little trick actually reinforced and enhanced my awareness. Without this kind of awareness and rationality, I would have been overwhelmed by my seeing."

"Your parents and your schooling provided you with the ability to organize your experiences in a useful way," Court said. "They helped you to focus and round up your attention at an early age, and you kept at it through your own persistence. What else did your parents do that fostered your early abilities?"

"Well, they kept me calm and well-rested, and limited my television watching in amount and content. My mother was still in college when I was a child, and I spent many afternoons playing on the college grounds. My favorite place was a rectangular grass bowl that was about two feet deep and maybe twenty-five feet long. I used to run up and down the sides like an airplane, and fall down the slopes with my younger sister."

I told Court that my dreaming, however, afforded me the real playtime. I loved to go to that grass bowl in my lucid dreaming and slide down the slopes with my body just inches above the grass. In my dreaming, it felt like I was swimming along the bottom of a giant swimming pool, molding the length of my body to fit the curves along the bottom of the sides, or along the giant slope that went up from the deep end. I would spend what seemed like hours caressing these grassy slopes. Then, I would pick up speed along the bottom in order to be catapulted into the blue sky above the towering eucalyptus trees.

I went on to tell him about another particular dream that had a quality of feeling that far exceeded anything I had experienced in my daily world. In this dream, I suddenly found myself hovering next to the ceiling in the hallway of my house. It felt just like the thrill of weightlessness that I would experience when my parents would throw me up into the air, except that the tingling excitement that I was experiencing below my navel wasn't coming and going–it was constant. That created a sustained and almost unbearable excitement in my lower abdomen. In this dream, I was staring at something that seemed vaguely familiar, except that I was looking at it through fish-bowl glasses. It had a sort of amber glow, and it was blocking my way. I finally realized that it was the light on the ceiling. Once I recognized it, my fixation was broken and I was able to pass it. I then continued along the hallway ceiling, 'swimming' around other obstacles, and in and around each of the bedroom doorframes and walls. When I woke up, my whole body was tingling from the exhilaration of my adventure, and I relished in the most pleasant sensation of utter relaxation that followed. I lay there for an hour, watching the amber colors float across the room.

I recalled, too, that there were bad moments. Being sick was horrible, and unfortunately it happened frequently. Most of the time it seemed to be the food that I ate. It wasn't necessarily bad food–it was just too spicy or rich for my body. It was also confusing and upsetting to my body not to eat on time. In addition, my parents liked to put me to bed around seven o'clock in the evening, even in the summer, while all of my friends were still playing outside. Because I wasn't even remotely sleepy, I would lie there for an hour or two, disturbed by the heat. The combination of all of these things led to many experiences of fat, thick hands and strange colors swirling around my head. My legs would get thick or thin as I lay in bed, and this was always accompanied by a metallic taste in my mouth.

Court stopped me and suggested that we go and get some dinner. We walked a few blocks over to our favorite Thai restaurant and ordered pineapple chicken to go. He greeted a few friends while we waited for our food, and then we headed back home. There was another beautiful night breeze blowing through the trees, and it followed us into his house. Court got some plates and silverware, and we helped ourselves to the steaming food. I could feel the warmth of it fill my belly and a pleasant wave of chills went up my spine. The presence had entered his house on the wind and it grew in the silence. I was suddenly transported back in time. I spoke out loud as I remembered a very vivid event.

"I am lying in the tall grass that has overgrown the strawberry patch in my grandmother's backyard. Today, it is breezy, with a slight hint of summer in the billowy white clouds that float lazily in that ominous blue sky. The cottonwood trees shimmer and whisper in my buzzing ears. I am filled with a quiet and lusty sensuality, for I am awaiting my lover who will be arriving very soon. I am filled with anticipation and excitement. My heart is on fire. I am three years old."

Court burst out laughing and started choking on his dinner. Then he sneezed loudly. "You thought that you were waiting for your auntie, didn't you?" he said sarcastically.

I hardly heard him. I was still engrossed in this bewitching memory. It had never surfaced so thoroughly before. In the past, I had only perceived vague shadows of this long-lost part of my life. These shadows would wash over me like a translucent curtain in a tropical breeze. I would just see my grandmother's house, or her bedroom on a lazy early summer afternoon, and time would slow down for a brief moment. Now, my body was thoroughly enraptured by the feeling and I could not, and would not, shake it. I wanted that feeling more than anything. I knew it was the magic and mystery that I had been searching for. I could sense Court watching me. After a few minutes, he leaned over and whispered in my ear.

"What are you *seeing*?" he asked intently.

"My dreaming body," I replied, still transfixed. I was still at my grandmother's house. "I feel like a ghost or an apparition," I said with a faraway raspiness. "The room is *alive*! The air and the summer wind are speaking to me." My hands were perspiring.

"What are they telling you?" Court asked me.

"Not to forget, no matter what," I said. I was beginning to shake. "They are filling me up with memories of their presence, with knowledge of their essence. They are memories without pictures, without image. I love them with my whole being. They are what I live for–they are what drive me to *know*. They are the Unknown, yet I know them better than I know you, my friend." My heart was on fire now and it was fueling the rest of my body. "Nothing else matters," I said. "Nothing."

The vision faded and I found myself back in Court's living room. I was very sad. I did not want that to end. Court looked at me.

"My only enemy is fear," I said. "Fear keeps me from joy, affection, love and life. It ruins the food that I eat, disturbs my health, takes away my dreaming, and clouds the vision of my true path." I stared down at my food. It was cold.

Court quietly took my plate from me and went into the kitchen. He reheated our dinners and came back. I felt better, but an intense longing remained. I ate some hot food and it warmed my belly.

"For thirty years I struggled with the idea that that memory may have been one of those sordid stories about childhood molestation," I said. "But I could never remember a face. I was almost certain that it had been some kind of sick and twisted mini-drama."

"It didn't have anything to do with your family though, did it?" he asked me.

"No," I said. "This was one of my first memories of lucid dreaming. For some reason, when I was asleep and out of my body, I liked to go to my grandmother's house and lie in the strawberry patch under her bedroom window. That house had some kind of power, and it feels like I went there every chance I got."

"The feeling of being sexually aroused existed in that dream because the energy used by your dreaming body comes from the same energy center as your sexuality," Court said. "The energy from your sexual center is used for power and control when on a dreaming adventure." He took another bite of food.

"Her house was always a great source of mystery for me. I'm not sure if it was the power associated with that spot, or if there were ghosts in her house. But even in the waking hours of my youth, I would feel a sense of foreboding and dark mystery every time I went there."

I remembered that it was an old, turn of the century wooden house, with a creaky front porch constructed of warped and splintery floorboards. It was painted on the outside in a light, hospital green. Immediately inside the front door was an old grandfather clock, which, for a three year-old, was creepy and alive. The front room always had the curtains closed because it faced the sun, and the dust used to glitter and move in strange patterns in the musty light of the room. There was an old, brown wooden record player console that had built-in speakers and records stored under the sliding lid. I used to slide the lid to the side and peer in at the record player. I had no idea what it was, and that only added to the mysteriousness of the room. Off of the front room was my grandmother's bedroom, and under her bedroom window along the side of the house was the strawberry patch.

Her kitchen always smelled like gas because of the leaky gas stove. It had an uneven rubber floor and a very deep sink where the water always dripped. At the back of the house was a screened-in service porch. It had plywood window flaps outside that were always propped open, and a spare bed. But the greatest source of distress for me was the basement. It was dark and musty with a narrow, steep staircase and a cold, damp earthen floor. The low wooden beams above were always covered with black widow spider webs. There was a single light bulb attached to the rafters, and my father was always swallowed up by the darkness as he went down into the basement to search for the electric cord and outlet that he had to plug the light into. As the dim light began glowing, I could see the old boxes of thick, rusted iron and steel tools. In my dreaming I remembered an attic, even though there wasn't one. I think there was a crawl space above the ceiling. I looked at Court.

"There are so many quasi-memories from my early dreaming that are still inaccessible. The basement, which I hardly ever went into, was the gateway to the older realms and the attic was the gateway to the mysteries."

"Your memories will become clear as you store more energy," Court said. He had finished his dinner now and was quietly rolling one of his favorite cigarettes–a combination of clove cigarette and pipe tobacco. People always thought that he was rolling big joints. He had fashioned a hollow pipe out of bamboo to hold these cigarettes, and now he inserted the cigarette into the end of the pipe and lit it. It took him a few minutes to get it going, and then the room filled with the rich aroma.

"What we're doing, by remembering your past in this manner, is reinforcing your connecting link to the Spirit by purposefully recalling events that show the presence of the Spirit. Your sudden and complete remembrance of your early dreaming adventures confirms that it is working. It is a recapitulation. Recapitulation is used to release trapped energy so that it is available for use again. People get old before their time because all of their available energy is locked up in various dramas from the past. Because they have no available energy, their lives become monotonous and they stagnate. Trapped energy creates disease and disease creates death, or a version of life that is similar to death. These elements push a person's dreaming body so far away that the person becomes empty. These are the ghouls that nightmares are made of. They are as good as dead."

He peered at me in the dim light. "But you haven't told me anything about your love life yet. Didn't you have any experiences with women that demonstrated the presence of the Spirit?" He winked at me and chuckled.

I smiled and thought for a minute, and then I remembered an unusual event. I told Court that during my seventh grade year I had a massive crush on a ninth-grader named Lisa. She was homely and slightly overweight, but very pretty. Her hair was shoulder length and feathered for that fabulous period of style that existed just before the eighties. She was simple and soft, and I could tell that she was curious about the intensity of my obvious crush on her, although her status as a cheerleader forbade her to have any contact with me. I was too young and too short, and practically a complete social outcast. I was one of the few seventh graders in her pre-algebra class. I remembered how my crush on her was antagonized by the fact that she only lived two blocks away, and my best friend lived on the same block that she did. I also had a part-time newspaper route that included her house. I even wrote her love-letters, which only embarrassed her more.

One night, a girlfriend of hers had a party. The party was at a house that was only one block away from mine. This was to be my big chance to spy on her. For some unknown reason, I decided to get dressed up in my Halloween costume to conceal my identity. It consisted of a really obscene rubber monster mask with fluorescent blue hair, and a torn-up sheet that I had painted some strange symbols on. I thought that I would sneak over and scare them all. Apparently, my early-adolescent hormones were orchestrating the whole event because I was sure that they would all run away at the sight of me, leaving me alone with Lisa. I would finally have the opportunity to profess my deep love for her.

Friday night came, and I told my ten-year old neighbor friend, David, what I was up to. He decided to follow me over on his bike and see the action. We arrived at the house, and I saw her mingling with her friends in the back courtyard. The property around the house was quite nice with high, red brick fencing and ivy growing all over the walls. The only way for us to get close enough was to sneak up the driveway while trying to hide behind what little shrubbery there was.

After getting about twenty feet up the driveway, a couple of the boys at the party snuck around and cornered us. I looked around but there was no way out. They yelled at the rest of the group to come over. As the rest of them approached, I felt that cold sinking feeling that used to come with the fear of being humiliated, and I knew that I was hopelessly doomed. The woman of my dreams was about to see me embarrassed and exposed!

I think, however, that they were still not sure of who I was because they didn't recognize David. One of the boys stepped forward and said to another, "Take off his mask!" And then everything around me darkened and went into slow motion.

My fright was the prominent factor now and I knew that something in me had shifted. As the hand came for my mask, I heard a strange and deeply unfamiliar voice yell in slow motion, "No, not my mask!" and then somehow I ran right under, and past, all nine of them. My body accelerated without effort in the darkness and I moved with precise steps even though there were no streetlights. I remember very vividly seeing the sprinkler holes cut deep into the grass. I also remembered that somehow I was able to see all of the high and low spots in the lawn, David's bike laying on the grass, and the ankle-twisting spaces that someone had cut with an edger between the grass and the sidewalk. I knew that I was not seeing these things with my eyes, however. They were unfocused and pointed ahead into the horizon of the next block where I lived. In addition, my rubber mask kept sliding around on my perspiring face, obstructing my vision.

I was traveling at a very great speed and yet my body felt absolutely exhilarated–not stressed or fatigued in any way. After

I had run about three-quarters of a block like this, I turned around to see how close they were, but no one was even in sight. I ran a little further, and then slowed to a fast walk. A few minutes later, David came riding up very quickly on his bike.

He exclaimed, "How did you do that–run so fast like that?" He was huffing and puffing.

I said, "I don't know. I guess I was just scared." David just stared at me, not sure what to make of what had happened.

"How did you get past them?" he asked again. "Two guys held me down and kept asking me questions. I was really scared. They wanted to know who you were, but the girls told them to leave me alone and let me go. I ran to my bike but you were already gone."

I had absolutely no answer for him. We continued back to my house in silence.

Court said, "There went your dreaming body again, leading you out of danger and helping you to see in complete darkness. Fear seems to be your greatest ally."

"It was, except for one year when I was a teenager," I said.

I told him that at the age of fifteen I entered into a serious state of depression that lasted for almost one year. I would wake up every night at about two o'clock in the morning and feel so scared that my blood would run cold. I was afraid of every strong emotion, especially anger and violence, and if I saw anything that had to do with anger or violence on television I would leave the room immediately and hide in my bedroom. When I woke up at night, I would listen to music with my headphones on to try to calm myself down. I was terribly afraid of dying, but it wasn't that I was considering suicide. It was something I couldn't figure out.

"Did you ever figure it out?" Court asked me.

"Not until recently. I realized that I had suppressed my rage and extreme frustration, and that this had created my depression. The frustration came from not being able to release my rage."

I described to Court how I had initially felt fear because I was neglecting my dreaming body in order to focus on my schooling and socialization. I was not learning to listen to it or become sensitive to its nuances. I was being taught to be a thinker with a western mind and to listen only to rationalizations. I was unconsciously afraid of losing my connection to the Unknown within me, of having my dreaming body reduced to a whisper. That fear had turned into anger, then rage, then frustration, and then depression.

To make matters worse, I had now become so conditioned by my religious upbringing and by society that I truly believed that the expression of my anger was not allowed–that it was a sin. I noticed at this time that I started having intimations–feelings about people or events that would come true. This made things unbearable as my anger increased and I felt it spilling over into my intimations. I was afraid of becoming violent, or of violent things happening to my friends and family, and so I began to pray very hard at all hours of the night and day. Praying further reduced the energy available to my dreaming body. I was very afraid of not being liked or accepted by family and peers if I did not continue to be pleasant and humble.

This choking off of energy to my dreaming body and its mysteries led to my rage, which I tried to release through skateboarding, or by playing and writing angry music and lyrics for the heavy metal band that I was in. This wasn't enough, however, and when my dreaming body realized that it was not going to get to express itself or release its anger, it became supremely frustrated and turned that sour, pent up energy into a serious state of depression.

"Did you know that you could've released all of that anger by confronting your belief structures, the things that angered and imprisoned your dreaming body?" Court asked.

"No, I didn't know that at the time," I said. "I was too afraid of authority and anger back then. I was incapable of confronting anyone or anything. I believed that I could hide from anger and conflict by being a nice person, and by allowing others to take advantage of me without offering any resistance. I was naïve, and believed that nice, humble people were always recognized and rewarded by others for their humility."

"You didn't realize that your humility was arrogance in disguise, did you?" he said in a penetrating voice. "True humility is not found in meekness, but in the elimination of your self-image or ego. You didn't understand that you quietly believed that you were superior to others. You believed that if people didn't recognize your superiority they were inferior to you."

I sat there, feeling the memories of the rage and depression welling up inside of me. "I didn't realize that I thought that I was better than everybody else," I said dejectedly. "I hadn't yet seen the face of arrogance hiding behind my façade of humility. I hadn't seen that I demanded automatic recognition from others as a sign that they were of the same level as myself." I shifted uncomfortably in my chair. "But what does this have to do with my depression?" I asked defensively.

"It was your own arrogance that kept you tied down. You firmly believed that you would be rewarded for your humility, and so you waited for the person handing out the rewards to come to you and relieve you of your fear, anger, rage, frustration and depression. You waited and waited, and that person never showed up. No one saved you and no one rewarded you. You were a perfect victim."

"You also did not know that you were burdened by the emotions of your family and friends," he continued. "As your awareness and ability to *see* began to grow, you literally bore the fears and frustrations of those around you—you felt the weight of their attachment to you. But you weren't aware of this and you didn't know how to get rid of it. What do you think the phrase means: *And he bore our sins?*"

He paused for a few minutes while I recapitulated. Then he asked, "How did you finally release your depression?"

"I fell in love." We both exploded in laughter. "It was my first experience with serious dating, my junior year in high school," I said. "One year later when it was all over, I cried everything out."

"That's pretty convoluted, but at least it worked," he laughed warmly. "When did you have your first sexual encounter? Your energy seems to have remained untangled for a long time."

I laughed. "Not until I was twenty-two."

"I'm sitting here with an honest-to-God prude!" he quacked.

"Not only that, but she had to get me drunk first and then practically attack me."

He encouraged me to continue with a nod.

I told him that Leslie and I were traveling with a music group one summer. She was a little smart-ass from the deep South, very pretty, and very engaged to be married. That was enough to keep me away, but I had never been up against anyone so persistent. She kept asking me to marry her, but I was still in college and wasn't the least bit ready to settle down. She followed me everywhere and teased me everyday. Eventually, we started kissing and hanging out away from everyone else. She was relentless in trying to get me to make love to her. She had even told me that if I would marry her I could still have sex with other 'blonde bimbos,' which was her way of referring to southern California girls.

One hot night in Texas, after a twelve-hour day of marching in the sun, a group of us went down to a local bar. I thought that we had managed to avoid being seen by Leslie when we left, but she and her girlfriend caught up with us on the road. Alcohol was still new to me, and so after one stiff drink I felt very relaxed and started to nod off. I decided to head back to the school gym where we were staying. I was barely out the door when she ran up behind me with her hormones in an uproar.

"Come on, it won't hurt a bit," Leslie teased.

"Look, Leslie, you're engaged," I said.

"Yes, but I'm not married," she said, emphasizing the last word.

"But why get engaged if it's not something that you're sure about?" I asked.

"Because he's the best one I've found so far, besides you. But if you won't marry me, then I'm not going to lose him."

"But you don't know what the future holds. How can you think like that?" I asked with more than a hint of exasperation.

"He's all I've got and he treats me well. I'm not going to lose him for nothing," she declared firmly.

We walked in silence for a bit and then she jumped on my back. I carried her for a while. In those days, love was pure enjoyment without all of the complications and unspoken attachments and expectations. I truly loved being with her.

We got back to the school and walked through the playground. She was teasing and pleading again. I was nervous, but I wasn't sure why. Suddenly, she took a running leap and knocked me off balance into the grass. She was on top of me and I was starting to give in. She knew it, too, and so she ran into the gym and got her blanket. It's still so funny to look back on that moment. It really wasn't anything transcendental, and yet it was magical. Here we were, naked under the most beautiful, starlit sky. I had no idea how exciting her naked body was, or that the smell of her hair and the bursting energetic richness of her bare skin against mine would remain with me for many years. What lasted for me back then was the idea that I had had sex, and the sixty-two mosquito bites covering every sacred vestige of my body.

Court said, "Your energy was still tight. It doesn't become loosened during sex unless you're attached in some way. Obviously, you weren't attached to her."

"I can only remember being attached once up until that point, when I had that girlfriend in high school. But we never had sex."

"Leslie became attached to you though, didn't she?"

"Yes. When she left a couple of weeks later, she cried. I cried a little, too, but I wasn't sure why. It seemed that I was crying because of her sadness, which was real to her. I didn't feel like we were losing each other. I knew I would see her again. We wrote to each other over the years. She even still married the same guy. I remember how much I secretly admired him because of his detachment. He was one of my first real examples of detachment in action. Whenever he and Leslie were in town, he would drive her over to see me and leave us alone for the day. I knew that he knew that she would try to get me to make love to her again, but I wouldn't because…"

"Because you were a prude," he laughed.

"No, because she was married! It wasn't only that I was rigid in my morality then, but my dreaming body sensed that her decision to get married was an energetic contract, and that she was the one that needed to void it before we continued our relationship."

"She wasn't strong enough," Court sighed. "Leslie compromised her life by clinging to what was in front of her instead of holding out for the realization of her fulfillment. It's sad to hear stories like that."

I looked out of the corner of my eye at him and fidgeted with my finger on the coffee table.

"Spill the beans," he commanded.

"I secretly hoped that she would hold out, too. But I've wished that for all of my girlfriends. I've wished that somehow we would all see through this dream and realize just how much is at stake. Leslie settled for less than what she was capable of. I've never understood that about anyone. How can anyone compromise their entire life for a security that inevitably leads to boredom and frustration?"

Court leaned forward, looked into my eyes and said, "It's not over until they're dead."

THE SPACE BETWEEN THOUGHTS

The smoke from the burning sage brings back many memories, yet they are memories that I cannot completely grasp. The first time that I ever smelled sage was on the night that I met Carol, in a story that almost never happened.

Carol worked with my sister in southern California, and lived in a cabin in the mountains outside of town. I had been living with my sister for the past couple of months while I saved up enough money to move to Seattle. My sister said that Carol was just my type, and she encouraged me to meet her.

One night, Carol called, and my sister handed me the phone. Carol's voice was very playful and melodious. We introduced ourselves and engaged in small talk for a few minutes, and then she asked me if I would like to stop by her cabin before I left town. I said that I might come by the next evening, and she gave me directions. I was curious about her, but since I was leaving for Seattle in a few days I was hesitant about starting up a new friendship. I wasn't sure that I would ever return to southern California.

The following night I was very tired and drained. I had just finished my last day of work at an aerospace firm where I had continually submitted myself to mind-numbing monotony for money. After I ate dinner, I decided to go to bed and forget about Carol. I brushed my teeth and got undressed. I had just climbed into my bed when something in me pushed very hard. I had never felt such a strong and relentless compulsion. I sat there for a few minutes waiting for it to die down, but it didn't. Instead, something inside of me came alive. It reminded me that life was short and that opportunities were challenges. I knew that the Spirit wanted to know if I was listening.

I accepted the challenge. I put my clothes back on and headed out. I felt a sudden surge of energy from my intention to pursue something beyond what was known to me. I remembered that my sister had told me that Carol was very alluring and deep, and I felt my dormant hormones come alive. I pushed down harder on the gas pedal.

After twenty minutes of driving up a very steep and dark highway, I reached the road that her cabin was on. I turned and followed the windy road down for a few miles. The shadows of the towering pine trees closed in above me as I strained to locate her cabin. There were no streetlights anywhere and I got completely lost. I wound up doubling back a few times before I finally found her dark green mailbox with the white, painted numbers on it.

It was now about ten o'clock and I wondered if she might already be asleep. I pulled quietly into the narrow dirt road and drove back to her cabin. It was completely dark. I turned off the motor and sat there, hesitating. I thought that I should call her, but then I remembered that she had no phone. She had called me the other night from a payphone at the store off of the main highway. After a few minutes, I noticed that there were lights on inside. The wooden storm windows had been closed from the outside and had almost entirely blocked out the lights inside. I sat there for a few more minutes, debating. Then the porch light flickered on and the front door opened. I saw the shadow of a young woman. She stood there, staring at me through the screen door.

"Carol?" I asked.

"Yes," she said hesitantly. "Are you Matthew?"

"Is it too late for me to be here? There was no way to call

you," I said. She stepped outside and approached me as if she were gliding.

"No, it's fine. It's nice to meet you. Come in."

She led me through the darkness to the front door and into the cabin. It was obviously built around the turn of the century. It had no insulation and I could feel the cool air leaking through the thin, wooden walls. Very dim, yellow lights hung from the ceiling beams and cast diffused shadows in the corners.

My eyes were slowly adjusting to the lack of light as I followed her into the cabin. She led me through the kitchen and into the living room. There were candles burning on the fireplace mantle and around the room. Sage was smoldering in an abalone shell on the bookcase. It was completely quiet and still inside, and also in the mountains outside. A very impersonal presence permeated the room. It was only slightly tempered by the warmth of the candlelight and her company. I felt a pressure below my navel that I had recently begun to recognize as a pressure associated with power and fear.

She stopped in the center of the living room and turned to face me. Our eyes locked; her beauty stunned me. She was a few inches shorter than I, with golden skin and a long, thick, wavy golden mane. Her eyes were friendly and inviting with a hint of mirth. Her features were beautiful yet strong. I was absolutely attracted to her.

She looked at me and then embraced me as if I were a long-lost friend. She offered me the old couch. She curled up in her overstuffed armchair across from me with a well-worn, woolen Indian blanket. We immediately hit it off talking about our favorite books. Time stood still for the next hour as I relished in a dream come true. I couldn't believe that I had almost stayed home! Here, for the first time in my life, was a woman who shared my interest in the Unknown.

She got up to make some chamomile tea and light some incense.

"Tell me about your upcoming trip, Matthew. Why Seattle?"

"I don't know, except that I feel something pulling me there. I'm tired of all of the noise and congestion in Los Angeles, and I want to be silent for a while. I may even make my way to Montana, or maybe even to Alaska. The highway through the Yukon is supposed to be spectacular."

"Yes, I've been to Anchorage. I loved the stillness there, but it was very cold. I like it here more. I'm more suited to the sun and the ocean."

I looked around the living room while she finished in the kitchen. The fireplace was made of smooth, round rocks from a creek, and on the mantel were various stones and crystals. I noticed that the plywood panels in the ceiling above were warped and pulling away from the beams. Carol walked to the end of the kitchen and lit a small fire in the wood-burning stove to take the edge off of the night. Then she came back into the front room.

"What are you looking for?" she asked as her eyes penetrated into mine. Her gaze made me warm inside. She handed me a mug of hot tea.

"I've searched my entire life for things to fill me up," I said. "I've tried women, music, jobs and money. But there is still a hole–something is missing. The books that we've been talking about point towards a truth that I can intuit, but can't quite grasp. Nothing comes close to satisfying the fire that burns inside of me except the presence that I feel here in this cabin with you."

"The presence of the Spirit?" she asked.

"Nothing else matters to me," I said. "No matter what I'm doing or where I am, and no matter how much I try to lose myself in people or things, that presence comes in and shatters everything to bits. I find myself with nothing. But as the debris settles, I feel the most intense fire in my heart and I long to embrace it like nothing else."

"Then this trip is a quest for you," she said mysteriously. "It is a solitary adventure. Don't let anything stand in your way."

I met once more with Carol before leaving town. Our meetings were very puzzling to me because we only talked about our dreams and endless possibilities–we rarely talked about our personal histories. Yet, I felt that I knew her more in those two meetings than I had ever known my most intimate girlfriend.

About six months later, I returned from my solitary journeys through Washington, Montana and Alaska. I was staying in my truck at her cabin in the mountains. It was summertime. She had been gone all night working as a counselor for a teenage girls' rehabilitation home. It was now mid-morning, and was already very hot and stifling. I hadn't slept well in the stillness of the heat and was in a daze. I wasn't sure what time she would be back, so I decided to go for a walk.

I walked up her street to a small bridge in a bend in the road. It passed over a small creek where it was cool and shady. I stopped there for a few minutes to enjoy the sound of the water singing over the round rocks below. Then I walked a little further to a dirt road that passed by a cattle fence. I watched the hills in the distance ripple in the heat, and then a golden retriever quietly appeared and welcomed me. A small, caramel brown horse came slowly up to the fence to spend a few moments with us, too.

I went back to the cabin and then behind it to the creek that I could hear running in the distance. I was trying to shake off the stiffness in my body. It was getting hotter by the minute and I started wondering again what time Carol would come home. In the heat, the presence that lived in that area became very suffocating and heavy. I could feel it compressing my body and pushing mercilessly on my solar plexus and lower abdomen. Then I heard a voice whisper inside of me that Carol was home. I saw her face. A hawk immediately cried above me and then circled over her cabin. I headed back.

"A voice told me that you were home," I said as I walked in the back door.

She smiled at me. She had beads of perspiration on her forehead from driving up the mountain in her old pickup.

"Let's go for a swim in the creek," she said.

"I was just down there and there's not a whole lot of water left," I replied.

"I know a deeper spot further up."

She grabbed some towels from a cupboard and then we made our way back to the creek. I had been unable to shake the fog in my head and the stillness had become deafening. I followed her in silence up a hidden path until we reached a place in the creek where the water had pooled. A very old and very tall oak tree shaded part of the water and the bank where we stopped. We swam together in the cool, muddy water and rubbed each other's backs with tanning lotion. The wind came to us as we stood on the bank of the river, and bathed us both.

"Everything is already perfect," said Carol. "Peace. Quiet. Contentedness."

After relaxing in the patchy sun underneath the tree, we headed back to the cabin. The presence and the heat were now too much for me. I went into her bedroom and lay down on her bed. A few minutes later, she came and lay down next to me. It was so pleasant to be with her. We talked some more of our dreams and held each other. I caressed her hair as she rubbed my back. The philter of her breath held me captive. I was intoxicated by the mood and my arousal was becoming more obvious. Before it became too apparent, she spoke.

"I've got to go and run a few errands now, but let's meet in town for dinner at six o'clock," she said quietly.

"Alright. I'll see you there," I said dreamily. I was happy to be spending any time I could with her. I rolled around on her bed for a while longer, making peace with the presence that pursued me.

I got up slowly and spent the next hour struggling to bathe myself in her makeshift bathroom. There were ants all over the toilet, but she refused to spray them with bug spray. She told me that they wouldn't bother me if I left them alone. The shower didn't work because the septic system was full and something had lodged in the drain. I decided to take a sponge bath in the sink instead. Then, before making the trip out of the mountains and back into town, I pulled a book from her bookshelf and read for a while.

I arrived at the pre-arranged corner downtown a little before six and waited, watching the tourists milling around. The sun had disappeared behind the mountains and the coolness of the ocean nearby was refreshing. Carol arrived a few minutes later and we hugged each other. I was really looking forward to some romantic conversation. She looked at me and smiled deeply.

"My friend, Court, that I told you about is going to meet us at the restaurant. He's the one who's been teaching me about souls and their histories. I think you'll really like him." She was very obviously excited. "Come on, we'll take my truck."

I stood there, devastated. I tried with all of my might to keep from getting really upset. I remembered our phone conversations while I had been in Seattle and Anchorage, and how it seemed as though she had always been chasing after various spiritual men. That was frustrating because I wanted her to admire me. I was definitely not in any mood to share our quality time with some wannabe master, especially one that I had never met.

We got into her truck and drove in silence. I struggled not to let her notice my sullenness. We arrived at the Thai restaurant a few minutes later, and she ran up to Court and gave him a big hug.

"Courty, this is Matthew, the guy I was telling you about."

"Hello," I said. I was smugly polite, and noticed that he seemed to be somewhat slow-witted in his dirty black dinner coat and flip-flop sandals. Suddenly, another young woman came running up to him yelling his name and practically jumped into his arms while he swung her around. I fought desperately at this point to keep from being consumed by my own jealousy.

"Oh, Court, I can't thank you enough," said the young woman. "You've helped me so much and I feel so happy!" He seemed genuinely happy and not too overcome with himself, so

I dropped my judgments and tried to figure out how I was going to be polite at dinner without being too obviously dejected. I did not want Carol to think less of me for ruining the evening.

The host showed us to our table and I, much to my chagrin, found myself sitting across from the two of them. It was becoming apparent to me that they were an item already. I decided that I would go to the bathroom and compose myself so that we could all have a nice meal together. I started to stand up when I heard someone whispering in my ear. I thought it was the waiter, but I couldn't understand what he was trying to say. At the same time, I realized that something had a strong grip on my umbilical region. This all happened so quickly that I experienced a moment of limbo as my entire body froze on the spot. Then, something in my stomach area took control and I found myself back in my seat staring at Court.

"…And you were a seventh-level old soul," he said. "But one year ago you had a walk-in, and now you are a graduate soul. The three of us were all alive together as friends during the lifetimes of Lao Tzu, Buddha, Krishna and Christ. The last life of your previous soul was in 1944 as a German woman. Your life, up until this point, has served as atonement for the four murders committed during that lifetime. Now that that is finished, this graduate soul has come here to fine-tune your body and mind for the work that lies ahead. You are protected and you are very clear. Yes. Very, very clear."

I sat there absolutely numb with the biggest, stupidest, shit-eating-grin on my face while Court stared back at me with the warmest, most friendly eyes I had ever seen. Where had my anger gone? It had absolutely vanished without a trace. Here before me sat an old friend, someone I had known beyond this space and time, a man who had touched my dreaming body with a force that I could only call true affection. I began to laugh, and Court and Carol joined in. Our laughter filled the restaurant and everyone in it.

"What do you mean by *souls*?" I asked after we had calmed down somewhat.

"There are seven levels of souls beginning with *Infant* and going through the *Old* soul level," he said. "Each soul lives as many lives as is necessary in order to complete each of the seven stages. The soul that has recently come into you has already graduated from the physical plane, but has returned to give you a tune-up."

"How does your system of souls relate to the concept of the dreaming body?" I asked. "This is confusing to me. I mean, it makes sense, but the two concepts seem to be on two different paths."

"Exactly," he replied. "A path is just a path, and syntax is just syntax. Clinging to one or the other is an unbelievably useless waste of time. I say, *soul*, you say, *dreaming body*. Now we go and get some bows and arrows and kill each other over it."

He looked at me with a penetrating stare. "The Unknown says the same things to me that it does to you. The way that you or I interpret or speak about these things, however, is colored by our perception and syntax. Everyone who *sees* hears the same voice. Some syntaxes are more accurate than others, but in the end none of them mean a damn thing. Syntaxes are cumbersome. Fearful people cling to them and construct their world based upon them. All that matters is energy. Neither you, nor I, nor Carol, can deny the fact that we feel a magnificent connection to each other. So, we should leave it at that. If you want to talk using your syntax, I will oblige you by responding within that mode of terminology. If I talk to you using mine, you will understand the Truth of what I am saying, even if you don't like my syntax."

Carol chimed in. "Language and syntax are just manifestations of energy. Our upbringing, our socialization, our likes, dislikes and temperament determine which path we choose and, therefore, which system of beliefs. The energy at its purest sense, however, remains unchanged. If you listen with your heart, or with your soul, or with your dreaming body instead of with your ears and your brain, you will find that we are all talking about the same thing."

I nodded in agreement, and was overcome once again with a wave of affection for my new, old friends.

Court continued. "Even if you or I could prove the validity of one of our systems, there would still be many unexplainable gaps and potholes along the way. Systems borrow from the modality of the time and people cling to them because they don't have enough energy to create their own system to describe the phenomena they're witnessing. Most people run around regurgitating the same crap over and over in order to tie themselves to a particular group instead of being authentic. They are lost in the confusing maze of information that is our society. Syntax should be temporary, created and recreated as life progresses. Modes of perception should be unlearned in order to adapt to new scenarios. Perhaps our challenge is to merge a few of these paths together to make a more accurate road map, and then be fluid, dynamic, and flexible enough to throw it all away if we find it interfering with what we feel inside."

We smiled at each other, and I could tell that he was challenging me with a look in his eyes.

"You have the energy to undertake a task like this," he said. I could feel the pressure increasing on my umbilical region as his eyes turned glassy and retreated into the depths. "You will galvanize a common thread of energy among those who long for and seek the Truth, but don't know what to do with it. You will give them a purpose, an objective, and will help them put it all together. But first you must lead yourself."

After dinner, the three of us piled into Carol's pickup. I sat in the middle. We drove for a few blocks and Court asked Carol to let him off at the next corner. She pulled over and stopped at the curb. I turned to give Court a hug, but something else took over inside of me. Apparently, it had also taken over Court as well. Court and I turned toward each other like a couple after a romantic night out, then both jerked back from each other at the same time and stared at each other wide-eyed!

Carol exclaimed, "Did you guys almost just kiss each other?" Court and I burst out laughing while Carol giggled nervously behind us. The funny thing was that I couldn't admit to myself that we almost did. I didn't understand that there were no gender lines here. There was only the unmistakable feeling of a relationship that extended beyond time. Court and I embraced each other, and he stepped out of the truck and into the night.

Court chuckled quietly as I finished my account of our first meeting. He was sitting on his makeshift foam bed in his upstairs bedroom, and I was sitting in an old rattan armchair by the door. It was dark except for a small lamp next to the bed. The two parrots that he and Carol had inherited from their self-absorbed owners were fast asleep in their cages.

"We are our thoughts, beliefs, and expectations," Court said. "It's truly amazing that your meeting Carol and, therefore, our meeting each other was so dependent on your overactive hormones. But I was young and driven by my senses once, too."

"You've never told me about your soul history, Court," I said. "What thrust you into your current way of life and ability to see?"

He blew out a steady stream of smoke and looked at his clove cigarette thoughtfully. "My last life ended with the blast in Hiroshima, and this life began in the throes of nuclear hysteria some fifty years ago. I expected annihilation on a daily basis. I took refuge from the insanity of the world in the arts and went nearsighted in the third grade to blur the faces and looks that were full of fear and frustration. This ensured my creative trance. I grew up fully expecting the world to end, and this dampened my enthusiasm for life, art, and fatherhood. My modern education amounted to twelve years taken from me which I will never recover."

"Once the school box had had its way with me and finally

surrendered its implied ownership of my person," he continued, "I quit in order to face the war machine. The military refused me, however, stating that I was a schizoid person. I played at being a starving hippie artist throughout my twenties. I then began to cover much ground in various art mediums up until I turned thirty. I started drawing for a living. But lacking a foundation of self-esteem, I allowed cocaine to enter my life, often spending more on drugs than I was making on contracts. Misery and self-indulgence led to my death at thirty-three. But a woman I had not seen in months came in the early morning to turn off the gas in my cabin, and to see that I returned to my body and consciousness. Apparently, the Spirit was not through with me yet. I felt like another Lazarus."

I sat quietly for a moment. "Pursuing a path with heart is so difficult. Everything seems designed to destroy any kind of connection to the Spirit. I know people who actually look forward to routines and predictability because they think that they have nothing better to do. And how could they, since their connection to direct knowledge is long gone?"

"Yes, the world is on a fast path away from the pursuit of the Spirit," he replied. "It's becoming more and more analytical. Our electronic world disturbs the natural energy of the body. Our brains are filled with synthetic images and noise. It's almost impossible for a person to experience restful slumber when his or her mind has been imprinted for eight or more hours each day with electronic images. Even music has become more linear. There is very little substance left. We are faced with quantity, not quality. We need space to breathe in."

Court thought for a moment. "People believe in conspiracies, not because of the government, but because of the very quiet realization of their dreaming bodies that everything that is popular in this world is designed to take us further from the mystery of the Unknown. It's become very in-vogue to be so busy that we have to talk on the phone while at the grocery store or while in our cars, or while walking down the street. We are constantly engaged. How can we possibly hear the knock of the Spirit when we are completely preoccupied? The whispering voice of the Unknown can only be heard in the space between noises–in silence. We can't *see* if we are talking."

"Our children suffer the most, however," Court continued. "They are only looking for a moment of silence. They want to stop the world, but no one will listen. The recent increase in childhood disorders and other diseases is simply a natural response by our children to the excessive stimulation that constantly places them in a fight or flight mode. Excessive noise is a form of torture. So is overcrowding, or the reality of always having someone interfering with your energy. It creates unwarranted stress. An old-soul child will simply withdraw, and may be labeled as slow-witted or excessively introverted. Children who don't know any better will express themselves through unthinkable acts of violence."

He looked at me with a hard stare. "What happens immediately after one of them shatters the world with violence?"

"The world stops for a moment," I replied.

"Just for one moment, the world stops what it's doing and looks with incredulity at what is on the news," he said. "War is what we used to use as a way to stop the world and to give people a chance to reevaluate their current way of life. We can't do that anymore because of our weapons of mass destruction."

"I saw a documentary on television about kids that kill at school," I said. "I became engrossed in studying their energy. The show pointed out that they were all outcasts and it reminded me of my own experiences. I never could understand why I, and others like myself, were bullied, harassed and shamed. It didn't seem to bother me as much as some of the others, though."

Court sniggered quietly to himself.

"What's so funny?" I asked.

He laughed some more. "You weren't bothered as much because you were a Catholic!" He bent over in laughter. I laughed, too, because I knew it was true. Martyrdom was a common theme for me and was part of my original arrogance.

"I also had ways of releasing some of that energy which they did not," I continued amidst his annoying chuckling. "I used my anger to further my studies, my guitar playing, my skateboarding and my will. The girls did not embarrass or snub me as much as the other boys, who wound up feeling inferior and humiliated. The girls seemed to feel something for me, despite my awkwardness. I realized that I had found role models that embodied power and leadership in the males of my religion. The killers, however, seemed to be lacking in strong male role models and their female classmates were intuitively aware of that. A woman will squash a man's power if he lets her."

"There is a strange lack of virile and competent male leadership in our world today," Court replied. "Men are becoming weaker at an alarming rate. Without mature role models, the boys struggle and the girls trample on them. It's just energy versus energy. Power is a natural trait that needs nurturing just like any other trait. It's easier for women to find and hold their connection to power because their source of power is the earth. Their energy also develops and matures sooner. The boys, however, can't easily find their connection to the energy from the universe because they are so distanced from it. There's no one around to point to it and to show them how to connect with their source, or how to command it once they do."

"What really caught my attention on this documentary was that all of the killers said the same thing: When they killed, they all felt as if it was a *dream*," I said. "They showed no emotion during the crime. I *saw* that their dreaming bodies had been driven out of their physical bodies by the fear of humiliation and impotence. I remembered how I used to experience that, too. I knew that their fear of not being loved had turned into rage and frustration inside of them. I remembered that fear and religion had protected me from violence. I understood that I also did not grow up surrounded by the incessant sensory input that antagonized them."

"Most of them also said that they heard a voice in their head," I continued. "The voice told them that they were nobodies, that they were worthless. I heard that voice when I was a teenager. I knew that it came from outside of myself. I remembered that the voice increased in intensity and frequency when I caved in to my fears and got caught up in my thoughts, or when I was overly tired. When I put the pieces together, I realized that the killers were acting on their fear and rage because they were too disconnected from their dreaming bodies and the Spirit to know any better."

Court sat quietly, staring into the sky through the window. "Men explode outwardly with rage and action, but women implode with bitterness and depression and hurt themselves. We seldom see women kill each other. When we are filled with anger and frustration, we become bullies and injure those that are weaker than us in order to release that energy. Or, we injure ourselves out of guilt for past wrongdoings. Children injure each other or themselves all the time, or they take it out on animals or bugs. They never realize why they do these things, and so they continue to hurt others as adults but in more 'respectable' ways. But no human can kill another if their dreaming body is present and connected to their physical body because their dreaming body is the source of all life–it *is* life–the Unknown."

"The boys wanted to be propelled forward by their peers, not held back by their limiting thoughts," I said. "The voice that these boys heard showed them the way out of the predicament that they perceived as threatening to their self-image. They removed the impediments, the obstacles in their way. They took back their power in ways that were dictated by their perception."

"Every soul comes into this world individually gifted and intending to deliver something of its true essence," Court replied thoughtfully. "None of us, however, escape the initial scathing process. Few manage to shed the effects of human trauma and shaming. Fewer, still, have any idea about the difference between the practice of fear and the practice of love. We all struggle to manifest essence in this life."

"The greatest paradox of the human condition is fear of joy," he continued. "Our children used to be such a blessed gift of inspiration. Look at the way they ride the current of the Spirit so naturally as they play with their friends! They flow with the wind, flying on the swing here, jumping off to kick the ball there, and then running over to greet another with a smile and a laugh. Now we lock them up and shut them down without a hint of guilt. Twelve years in a school box is a betrayal of a child's essence. Owned by their parents and the state, they learn to give up giggling and wiggling for the documents of intelligence. Do we then give this right back to them with a diploma and a handshake? Isn't a diploma nothing more than a declaration that the child has now been trained to spend the rest of his or her life in the subjugation of joy to reason?"

We both sat in silence. My mind was spinning from all of the implications: Violence is nothing more than a cry for help from our children trying in a most desperate fashion to reverse the path that is taking them further from the Spirit–it is an attempt to stop the world. Our children are simply looking for some silence, some space between sensory input. They are overwhelmed with noise and bombarded with too much sensationalism. They just want to hear the voice of the Spirit and they intuit that it's there, more than the adults, because they are still closer to it.

We lock them up in square rooms all day long and call it education. We drive them around in square boxes filled with talk radio. We lock them in their rooms with violent video games and neurotic music videos. We engage them constantly in competition and comparison. When do they go outside? When do they use their innate ability to connect with the Spirit and bring fresh ideas into this plane? When do they learn to take care of themselves and assume responsibility for their choice of actions?

There is no energetic frontier for them, nothing for them to explore on their own. Instead of allowing them to find out things for themselves and develop their own intelligence, we try to force-feed them the voluminous data that we have already gathered. This is an extraordinarily arrogant presupposition—that we have already evaluated, judged, and delineated the meaning of everything in this universe, and that we are so sure of ourselves that we do not allow our children the opportunity to navigate any alternative or original interpretations.

Court looked at me in the dim light of his room and said, "There is a tremendous sadness that exists in this world. It is the sadness of so many unfulfilled lives, and we are afraid of it. We are afraid to stand up and take responsibility for our lives and then change them. We think that we can escape from all of it by making ourselves too busy, by filling our minds full of opinions instead of energetic facts. But the sadness will get us in the end."

He opened an old book that was lying on his bed. I saw that it was one of his favorites, *The Gospel of Thomas*. He read aloud.

> *If you bring forth what is within you,*
> *What you have will save you.*
> *If you do not have that within you,*
> *What you do not have within you will kill you.*

"How can we bring forth what is within us if we can't even hear it?" he asked. He closed the book, and retired for the evening.

A few days later, I found Court sitting alone in the coolness of his living room reading a book and eating chocolate, another one of his home remedies.

"Chocolate has an alkaline property and is good in small doses for flushing the lymphatic system," he said. "It also provides lecithin which coats the wall of the large intestine and protects it from irritation during the cleansing process."

I sat in the armchair and relaxed. It was a beautiful morning outside, with the marine layer of fog blanketing the southern California city. He looked at me.

"Do you choose life or do you choose death?"

"I choose life," I said, a bit startled by the question.

"I think you would be surprised at how long it takes some people to answer this question, and what their hesitance implies."

"Do you go around asking people that question a lot?" I asked. I was worried that he might be frightening people needlessly.

"Of course I do. If I cannot help them to live, then I will help them to die."

I felt a shiver run through me. I could feel the ruthless power behind his statement and the tremendous accountability that accompanied it.

"Don't you realize that once you become a man of power you must also assume responsibility for the fact that you are an instrument of the Spirit?" he asked me. "The Spirit does not waste time. Your actions in the world of men will have lasting effects on their lives and will alter their paths forever because you are no longer engaged in self-reflection. You are a mirror for the power of the Spirit. All men of power experience this effect. Jesus may have been one of the last great men of power to roam this earth, and one of the most truly successful. Listen to this quote that I was just enjoying from *The Apocryphon of James*:

> Now the twelve disciples were sitting all together and, remembering what the Savior had said to each one of them, whether secretly or openly, they were setting it down in books. And lo, the Savior appeared, after he had departed from us while we gazed at him. And five hundred and fifty days after he arose from the dead, we said to him: "Have you gone and departed from us?"
>
> And Jesus said: "No, but I shall go to the place

from which I have come. If you desire to come with me, come."

They all answered and said: *"If you bid us, we'll come."*

He said: *"Truly I say to you, no one ever will enter the Kingdom of Heaven if I bid him, but rather because you yourselves are full. Let me have James and Peter, in order that I may fill them."* And when he called these two, he took them aside, and commanded the rest to busy themselves with that with which they had been busy.

"Since I have been glorified in this manner before this time, why do you all restrain me when I am eager to go? You have constrained me to remain with you eighteen more days for the sake of the parables."

"Become zealous about the Word. For the Word's first condition is faith; the second is love; the third is works. Now from these comes life."

Court looked at me and smiled. "Do you understand what this passage is telling us?"

"It's telling us that intention, affection, and action are the keys to succeeding in our paths."

"Exactly," he said. "But what about the indirect message?" I looked blankly back at him. He smiled intensely at me. "It says that *five hundred and fifty days* after he rose from the dead he was still with them. Then Jesus asks them why they are holding him back. Don't you see? Even after his crucifixion he remained with the disciples because they were keeping him in this world— *Jesus did not die on the cross!*"

I experienced a vacuous feeling in my head, and then I got terribly excited. "What are you saying?" I exclaimed.

"Jesus was the ultimate man of power," he replied with consuming passion. "He put himself to the supreme test and allowed others to torture and crucify him in order to push his dreaming body completely out of his physical body. This maneuver gave him further insight into his own hidden abilities." Court flipped rapidly through the pages in his book. "The Gospel of Peter says that Jesus was silent as they crucified him, as if he was experiencing no pain–*as if he wasn't even in his body!* Do you see? He used pain and fear to thrust himself deeper into the Unknown."

"His timing was impeccable, too," he continued. "Because of the proximity of Passover, he also knew that they would have to take him down off of the cross in a hurry, before sunset. Judas was actually Jesus' cohort and was given a chance to perfect his skills as a man of power, but in a different role. His role was to 'betray' Jesus to the authorities at the exact moment that would assure crucifixion on the day before Passover. Judas and Jesus succeeded in convincing everyone that Jesus was the ultimate threat to the Roman government and the Jewish religion, and that the crucifixion could not wait until after the religious holiday."

I sat there with my mouth open while he continued.

"Death by crucifixion was an agonizingly slow process. It could take days for a person to die. Pilate was surprised to learn that Jesus had expired within a *few hours*, and dispatched a soldier to confirm his death. Remember that the gospels say that no bones were broken and that his side was pierced? Jesus' body had entered a deep state of shock brought about by pain and the loss of blood. Many ancient people practiced controlled bloodletting to bring about such a state. This incapacitation of his physical body allowed his dreaming body to take command. The physical shock lowered Jesus' vital signs so quickly and completely that he appeared dead. The soldier pierced his side to confirm his death, and Jesus' body did not respond in any way. The soldier did not believe that he needed to foster death by breaking his bones. The two criminals that Jesus was crucified with had their bones broken because they were still very much alive. Once Jesus was removed from the cross and placed in the borrowed tomb, he was free to heal his body in dreaming and replenish his physical life force. Then he moved the stone away and revealed himself."

I suddenly remembered something from my studies in college. "Some scholars considered Jesus to be a magician or sorcerer," I said. "Sorcerers and magicians were a more tolerated part of society during that time. It's a tragedy that people today allow themselves to believe that shamanism is evil. It's one of the only surviving practices that retains any knowledge of our possibilities."

"Those people believe in evil because they are afraid of power and self-responsibility," Court said. "People who believe in evil are the ones who expect to be saved by someone or something else. They don't understand that all—and I do mean *all*—ancient religions were founded on the basis of salvation through the *self*. Salvation is not a passive mode; it is an active mode. Our religions today are all institutionalized. Men have declared that the only way to God is through the institution. Shamanism is, and has always been, an active mode based on the success of the self."

"The passages that you've been reading to me come from the Nag Hammadi library," I said, remembering more of my studies. "Nag Hammadi is in Egypt. Syrian-Egyptian Gnostic sects wrote the texts. Gnosticism is rooted in individual transcendence and direct contact with the Spirit. The Gnostics believed that Jesus was not confined to his body until death, but was free to do as he pleased. They believe that he was not present in his body at the time of his crucifixion, but was actually standing in the distance laughing at the ignorant crowds. It's theorized that Jesus spent his lost years studying in Egypt before he began his public teaching at about the age of thirty."

"Quite a few of the gospel passages bear an incredible resemblance to the magical writings of the shamans of his era," I continued, "such as the Spirit descending upon him as he was baptized, his withdrawal into the wilderness in order to be tempted, and the use of spittle as a healing substance. The Gospel of Mark exhibits telltale signs that passages regarding deeper truths have been removed from the text that we have today. Mark speaks of a young man wearing nothing but a linen sheet when Jesus was arrested. A young man wearing nothing but a linen sheet was common in secret initiations."

Court nodded. "Even more recent men, such as Carl Jung, spoke of salvation through the self–through the process of individuation–and believed that the unconscious is a source, like a well. Jung said that it is our purpose to draw as much as possible from this well and bring it into our consciousness in order to obtain more of life. He believed that the unconscious is the real entity and that our consciousness is the dream. He said that we should not be afraid to make mistakes, and that we must be detached from emotional ties that force obligations and constraints. His syntax was rooted in the language of psychology."

"So why and how did the disciples keep Jesus here in this world?" I asked. "Was it the power of their thoughts?"

"By appearing to have died on the cross, Jesus had successfully disconnected himself from his followers' beliefs about him," Court answered. "He had entered into uncharted territory where their minds had nothing to cling to, no system of beliefs to fall back on. When he appeared to the disciples after his death, he had become more powerful through the supreme manipulation of his dreaming body and physical body. He now had the power necessary to reveal his dreaming body to them. This, coupled with their shock over seeing him alive again, forced their perception to shut down and their dreaming bodies to *see*."

I then remembered a line from the gospels about how a prophet was honored everywhere, except in his hometown and by those he knew. I realized that by knowing the personal history of Jesus, his friends and family were unable to allow him to be anything other than a carpenter's son. It would've been impossible for him to completely reveal himself to them before his crucifixion because the fixation of their thoughts on his past had literally trapped him and kept him from becoming something more. He would have needed an unimaginable amount of energy to convince them that he was otherwise. His apparent death, however, shattered their limiting thoughts and beliefs.

"Remember how they all saw him bathed in radiant light?" Court asked. "That was the glow of his dreaming body that they were all seeing for the first time. A man of power strives in his lifetime to erase his personal history and to make himself unavailable to others in order to be free to leave this earth when he chooses. The power of other people's thoughts should not be underestimated, however. The longing and sadness of the disciples and close friends of Jesus was so powerful that he chose not to leave this earth immediately after his crucifixion. He says in *The Apocryphon of James* that he placed himself under the curse of remaining in physical form in order to help them be saved. He remained with them for almost a year and a half, teaching and encouraging them to fill themselves with power. Finally, he leaves them behind in order to strip himself of his physical body and clothe himself in the Unknown. James and Peter saw his dreaming body leave amidst a trumpet blare and great turmoil. They watched as his dreaming body consumed the energy of his physical body."

"I feel that a man of power like Jesus enlarges other peoples' perception by increasing the energy available for awareness," I said.

"Sometimes the proximity of a man of power is all that is required for perception to be enhanced," he replied. "The dreaming body of each human being is already connected to everyone and everything. It is a microcosm of the Unknown. The truth is that if we save enough energy we can actually enlarge our perception so that it can accommodate more of the energetic world as intuited by the dreaming body. We have limited our perception by our thoughts, beliefs, and expectations—we have gone from being at one with the universe as infants to being only aware of a miniscule portion of it as adults because of our socialization and fears. We are the ones who have limited our perception and ourselves." He looked at me. "As your energy increases and you vanquish your fear, your perception will increase."

We sat together in silence. The parrots upstairs were squawking madly as the sun went down. Court went upstairs to feed them and put them to bed. My whole body felt tight and focused. I felt a force pulsing inside of me. I sensed a core within that existed independently of my emotional turmoil. I wanted more of that force.

I suddenly remembered how I had struggled with my inability to find a path with heart. After college, I went to work as a purchasing assistant for a company that bought spare parts for the military. One day, I looked at the other two young people in my office and everything stopped. I was appalled that we were so consumed by our work when I knew that none of it mattered. I was in the present moment, and in that moment all that mattered was that there were three energetic beings gathered in a room together. We could be using our energy to bring ourselves closer to understanding our purpose in this world, or something useful. Instead, the three college graduates were spending eight hours a day trying to get vendors on the opposite side of the country to send us paper toilet seat liners and spare springs for toasters on battleships.

I spent almost fifteen years after that trying various jobs, thinking that it was just the type of work that was bothering me. Eventually, I realized that what was bothering me was that I had to shut down my heart energy center in order to put up with the monotony of the work I had selected. It was a way of keeping myself from remembering that joy was the primary reason for living and that there was no joy in the repetition that I had surrounded myself with. It was an excruciating and self-defeating feeling.

Once I had shut down my heart, it was much easier to continue day after day in the same old routine, internalizing my frustration in order to make a living and remain pleasant to others like myself. But my intention to find the right way of living continued despite my cowardice. The energy that I had, and the awareness that I had been cultivating, started screaming inside of me. At first, I behaved like most post-graduates did and went out and partied every chance I got. This only made me more tired and worn out. Even in my drunken stupors, however, I could *see* that what I was feeling and expressing was not true happiness. It was, instead, a reaction to being frustrated all day. It was an opening of the steam valve and an outpouring of the rage locked inside of me.

When my heart energy center was shut down or restricted, my energy backed up in both directions. Ideally, my energy should have flowed evenly through all of my energy centers, creating a very stable and solid feeling. But when my energy was pinched off at my heart, it built up both in my solar plexus and in my throat. This abundance of energy in my solar plexus created power issues that manifested as anger and frustration. This anger and frustration turned into antagonism towards myself, and then others. The abundance of energy in my throat energy center led to very vocal behavior—excessive laughter and noise.

Getting drunk was an easy way of releasing the overabundance of energy in these two centers, but did not remedy the shutting down of my heart energy center. It was the experience of working in dozens of jobs that allowed me to understand this, not with my mind, but with my dreaming body. It was then that I realized that I had to live a path with heart. Otherwise, I was destined to grow old and develop all of the typical diseases that plagued the people who had given up.

As I sat there remembering all of this, it occurred to me that energy flowing in an unrestricted manner throughout my body would create a situation where no single emotion was favored above another. Tranquility, not happiness, would be my ultimate condition. All emotions would be equal. I saw that tranquility was joy—a state of being in which energy flowed through my body without restriction. It was creativity. This was the creativity that would lead to my fulfillment. It was a creativity that would allow me to develop my dreaming body and its hidden resources, and allow me to experience something other than this daily drudgery.

Court came down after awhile, turned on his lamp and sat down. I immediately tackled him with my realizations. He said that my realizations were the result of my dreaming body's need to fulfill itself. Our conversation, he said, had stirred the available energy inside of me. Now my dreaming body wanted to take advantage of that opportunity. It wanted to correct my faulty perception regarding my selection of a path with heart. It was going to fulfill itself with or without me.

"Hearing about a man of power like Jesus reminds something inside of me that a real path with heart is possible," I said. "I've never been comfortable or solid in any other capacity except with the energy that we're embracing now. I have struggled since graduating from college with how to make my path with heart come to life. How did Jesus and those like him do it? How did you do it?"

"You cannot just consider or talk about a path with heart," Court replied. "You must pursue it against all odds. If something rings true for you, then nothing and no one will be able to keep you from it. I am not afraid to live my Truth."

"Do not subscribe to the notion that your life work is something that must be contrary to your heart," he continued. "Living a path with heart colors your world with joy. You become one with your path instead of at odds with it. You become light instead of heavy. The joy motivates you and cuts through fear. It invigorates you and adds incalculable happiness and flavor to your life. The Spirit wants us to enjoy prosperity and fulfillment but we fight with it constantly. We choose to live in lack."

"Fear can stop you cold from engaging the energy necessary to stand up and take charge of your life, and not be a victim of unseen powers," he said. "Being a victim is a choice, not a position that is assigned to you by some mysterious force. Defy your fear! One day you will be on your deathbed and you will have to face the fact that the only one who has determined the outcome of your life was you. Do you want to be responsible for a wasted lifetime? Do you want to be face-to-face with the realization that you allowed your fears to keep you from everything fulfilling in your life? Do you want to realize that you have been nothing more than a coward who wasted his energy creating excuses for why he never did the things that could've fortified his heart and therefore been a source of encouragement and inspiration for everyone else that he came into contact with?"

"You believe and expect that everything should become perfect when you make one paltry attempt at correcting your flaws," he hammered. "That's childish. Don't be so black and white in your expectations and perception. Your self-image is killing you. Look at how you want to give up if you can't do something perfectly the first time! That is your false-self wanting to always look good in front of others. People might ridicule you. You might look stupid. You might become embarrassed and stop trying. Then, to save face, you will blame forces outside of your control. But nothing is outside of your control. You just *can't* be afraid to learn. Screw everybody else! Look like an idiot, and don't give a damn about what they think of you. Learn everything that you possibly can in order to find fulfillment. Take the time to start completely over, if necessary. Push yourself and persist, and eventually you will prevail. Your life and freedom are an investment. Every penny of energy that you put into this investment will eventually add up. Do it for yourself. So what if it takes a lifetime? Do you have something better to do?"

He looked at me with a penetrating stare. I automatically recoiled. "What have you got to lose?" he queried. "You're already unhappy. You are already full of fear."

I was stunned. I sat there silently. And as I did so, I could feel a thick presence in my heart. It was a strangely pleasant mixture of coldness and heat, and the more I accepted the responsibility for my life and my current situation, the stronger it became. I had always been silently aware of the fact that I was the only one keeping myself down. I was aware, too, that a lot of my false starts and rapid decisions to make life-altering changes were the result of realizing that I was not following a path with heart. But in the back of my mind I recognized that I had known all along what my path with heart had been. I had simply been wasting time trying to get to it quickly by cutting corners and by not doing the work necessary to correct my imperfections in order to appear better than I really was. I had not allowed myself to express or feel the joy of spontaneity like other people did in order to feel superior to them. My arrogance and pride wanted me to stand out in a crowd, not because I worked hard and excelled at something, but because I did the things that no one else wanted to do. I saw how I had avoided committing myself to the effort and time necessary to make the changes. I had been irresponsible. I lacked focus and persistence.

"It seems like there is always something in the way, or something that I must take care of before I can begin," I said quietly.

"You give up when you should hustle!" He was adamant. "You can't wait for the perfect moment because there will never be one. The path with heart will always be fraught with excuses–the 'should haves' and 'could haves'. Stop using your brain to find your path and simply trust the Unknown–the feeling that resonates within your heart and bowels. Don't question *how* it will happen! Instead, focus all of your energy on the *intention*, and then the Spirit will see that your intention is solid and real and will show you the way. Just do it, and you will suddenly find yourself in the midst of it–the means will suddenly materialize."

"I've tried so many times to get started on my path but I always seem to run out of money," I griped. "I'll save up some money or borrow it to give myself time to get things rolling, but it always seems like my timing is wrong."

"That's because you're always looking for a safety net or some backup plan in case you fail. Don't you see? You fail before you even get started. That's what *trying* is. Trying is not *doing*. Tell me, why did you find it necessary to have a backup plan of some kind?"

"In case I didn't make it," I said slowly as I looked into his eyes. They were calm and powerful.

"If you believe fully in yourself you won't even think about having a backup plan," he stated quietly. "If you really know in your heart that you are doing the right thing, there will be no doubt. If there is doubt, then either it is the wrong path or you are not ready. Your fear is what makes you doubt yourself, and it is this fear that you must overcome first. This fear makes you look for security. The need of a safety net says that you don't believe that you can make it. That creates a self-fulfilling prophecy. If there's no question in your mind then you will proceed as though you've already made it." He paused briefly, and then continued.

"Power only acknowledges power. The Spirit only recognizes action. If you don't invest energy you won't receive energy. When you make a complete energetic commitment to yourself and your path, you have invested energy. But the decision must be final. Making a decision is one of the most difficult things you will ever do. You cannot look back if it is truly a final decision because you will have altered your life forever. If you don't commit one hundred percent then you are not committed, and your energy will not be there to back you up."

"Once you have made the decision, then you can take the first step—and it must be just as strong. The boldness of that step will release hidden reservoirs of strength and create forward momentum. Your dreaming body will be activated. Only a fool would approach power filled with fear. In the world of predators, one who is full of fear will run away until he believes in himself. Otherwise, the more powerful predator will steal his power—his life. When you have vanquished your doubts and fears through smaller challenges and have established a solid connection to your path and allowed your power to rise up within you, then you will enter the arena of power to claim that which is rightfully yours. Then you will dominate, or at least be accepted as an equal."

His words made me feel strong inside. I liked that feeling. I did not like being less than I was capable of. "I see that my own inferior thoughts, beliefs, and expectations have kept me from my true path."

"Not only that, but you have failed to remember that the means does not justify the end. You can't get to a path with heart by pursuing a contrary path! Your thinking says that you should keep all options open and not close any doors. But you can't do that. You can't live a path with heart by doing something that you hate in order to get there, because the path that you tread *is your path*. You *have* to close doors–you *have* to turn your back on the things that don't bring you fulfillment. Otherwise, your intention will not be clear and your energy will not be focused on your goal. You will spend years chasing your own tail. You either are what you're meant to be, or you're a fake. You either focus on the Spirit or you don't. There is no in-between. There is no process to get from where you are to where you want to be. If you want to be something else, then change. If you say that you will gradually become what you wish to be then you are fooling yourself. The process of becoming is an illusion. Progress is an illusion."

"Isn't taking a step, or a series of steps, the process of becoming?" I asked.

"The process of becoming *what?*" he retorted. "The process of becoming a concept, an idea in your little brain? That is the illusion. If you are aware of something, you *feel* it in your body, not in your mind. You can *act* on that feeling. It is your awareness that dictates what you are capable of at any given moment. You can't act on something that you don't feel. Do you see? You are aware and you feel it. You hook yourself to that feeling and act. Suddenly, you are a different person. There was no process. Awareness is power; thoughts are not. A path with heart requires no thought."

I stopped talking because the force of that power consumed me. I knew that this power was deliberate and intentional. I knew instantaneously that I could command that power if, and only if, I let it command me. It didn't make any sense to my mind, but my body knew exactly what it meant. I felt a sudden shiver.

"Why is freedom so frightening?" I asked.

"Because there is nothing and no one restraining you," he replied. "There is no energetic tension. We are so unbelievably secure when we feel restricted. This entire world that we live in is structured that way. But in some ways it's necessary, otherwise we would blast off into infinity the moment we were born. We need these challenges in order to grow. We learn to recognize what is false, and by doing that we find the Truth." He looked at me sideways. "You are energy. You alone have decided what that energy is capable of based on your thoughts and fears. If those thoughts and fears are limiting you, then change them. You have everything that you need already."

"Then why do so many gurus say that you can find happiness in any situation, even in a miserable one, if you're centered inside?" I asked.

"Because they have never lived on their own and under their own means in our day-to-day society. Other people give them money, food, and the other things that they need to live. They have not experienced the fears associated with being fully self-dependent in this world—of having to *fight* to make a living in this world *and* pursue a path with heart. They are already secure. They are living a path that makes their followers and themselves perceptually complacent."

"Some of them, however, are genuinely following their path with heart," Court continued, "but are not aware of how injurious it is to be anywhere other than on a true path."

"Why aren't they aware of that?" I asked.

"Because they have never experienced any other path. They don't understand the tremendous sadness that exists in an office full of people who have already shut down their heart energy centers. They have never experienced the force of that negative energy pattern over the course of days, months, and years. They aren't aware of how it slowly eats away at your strength, bit by bit. They don't realize that there is no happiness away from your true essence, no peace. But we must also remember that the people in those offices have *chosen* to be there, and the gurus have not."

He paused for a moment. "Being happy wherever you are has nothing to do with some phony ideal of being centered inside," he said. "It's that line of reasoning that leads so many astray. You are *not* happy inside if you're *not* following your heart. That is a fact. Living what is in your heart is what makes you happy wherever you are."

Court stared outside into the darkness and listened as an owl began hooting. The sound of it resonated closely on the nighttime coastal fog. "Do not be trapped by belief in mistakes. There aren't any. Nothing is a waste. There are no wrong choices. Everything that you have learned from your random adventures in this world will be useful to you here and in your dreaming. Clinging to your mistakes comes from fear of failure, fear of looking stupid around your peers—there's that damn self-image again! If you let other peoples' opinions about you hold you back then you are dead before you are in the ground. Let the past go free. Then your mistakes become lessons on a never-ending journey to freedom."

"This world is the training and proving ground for other worlds that you will encounter in lucid dreaming," he continued. "An infant is not given a ship and sent off to sail around the world. It has to learn how to walk and talk and fight and feed itself and take a crap over the side without falling into the ocean. You have to learn how to function and survive in this world, first. Then you can sail off on other adventures in dreaming. This world is like a safety valve to protect you from your own ignorance and stupidity. If you can't survive in this world, you won't survive in any other. If you can't behave in this world, you won't be allowed to endanger another. So many people choose to live a miserable life here, and then want to go to sleep and have wonderful adventures in heaven. They are completely missing the frigging point! You have to intend *this life* to perfection before you can find happiness anywhere else. If you can't accomplish anything in this dream, what makes you think that you can accomplish anything in any other dream? You must pursue your dreams here and now—you must accept your birthright—you must make this world work first. You can make as many mistakes as you want provided you don't get old and die in the meantime. If you keep your eyes open you will learn, and you will gather weapons and knowledge from every adventure that you undertake. Nothing will be wasted."

"Always make sure, however, that you take care of your physical body," Court said. "It is your vehicle in this manifestation. How would you like to go to the moon in a dysfunctional ship? Tune up and perfect this vehicle, this body, first. Experience the earth, go barefoot outside, dig a hole, plant a garden, lie on your back and watch the clouds float by, fly a kite, and stop your internal dialogue—your thoughts. Relax and enjoy your adventure. The time to live is now."

He reached out for his yellowed book and flipped through the pages. "This passage is from Thomas:

> *If you do not observe the Sabbath as a Sabbath you will not see the Father.*

"The Sabbath is a day of rest. Rest is just as important as eating to the body because rest brings calm and quiet. You will only see the Spirit and your path with heart if you rest, if you allow silence into your life. People want to rest, but are afraid to. They're afraid that their world will come apart. And they are right—it will come apart. Here's another:

> *They said to Jesus, "Come, let us pray today, and let us fast."*
> *Jesus said, "What sin have I committed, or how*

have I been undone? When the groom leaves the bridal suite, then let people fast and pray."

"He is also saying that punishing your body is wrong. Experience the joy of living *while you are alive*. You will find what you are looking for if you follow your heart." He winked at me. I nodded. "I know. I forget that a lot," I said. We sat in silence for a few minutes while he thumbed through the *Tao Te Ching*. He cleared his throat and read:

> *He who devotes himself to learning seeks from day to day to increase his knowledge; he who devotes himself to the Tao seeks from day to day to diminish his doing.*
>
> *He diminishes it and again diminishes it, till he arrives at doing nothing. Having arrived at this point of non-action, there is nothing which he does not do.*

LELA'S SHADOW

Now for you there is no rain
For one is shelter to the other.
Now for you there is no darkness
For one is counsel to the other.
Now for you there is no pain
For one is comfort to the other.
Now for you there is no night
For one is light to the other.
Now for you there is no cold
For one is warmth to the other.

Now for you the snow has ended always
Your fears, your wants, your needs at rest
It is that way—today, tomorrow, forever.

Now it is good and there is always shelter
And now there is always warmth
And now there is always comfort.

Now there is no loneliness
Now, forever, forever, you are as one.
There are two bodies
but there is one heart in both of them
And you are the same person.

-Apache Wedding Ceremony-

A couple of weeks later, I returned to Court's house. It had been raining for three days straight. The ground was saturated with water and glistened in the amber glow of the street lamp. I could still feel the weight of the thunderheads above even though I could not see them in the blackness of the night. Their pressure pushed me deep inside of myself, closer still to the indomitable mystery. The faraway flickering lights in the heavens told me that this was going to be an irrevocable night.

As I approached his front gate, I could smell the sweet aroma of the water-laden banana and pine trees in his front yard. There were no lights on in the front room, but I knew that he was home. I paused for a moment just below the front steps and breathed in and out. I deeply cherished moments like this when there was not a trace of doubt inside of myself. I felt united and unbroken, instead of at odds within. My purpose was clear.

I slowly walked up the steps as I listened to the melodious ringing of the small, metal wind chime in a gust of that humbling wind. I reached up to knock, but stopped. I did not want to disturb anything. I sensed that I was nothing more than a receptacle, a chalice, and that my role was to appreciate with the awareness of my soul the unquestionable perfection of this peerless dream. I inhaled, filling every bit of my being with the Unknown, and then knocked softly.

A few minutes later, Carol shuffled up in her sheepskin slippers and opened the door. She greeted me warmly, and said that Court was in his drawing room working madly on a piece of scratch art. He had been this way for almost two weeks, hunched over his drawing table, not even ten inches away from another masterpiece. He would stay up until three or four o'clock in the morning she said, go to bed for a few hours, and then return to the piece. This one was called, *Smug One*, and was a reminder about pride and the fall that awaited him, should he indulge in it. Its purpose was to help him remember to nurture his newborn self-esteem like a seedling.

He peered at me over his glasses and decided to take a break.

He pulled up two chairs in the small, crowded room. The light on the ceiling was shrouded with some pinkish-red fabric. He closed the door and opened the window while he lit his clove cigarette. It was raining outside quite peacefully now. He changed his stereo to the classical station and we sat down. I could feel the presence come into the room, almost as if it had come in through the window or was stored in the smoke. A piece was playing on the classical station that I had never heard before. It was entitled, *The Lark Ascending*, by Ralph Vaughan Williams. The mood became absolutely indescribable.

We sat in silence while the presence thickened and moved through us. I felt transported to another place and time–something ancient–something mysterious. Court stood up to go and help Carol in the kitchen and I got out of my chair to let him by. He reached out and put his hands on the sides of my head and pulled my head towards his. The room vanished as he kissed me on the lips.

"I have been waiting for this moment since the first time I saw you," he whispered. "We have known each other so many times in so many other lives and we have been so very, very close. Tonight it is right."

My body was absolutely electrified. Something inside of me was pulsing and ringing. This friend of mine and I were older than time. I felt a long lost connection to him and the energy that was on fire inside of me pulled me backwards into the fog. I slipped out of this dream and felt the countless times that we had been together before.

I found myself back in Court's drawing room. He stared at me with untold affection while he continued to hold my head in his hands. I looked deeply into his eyes and my heart swelled within my chest. I saw that we were lovers in the truest sense. We hugged each other, and then he went to help Carol in the kitchen.

I slowly sat back down. The emotion of the moment had stirred up hidden memories, memories of a lost love that had abruptly ended just a few years ago. I suddenly found myself walking along Dockweiler beach late at night. Dockweiler beach was just outside of Los Angeles International Airport, and was the beach that the airliners flew in over when arriving. As the huge passenger jets flew in low and slow over the water with their landing lights on, the ocean lit up like a vat of black oil with silvery ripples in it. The nighttime fog made the whole scene into an eerie illusion.

As I walked along the beach that night, the Spirit told me that the woman I was looking for had a first name that began with the letter "L". I waited for almost three years for the woman to appear.

Court walked back into the room and I emerged from my remembrance. He smiled at me and said, "Affection is beyond the reach of time. Perhaps it is the only energy that can travel at will alongside our life force." He cleared his throat. "I think I've distracted you from the purpose of your visit, though."

I was still in a daze, but managed to rearrange my thoughts and feelings. "I wanted to find out more about Lela, the woman I almost married," I said. "The whole event has taken me years to recapitulate and unravel. I want to know why it happened. What was her power over me and where did it come from?"

He looked out the window at the distant lightning.

"How did you meet her?" he asked me.

I told Court that I had been participating in a discussion group that met weekly in West Los Angeles. We usually sat around and engaged in dull discussions about the works of a famous author that I hoped to meet someday. That fall, the man that ran the group called each of us and announced that he had succeeded in getting the author to come and give a lecture at his apartment. I was very excited–I was going to see the author in the flesh. He was coming to where I was.

On the afternoon of the lecture I was standing in the entryway of the man's apartment, hoping to introduce myself to the author when he came in. The door opened and I waited intently. Instead of the author, however, three women walked in. My attention was immediately riveted to the last one. As she walked by me, I felt something punch me in the solar plexus. It felt as though she had reached out with her hand and slapped me just above my stomach. Then she smiled and said hello. I was completely consumed by her and immediately began perspiring. She was very exotic looking, with lustrous brown shoulder-length hair, bold blue eyes, and creamy Hawaiian skin. She had very firm, yet sensuous lips, a voluptuous body, and intense energy. I was instantly hooked.

I had to laugh at the irony of the situation because her presence distracted me through the whole of the author's lecture. After waiting all this time to meet the great man, there was a distraction in the room. If only I'd known how true this would turn out to be.

Court smiled as if he knew the whole story already. "You must have known early on that this was going to be a stormy relationship. What a twist! Your intention delivers the great author right into your presence. But just before he arrives, the Spirit throws a monkey wrench at you!" He laughed in spurts.

"I guess at the time I thought that it was a coincidence," I said.

"There are no coincidences!" he exclaimed. "Energy attracts energy. She was sent to test you. The Spirit wanted to know if you were ready to move forward as a man of power, or if you still needed further lessons and clarifications. The Spirit was testing you to see if you had relinquished your own agenda—your own desires—or if you were still selfishly motivated. The Spirit wanted to know if you had gotten out of the way yet."

"How can you possibly arrive at that conclusion when I haven't even begun my story?" I asked defensively.

"It wasn't obvious to you at the time because you were on the inside—you were about to *become* the lesson," Court replied. "If you would've seen what was happening at the moment that you met her, you wouldn't have needed the lesson. It's only obvious to me because I've already been tested in a similar fashion. I have seen how the Spirit tests men."

"Why does it test them?" I asked.

"The Spirit tests men to see if they are ready to listen and follow its lead. Men of power are only given the keys to unlock the mysteries if they are free from selfish motivations. You tried to force the Spirit to accept this woman as part of his plan for you. You just can't do that. If you are not clear inside about your intentions, then you will be drawn into a lesson–you will become the lesson in order to see that which is hidden from your awareness. If you keep your eyes open during the lesson, then the debris that clouds your vision will be removed and you will see yourself clearly. Maybe *too* clearly." He chuckled annoyingly to himself.

"I do remember how I had the opportunity early on to let her go and to see an aspect of myself that I was unaware of," I said. "We had an enormous fight on the telephone and she hung up on me. I spent an entire day debating about whether or not to accept her shortcomings or to just walk away. I almost walked away. But I was too motivated by my lust and fear of loss. I lusted after her intense power because I didn't have enough of my own, and I was afraid of never experiencing the sex of an erotic woman if I let her go. So I tried to possess her."

"The Spirit packed your relationship full of lessons," Court said. "You came away with an abundance of power because you kept your eyes open. Every event, every moment in our lives is chalked full of opportunities–even more so if we make a decision that promotes the self above the Unknown. The Spirit wants us to learn. Now, finish your story."

I told Court that my relationship with Lela was difficult from the beginning. When we weren't covered in the sweat of sex, we might as well have been in a boxing ring. She was three years younger, but very set in her ways. She held onto her past with all of her strength, and it created a palpable density in all of her muscles. She was five pounds heavier and just a hair taller, but she did not look fat or even stocky. Lela's power over me was unquestionable. She was a maverick. Her power extended to all men, and women either hated or admired her.

I thought that she wanted the same things out of life that I did and I told her about my intentions to become a man of power. Because she listened so intently and seemed to agree with my plans, I thought that she would become my ally and release her excess emotional baggage. It quickly became evident, though, that she did not intend to let go of her past without a fight. But I had tons of strength and thought that we would unite under a common purpose. I thought that I could see a light at the end of the tunnel.

On one of our first dates, she took me on a nighttime hike to some rocks in the hills just north of Los Angeles. It was a perfect fall evening with a three-quarter moon, and we climbed slowly up the trail as the last of the gray blackness bade the earth goodnight. We were both a little uncomfortable, our relationship still being in its early stages. At one point I stopped, because something beckoned me to my left up a hill. It turned out to be a shortcut to the rock formations that she was taking me to for the first time.

When we arrived at the rocky peak, I noticed a giant rock that was shaped like a bird's head with the base of its beak level to the ground. It had a wind hole where its eye would naturally be, and in the waxing moonlight it was ominous. I walked over and sat up on the beak, and saw that over the left side was a substantial drop-off. Lela came up to where I was and then slid backwards on her rear along a channel on the right side that went into the eyehole. We both sat for a while, staring into the blackness.

"Why don't you try this spot out," she said with her deep, full voice. She slid out of the eyehole and I backed in, and then she went wandering.

I slid carefully inside the round hole and realized that it was perfectly sized. My back and legs fit exactly into the grooves of the cool rock, and my head was an inch from the top of the hole. It was very soothing. I relaxed in the calm night air and looked around at the city lights below.

After a short while, she called up to me. "Come on, let's go exploring." She took me to the various formations, and then invited me down inside a cozy hole that was in-between two giant rocks. I realized after a few moments that these two rocks extended out over a sheer cliff, and that there was a narrow slit in the side of one that looked out over the city. We sat together inside the hole for quite a while, admiring the view and each other in various tender and yielding ways.

Slowly, we relaxed and climbed out of the hole. She pulled two ripe peaches and a bottle of sage tea out of her backpack, cut the peaches, and fed the pieces to me with her warm, sensual fingers.

"This is quite a place," I said fondly to her as I licked the sweet juice off of my lips.

"Yes, I love it here," she replied. "I love to wander around in the night air and feel the earth."

I looked into her intense eyes and smiled. She smiled back. Our mutual attraction was unmistakable. After we finished eating, I rubbed her neck and shoulders while she sat in front of me.

"Let's go over to that next hill," I said. "I feel something pulling me."

We walked a short distance in the moonlight to the hill and stood there embracing each other. I was completely absorbed by my feelings for her, and the smell of her skin and hair stirred the depths of me.

Suddenly, I heard something snap nearby, and I turned my head sharply towards the sound.

"What is it?" she said with alarm.

I was disturbed and my body quickly filled with nervous energy.

"I'm not sure," I said warily.

I began to pace and hop around. Abruptly, someone with a

deep voice said, "It's coming." I realized that it was my voice, but it was very far away. Then, out of the corner of my eye, I saw the dark shape of a bird spring from the nearby rocks. It flew powerfully across my field of vision from right to left and vanished. Chills went up my spine into my head.

"That didn't feel like a bird," I said.

"If it wasn't a bird, then what was it?" she whispered hoarsely.

I was now thoroughly alarmed. What happened next sent my body into waves of uncontrollable spasms. To the absolute bafflement of my rational mind, I witnessed an enormous bird shadow emerge from the valley on my right, its wings fully extended on a sideways flight. It eerily soared along the same path as the previous bird, passing directly between the moon and us. It continued on up into the sky and landed right over the eyehole where we had been sitting earlier. Lela and I froze on the spot as we watched this silently threatening display. My eyes had seen something familiar, but my body had registered a solid black mass that resembled a four-foot long flying carpet. It was huge and slow, and very dark.

"Look," said Lela. "It's on top of the eye. It's a coyote."

I did not see a coyote, though what I saw was certainly as large as one. It was taller than the hole below it.

"It's watching us," I said. I was still trembling inside.

I suddenly had the overpowering urge to run towards it. I knew however, beyond a shadow of a doubt, that doing so would be a deadly mistake. I stayed where I was, tightly holding onto Lela while it silently watched us. Then, it crouched down and leapt up into the sky, shooting to the left into the darkness.

"I think we'd better leave now," I said urgently.

"I agree." She was shaking. "What time is it?"

"I think it's just before midnight." We left quickly, and the clock in the car read 11:51 p.m.

Court was staring past me into the darkness. "Power was following you from the beginning. It sensed that your relationship with her had extreme potential." He turned his eyes toward me and said, "Were you ever able to see the source of her power?"

"What do you mean by 'the source of her power'?" I asked. He seemed to be hinting at something.

"Did you ever notice anything unusual about her when you *saw* her?"

I thought back through my memories.

"About a month later, we were sitting in my room at night after we had finished dinner," I answered. "I found myself staring at her absentmindedly. I was slipping in and out of a trance…"

"What are you staring at?" rang Lela's sultry voice.

"I was just watching your face change shapes, and I saw many different faces that felt like they were from your past," I said to her. "Some were younger versions of you, and some seemed like other faces that you may have had during other lifetimes." I was still staring at her. Then a bubble of awareness burst inside of me and I felt a voice talking. The voice spoke to me.

"Those are the faces of her past lives or past incarnations." That comment seemed odd to me because I didn't believe in reincarnation for individual souls. In the past, I had seen that once a soul died, it journeyed to join other souls like itself, breaking apart into energetic units as it did so. These groups of souls were called entities, and thousands of these entities existed outside of this time and space. The souls within each of these entities were all related energetically, like a family. Each of the energetic units from every individual soul had its own unique awareness and energetic history. In death, those fragments, or units, were then rejoined with the other energetic units from other souls within that particular entity. In this state, they composed a single, unified awareness, and all of their individual life experiences enhanced the overall awareness of the entity. The individual soul ceased to exist as an independent awareness, and now existed as pieces of a larger awareness within its entity.

When a new person was born into this world, energy was selected from the available pool of energetic units stored within that entity, depending on the combined energy of the parents and other circumstances. If the parents had tremendous energy, then they attracted stronger energetic units from the entity, and vice versa. Thus, each new human being had an assortment of energetic units from various individuals and various lifetimes.

I told all of this to Lela.

"If that's true, then why do we have flashbacks of our past lives?" she asked.

"Sometimes, a group of these various energetic units have experienced tremendous emotional events in a past life and are still joined together by the energy of that event," I said. "This is what creates the flashbacks, and is also why we never have long sequences of memories."

"But we recognize people all the time that we seem to have known from other lifetimes," she said.

"These people carry with them energetic units that were once associated with some of the energetic units in us in some other lifetime," I said. "That's why we recognize them. But our past-life memories are always incomplete, aren't they?"

"That's true," she said reluctantly. "Are you saying that there is no way to escape this dissolution when we die—that we are trapped in this cycle?"

"We can escape this cycle by gathering enough energy and intending an alternative to having our awareness dissolved back into the entity at death."

"That's a nice idea, but I don't believe it," she countered. "I think that we are souls that live forever, and that we are reincarnated in order to enhance our own awareness on our path to enlightenment."

"Then why don't we remember longer sequences of events from past lives?" I asked. "It seems to me that we would retain some type of continuity. Maybe we would only remember bits and pieces, but they should have some kind of common mood or setting. None of my memories have a common mood—none of them have any continuity, whatsoever. When I look at you, I feel like I knew you from a lifetime colored with dark browns and greens–a time of great sadness and longing. But if I'm walking through an antique store and I see anything related to World War II Germany, I feel a tremendous surge of great power and white heat. The two memories are completely disjointed and make no sense together. They aren't sequential at all."

"Maybe those are different past lives for you," she said.

"Maybe I'm simply tapping into the history of the thousands of past lives stored in my entity, a history that anyone from my entity can access," I replied.

She shrugged her shoulders and stared at me, and I reentered my trance-like state. As I watched the various faces of Lela coming and going, I saw masses of blackness. It wasn't the color black, but was more like a vortex or an absence of light that gave the appearance of black. I wondered why there was no color to it, no hue like I had seen in other peoples' auras.

Court got up and stretched, and we moved into the front room. He sat in his old, overstuffed armchair and I opted for the one by the window.

"Remember the time you and Lela found Carol and I at the restaurant?" he asked me.

"Yes, that was really incredible," I replied.

"You never told me how that came about."

"Lela came over for dinner one evening," I said. "We were supposed to be going out, but we hadn't decided where we were going. As we were sitting in my room, I was overcome with a thread of intention."

"What do you mean by 'a thread'?" Court asked me.

"Whenever I feel something or someone pull on me, I call it a thread. It feels literally like a thread of energy connected to my will, just below my navel. This thread was coming from you and I knew that it was time to take Lela to meet you. She was hesitant, though."

"Why?" he asked.

"Because she was jealous of my admiration for you and also because I had been in love with Carol before. She swallowed her fear, though, and we left."

I told Court that this might have been an ordinary story, except that Lela and I had to stop at the store and go to the bank before getting on the freeway during rush hour traffic to make the two-hour drive to Court's town.

"When we neared your town," I said, "I felt your presence at a restaurant that you and I had been to once before. I parked the car, and Lela and I walked one block over to the restaurant. The thread was pounding inside of me now, and as we walked through the front door we saw you and Carol being served your dinner at a table with four chairs."

"I saw you coming towards us," Court said. "I felt such an overpowering surge of energy. We all burst into laughter, then. Everyone was shaking from the power of the event. Carol even excused herself to go to the bathroom because she couldn't stop laughing. We could hear her nervous giggling all the way into the bathroom."

"Moments like that are such powerful reminders of the connection that exists between all living beings," I said thoughtfully.

Just then, the front door of Court's house flew open and Carol walked in, damp from the rain. She had left to get some groceries while we were in Court's drawing room. Court and I greeted her, but she was visibly upset.

"What's bothering you, Carol?" I asked.

"I was driving home along the back road and there was this pickup in front of me," she said angrily. She was trying to control herself. "There were two guys in it. As we came around a sharp curve, I saw a rabbit sitting in the middle of the road ahead of them. It was blinded by their headlights and temporarily frozen with fear. I hit my brakes because I knew that they were going to have to stop quickly to avoid hitting the rabbit. You know what those bastards did? They sped up and swerved towards the rabbit!" She was shaking now.

I didn't say anything. I sat there quietly because the story seemed to be over.

Carol continued. "Then the most incredible thing happened. The rabbit squatted really low and twisted his body so forcefully that it looked like he ejected himself right out from under the car tire. He flew off the road and down into the bushes, completely unscathed. I couldn't believe my eyes. I felt like running those jerks off the road, but I knew that I had just witnessed a feat of personal power."

She excused herself to get ready for bed. Her story unearthed a sequence of memories and I narrated them to Court.

One evening, just before sunset, I was returning to my condo in the Burbank hills after going to a lecture at a bookstore in Santa Monica. I was driving up the long, winding hill before the tennis courts when I saw a small bird flailing about in the middle of my lane. I swerved to miss him and quickly looked in my rearview mirror to make sure that I hadn't run him over. He was still trying to fly with what seemed to be a broken wing, and other cars were driving right over him without giving it a second thought. I was very disturbed by the bird's situation and his helplessness, but as I continued up the hill I tried to comfort myself by remembering a story that I had heard of a person who had worsened the fate of a snail by removing it from a sidewalk. The story said that the outcome of such a situation was determined by one's personal power, and that the fate of the snail had been worsened because someone with less personal power had interfered with it. I decided to allow the bird to discover his own fate. However, I just couldn't shake my discomfort.

As I approached my driveway, the feeling of discomfort intensified. I swung the car around and drove quickly back down the hill. I fully expected to see the bird squashed in the road where I had left him, but he was sitting there very quietly. I pulled up behind him so that no one would hit either of us and parked the car in the middle of the street. I got out and walked up to him. He was very frightened, and was trembling and panting heavily. Twice, I tried clumsily to pick him up, but he fluttered and fell back down to the ground. But then I let go of my fear and he allowed me to pick him up. I held him gently in my hands and I realized that we were talking to each other. It was a feeling that my brain was at a loss to describe.

During our 'conversation,' people kept driving up the hill and swerving around my car in a very exaggerated fashion, acting like they couldn't see us. I could feel their anger at being inconvenienced and their attempts to bully me, but it didn't matter now. I was in a different time and place.

I took the bird to some shrubbery in an elevated planter next to the sidewalk, and set him on a ground vine. Then I stroked his head. I remembered that as a child I had always had a silent wish. I wished that if I was dying and there was nothing left to be done, that someone would take me and lay me on my back in an open field. There, I would stare up at the vastness of the blue sky. I would feel the presence of the earth and the flight of the cool wind on my face, and find comfort and strength. I remembered that this feeling had resurfaced after the death of my uncle who was found lying beside his grape vines, pruning shears in hand.

As I walked away from the bird, I wished him well and hoped that I had not interfered with his life in a careless way. Then, I felt a twinge, like a unit of awareness coming from the bird. It felt like he had asked me what he could do for me in return for my gesture. I looked back at him, and asked him for the same help if I ever needed it. I asked him to teach me to fly again, as I had done in my childhood dreams. I went back to my car and back to my home.

A few months later, I was returning to Burbank from a trip to Arizona where I had met Lela. We had been driving all night and I was utterly exhausted. I had just finished driving her back to the Los Angeles airport to pick up her car, and that had added another forty-five minutes to my trip. It was almost six o'clock in the morning and the sun was going to be coming up soon. I was driving frantically down the freeway and constantly drifting off to sleep. I had both windows rolled down, the stereo on full-blast, and was chewing anxiously on an old drinking straw that I had found in the glove compartment. I had put myself in the middle lane of the freeway so that if I dozed off again I would hit the raised lane dividers and get awakened. The last thing I remembered was being at home, in bed with my pillow, all curled up.

It was so nice to be home in bed. Everything was so peaceful and still except for the police officer that was leaning over my bed and hurting my eyes with the heat of his flashlight. If only he would leave me alone! I reached up to put my hand over the light when I suddenly realized that my pillow was actually my steering wheel and that I was still driving on the freeway! There was a truck right behind me, flashing his high beams on and off. The driver was experienced enough to know that sounding his horn would've been dangerous. As the gravity of the situation hit me, I caught a glimpse of a little bird driving the truck in my rearview mirror. I did a double take and felt the bird's presence. This was the return of the favor. I waved at the bird driving the truck, and returned home to my real bed, thankful and bewildered.

Court went upstairs to say goodnight to Carol. They did not share the same bedroom. My recapitulative trance was producing a stream of memories now. Court came back down and saw where I was. He made a comment.

"In the story of the snail on the sidewalk, it was the snail's fate that someone with less personal power had crossed its path. That means that the man that moved the snail didn't have the personal power at that time to make such a decision for the snail. You, however, had enough power at the time to make that decision for the bird. So accept it. Let's continue with Lela."

I told him that one month later, I met Lela again in Arizona and took her to the airport there to catch a flight to Europe. She was meeting some friends there to discuss a business deal. After dropping her off in the early afternoon, I began the eleven-hour drive back to southern California. It was one of those warm, late winter afternoons in the desert, and I was tired again.

Lela and I had been up all night fighting. She had an undying compulsion to gather the attention of other men, and she tested me constantly around them to see if I was strong enough to withstand their intention to take her away from me. I indulged in self-pity on almost every occasion and became weaker on a daily basis. Our fights were a result of my inability to be solid under her onslaughts. When I was strong she was my partner, but when I was weak she would take what little strength I had left.

Court had told me over the phone at that time that women feel a constant fear of loss when they are around their male sexual partners. Lela was always afraid of losing me, although she never would have admitted it. Instead, her insecurity spurred her to constantly seek the lustful admiration of men just to make sure she always had someone to turn to in case I failed. I discovered during these events that jealousy is very real, and that she could intend fear into me by flaunting her energy outwardly in a surreptitious manner. I realized that the idea of being unaffected by jealousy was a farce. The real issue was maintaining my own energetic integrity and focus on the Spirit so as not to be concerned with her behavior. When I did that, Lela was my cohort. When I did not, she was energy on the prowl.

As I drifted off to sleep again on the highway, I longed to be with her in the plane to Europe. The heat and the sun helped to reinforce my drowsiness. I entered a hazy world where my desire to be with her was a tangible force, a living entity. I wondered where I was. Something caught my attention and I looked to my right. There was an arm resting on the armrest of an airplane seat. I looked at the bracelet on the woman's wrist and recognized it as a solid silver piece that I had bought with Lela at a roadside trading post down by the Mexican border. A famous artist of that area had cut it and stamped it with various Mexican motifs. The arm moved and I recognized the way that it moved. It was Lela's arm! I could feel her body, and also the presence of an unknown passenger seated next to her. I felt a powerful bodily knowledge. It told me that I had just deployed my dreaming body to be with her on the plane. I was so excited that I woke up back in my car on the Arizona highway.

"Court, to this day, I'm not sure of the energetic reasons for feeling so lost whenever she left," I said. "I would get to the point sometimes where I couldn't even eat or sleep. I know I was attached and dependent on her, and that I had already lost a lot of my energy by being tangled up in her. But what was the unbearable emptiness that I felt whenever she was gone?"

"Where did you feel it?" he asked me.

"In my stomach and solar plexus," I replied.

"It was your ultimate fear–the fear of loss. The solar plexus energy center, or chakra, is where fear is felt."

"I thought that fear was felt in the base energy center," I said.

"The fear that you feel in your base energy center is animal fear related to self-preservation and survival. The fear that you feel in your solar plexus is emotional fear. As I said before, the Spirit packed your relationship with her full of opportunities. You took on a truckload of emotional issues all at once."

"Wasn't I mostly afraid of losing her because I was afraid of losing her power and support?" I asked him.

"You were afraid of being left alone," he replied. "You still had not assumed complete responsibility for yourself and for your position in life. You were still an irresponsible child who was unable to take care of himself. But let's finish this tomorrow evening. You're running out of steam." And he sent me home.

I arrived the following evening at dinnertime. His front room was filled with his friends. It was a potluck and they had all brought something. I found him in the laundry room. He was showing his friends the shirts that were being silk-screened with some of his drawings. I felt out of place.

"You didn't tell me that I should bring anything," I complained.

"I didn't know that there was going to be a group of people over," he said. "The Spirit is spontaneous. Look, there's a woman who was the model for the Statue of Liberty in her past life."

"What are you talking about?" I asked.

"The Statue of Liberty was modeled after a woman, and there she is in her present form. She's very striking. Look at her face. Look at the way that it's chiseled."

I could see the similarity. It had to do with the angular features and the disposition that she conveyed with those features. It was quite pleasing.

"Look at how the mood of liberty is conveyed by this woman. Liberty is freedom from attachment—it is independence, and the ruthless strength of self-preservation and self-sufficiency. It is a noble mood. And look over there," he pointed. "There is Abraham Lincoln's reincarnation."

The man definitely carried the same essence that I had felt when viewing pictures of Lincoln. I sensed a musty, or older quality when I looked at him, almost as if someone had dragged him out of the closet where he had been stored for all of these years, and then dusted him off for this gathering.

"Death in our world is life in another," Court said.

After everyone had gone home, Court and I picked up where we had left off the night before.

"Lela and I moved to the outskirts of the California desert and lived in a small house overlooking a barren plain," I said. "The loneliness that I felt from having lost my connection to the Unknown was accented by the barrenness of the high plain that we lived on. It felt like we were stuck in a dream somewhere, completely lost. I remember her eyes drifting far, far away as we lay together in bed, and the faintness of her voice as she asked me why we were here in this world. I felt so unbelievably deserted. That summer, there wasn't a single monsoon."

I paused, deep in thought. "Neither of us wanted to work, and each of us wanted the other to be the provider," I finally said. "We eventually ran out of money, and so we both had to get jobs. We had practically torn each other to pieces after only a few months, and we were both energetically weakened from our indulgence in our fears and insecurities. We both secretly felt that a child might add hope to our lives."

"Unfortunately, that is what most people think," Court said. "When our energy is low and our link to the Unknown has dried up, we become desperate. It's too difficult and it requires too much persistence for most people to begin retrieving their energy, bit by bit. But it's the only way. Having a child under those circumstances puts the child in an awkward predicament and weakens the energy of the parents even further because a portion of their life force is extracted to produce the child. The parents will always be waiting for the child to save them."

"I know," I replied. "I could barely hear the voice way off in the distance telling me to be careful. We never used birth control, and so the temptation was almost irresistible. Shortly after we had moved to our new house, we went to stay with some friends in northern California. We had both been feeling pensive for a few days, like a shadow was following us. Lela was not feeling well, either, and at one point her friend suddenly burst out, 'It's because she's pregnant,' and everyone knew it was true. Lela and I both concentrated very intently for the next two days and willed it not to happen. We were terrified."

"You both knew that your quest for freedom would be as good as gone if she had had the child," Court said. "You were too weak."

"It almost happened one other time as well," I said. "It was late on a very hot summer afternoon, and Lela and I were having sex in our home in the desert. We were sitting up, and I was looking out of a window that faced a nearby hill. Almost immediately after we started, a thunderstorm began forming. My thoughts were absent and I felt power filling the room. Then a flash of lightning ignited outside of the window and temporarily blinded me. I felt something like a fog or a mist around my head, and I sensed a foreign presence. It had surrounded us both but was only visible to me. It felt as if I was staring at an ancient puissance—a fierce entity, except that I kept flip-flopping between actually seeing someone or something that looked like a warrior, and literally being in the middle of a vaporous cloud or energy field that surrounded both of our heads. It spoke directly inside of me and told me that it wanted to come in—that it wanted to enter Lela as a child. I was disturbed, yet energized, by this entity because of its frightening power. I had flashes of the incredible strength of this being and how amazing it would be to have a companion like that in this world. But then something shook me out of it, and I said no. It left us and vanished, and the thunderstorm subsided."

"You must have rallied some of your energy before this episode because the storm and the foreign energy are an unmistakable sign of power," Court said.

I laughed. "I think we just hadn't fought in a couple of days. The desert was an incredible place for witnessing power. It almost felt like my energy was drained on the surface, but not underneath."

"That's not the case," he said. "You were definitely weakened. What you were feeling was your intention to keep the Unknown alive. It burns very strongly inside of you. Whatever energy you hadn't wasted was still keeping the thread warm, and whenever you stopped indulging it came alive again." He laughed. "Lela constantly challenged you, and yet she gave you magnificent opportunities. These situations gave you opportunities to learn how to solidify your will in the face of intense adversity. How did you manage to pull out of it?"

"I went to the bookstore one day in the midst of another argument. I was at my wits end. I was physically exhausted and had used up all of my reserve strength. I knew that I was on the verge of allowing something deleterious to happen to me in order to escape my failure and misery. I did not want to die, but I shuddered at the depressing thought of how much time and effort it would take to put myself back together again. I pulled a favorite book off of the shelf, and was instantly reminded of the need to intend my will to be one with the will of the Spirit. I saw that I had abandoned my connective trances to the Spirit because they made Lela feel insecure, as though I was leaving her. I had weakened myself so that she would not feel threatened by my strength. I was arrogant enough to believe that I could survive solely through her love for me. I actually believed that by suffering for her and by denying myself the joy of the Unknown that I had so carefully nurtured that she would see how much I cared for her and finally trust me. What a fool I was!"

"What a perfect martyr, what a saint! Can I touch you?" Court reached out timidly and poked me with his trembling finger. He recoiled immediately as if it had been scorched. Then he laughed at me as if I was the most pathetic man he had ever encountered. I knew that he could only laugh that way because he had experienced the same haughtiness in his own life.

"I finally learned that I could be of no use to others if I was of no use to myself," I continued. "I knew that my death would do nothing for either of us. I went back home and stated the facts to her, point blank. I succeeded for that moment in detaching myself from her and her troubled and erratic energy. I told her that we needed to take definite steps to improve our relationship by improving our individual selves *by ourselves*, and that we should begin at once."

"How did she respond?" he asked.

"She went to a friend's house for a couple of weeks, hoping to reawaken my fear of loss. It backfired, though. I had just enough time to retrieve some of my energy and become very angry. I made the decision to completely detach myself from her."

"You slew the dragon. You freed yourself from attachment at your weakest moment," he commented.

"With a quivering hand," I chuckled lightly.

"Did you witness any other acts of power in the desert?" Court asked me.

"Our dog, Ralph, was a manifestation of the playful side of the Spirit," I replied.

I told Court that Ralph was one of the most entertaining characters that I had ever known. He had just shown up on our font doorstep one morning. He appeared to be some type of wolf mix. Lela wanted to keep him, but I was thoroughly against it since we were barely able to feed ourselves. I was also trying to keep her from distracting herself with the silent hope that the silence of the desert would help her to see through her own fears. She tried unsuccessfully to find his owners, and then finally took him to the animal shelter. The shelter only kept strays for ten days before they were put to sleep. I knew this, but I felt that his personal power would decide whether he lived or died.

A few days later, we left town and didn't return for one week. While we were out of town, I felt Ralph come to me and ask if he could live with us. I didn't like dogs because they were messy and dependent, so I wished him well and put him out of my mind. Two days after returning home, however, I was out running some errands in the late afternoon when the message came in loud and clear: 'Go to the shelter now.' I immediately turned the car down a side street and headed for the shelter.

When I arrived, I noticed the unused syringes on the desk. I asked if they still had the wolf dog. They told me they weren't sure, and sent me inside the kennels to look for him. I could feel the darkness of death hovering. I hurriedly walked down the dank cement walkway between the two rows of cages. I wanted very badly to turn back because the desperation of the barking dogs was very agitating and made me feel ill. I could feel death pushing below my navel, trying to enter. I neared the last two cages. I didn't think there were any more dogs there because there was no barking. I was going to turn around and get the hell out of there, but something pushed me to keep going. Then I saw him. He was cowering in the very back corner of his cage. He was silent and very afraid. He just looked at me, and I looked back. I rushed out and told the attendant that I would be back the next morning for him when I had some money."

I stopped my story for a moment and looked at Court. He was breathing heavily. My awareness shifted back to the desert. I was standing outside with Lela. The sun had set and we had just experienced our first flash flood in the desert. It was glorious, with the reddish-oranges and purples stamped madly on the clouds in the sky above. The earth was bursting with water all over, and the wind chilled us in the middle of the scorching summer.

"I hope when it gets hot and dusty that you will remind me of how much I love it here in the desert," I said lovingly to her. "The intense quiet and aloneness, the wildflowers, the mice, snakes, tarantulas..."

"...Scorpions, swarms of wasps, centipedes, skunks, and jack-rabbits..." Lela continued.

"...Porcupines, roadrunners, and coyotes, have all welcomed us and made us feel at home," I finished.

"Remember the night that the coyotes surrounded Ralph?" she asked me as she looked up at me with her dark blue eyes.

"We were asleep in our home and Ralph was outside, sleeping," I replied. "It was last fall, and we had just brought him home from the animal shelter. There was that female in the coyote pack, the one that had a higher pitched bark than the rest."

"She was the boldest one," Lela responded.

"She used to lead the rest of the pack in their moonlight cries," I said back to her. "I remember that it seemed like she was always trying to lure Ralph out away from our home. That night, her bark was so crisp on the cold, night air. Ralph was barking like crazy, and then all of the coyotes started howling all at once. The entire pack had completely surrounded Ralph and us."

"I remember how nervous you were," she said.

"You were nervous, too," I said as I pressed her closer to me. "My friend had told us that coyotes liked to lure dogs out so that they could eat them. You sent me outside to get him. I practically crapped my pants when I stood amidst their simultaneous howls. I picked up two pieces of metal pole and started clanging them together in the hopes that they would be frightened away by the sound. Instead, they just howled more. It was terrifying and exhilarating to be in the midst of such power under the moon. I grabbed Ralph and pulled him inside."

"What about the time that we came back from dinner one night?" she asked me. "The female coyote was alone, nearby, and was yapping like a clown. Ralph went after her." Lela smiled at me with her thick, alluring lips.

I laughed. "It was pitch dark and I called him, but he didn't return. I heard him tearing through the brush in the distance. Then, suddenly, I heard a crashing through the bushes a few feet away. The female coyote ran right past me with Ralph at her flank. They were completely engaged and were so intense in their playful competition."

I stopped again and looked at Court. "Ralph was such a character," I said affectionately. "He would laugh and leap into the air. I think he was always trying to show Lela and me how to live. But we were always too busy."

"Where is he now?" he asked me.

"I left him with a dog rescue group. They told me that he was being given to a family with a young girl. That was perfect for him. He had roamed alone and at will in the beautiful desert, and now he was going to enjoy the companionship of someone who could be close to him."

I paused for a few minutes. I had never seen before how Ralph's spontaneity and sense of abandon had been a quiet source of hope and inspiration for me in my darkest hour. He had been a true friend.

"For three years after I left him, he hung onto his connection to me," I said slowly and softly. "I could feel him trying to pull me back into his life. And then one day I felt the connection break. He let go of me and moved on."

Court and I sat silently. I was feeling very pensive. I had not been thorough in my recapitulation of Lela because it was too painful. Every time I began, I experienced an uncontrollable longing. I remembered nothing but darkness. I remembered that I had decided to cancel our plans to get married because I was incapable of retrieving my strength with her around. There was nothing more that I could do except save myself. I knew that I had put my own life at risk by trying to bring her into my life against the will of the Spirit. It was not up to me to save her. That was up to her and the Unknown.

"Court, your statement that death in our world is life in another reminded me of something that happened just prior to the end of our relationship," I said.

Late one night, I was driving home from work. Lela was not living with me anymore. I was exhausted and apprehensive from trying to decide if I should remain firm in my decision to completely sever all ties to her. I was driving a little faster than usual down the road at the end of town when I saw a bird take off to my left. He had been sitting on the side of the road and was now flying towards my car. I thought nothing of it since it was something that happened fairly frequently, and the birds always managed to clear the car. In my tired state, I did not respond quickly enough when I realized that he wasn't high enough, and 'Smack!'– he hit the top of my windshield. I felt the all too familiar feeling of the blood draining from my stomach, and then my limbs went cold. I wearily turned the car around.

I pulled up behind the bird. He was lying on the opposite side of the road from where he had taken off. I left my headlights on as I got out and walked timidly towards him. He was lying on his back. I was afraid to look at him, but made myself anyway. His wings were outstretched, and I saw his beak opening and closing very slowly. I couldn't see the rest of his head and

I felt sick as I thought that the car might have smashed his head down into his chest. But there was no blood. When I got close enough, however, I saw that it was either a baby owl or a very small adult owl.

The small owl kept stretching out his wings and his claws very slowly. I got a stick, hoping for some non-existent moment when he would grab onto it and I could lift him to safety. I put the stick in his claw and he tried feebly to grab onto it. His grip was so weak and weary. I saw his eyes shift to my right and look way off into the distance and deep inside of himself, all at the same time. Then his chest heaved once more, and he expired. I kicked myself for my ridiculous fears about touching wild animals and I picked him up. His head was completely loose and fell backwards. I hesitantly reached up and cradled it with my other hand. I carried his lifeless body over to a bush and laid him down underneath it. There was nothing more I could do. I felt so worthless at that moment, and yet I was so quietly awed by the experience. Amidst my remorse, I was silently thankful for the opportunity to watch his spirit leave his body, and to see the look of infinity in his eyes at his last breath. His death reminded me of the mysteriousness of life.

A couple of days before, I had received a special-order in the mail of some of my favorite tobacco from Alaska. When I had tried to smoke it earlier that evening, I realized that I had no matches or lighter. I was not to be the first one to experience it. I took some of that tobacco and sprinkled it on the owl and apologized for my stupidity. And yet, I was aware that this owl had chosen me for some reason. As troubling as it was, I knew that I had been blessed. The owl had given me gifts–the gift of seeing in the darkness, and wisdom. I accepted his gifts, thanked him, and returned to the cold darkness of my empty home and my life.

Court looked gently at me. "Two words were given to me as you spoke: lachrymose and lamasery. The word, lachrymose, means tearful or mournful. Lamasery is a monastery for lamas or monks. You felt mournful at the passing of the owl and the passing of your life with Lela. Yet, you were blessed as one who devotes his life to the search for the Truth. The owl's death symbolically freed you from a life of seclusion and self-imposed barrenness. An owl is a night seer, a harbinger of dark wisdom. He was a gift–a spirit guide–to help you find your way in the dark until you returned to the light. In one of your past lives with Lela, you had given her an owl as a gift and she had rejected it. It was returned to you."

I stared at him with glassy eyes and he stared back. His look became very penetrating. I could tell that he was still looking for something in my stories about Lela. He moved in closer to me and spoke in a very forceful whisper.

"What do you know about ghosts?"

I shuddered, involuntarily. The thrust of his words propelled me back in time. I found myself sitting in my reclining chair in an apartment a few years back, thoroughly consumed by a book that I was reading. Out of the corner of my eye, I saw a cat run from one side of my room to the other before disappearing into the bathroom–except that I didn't have a cat. This had occurred so quickly that all I could remember seeing was a black shape, about the size and shape of a cat, moving about an inch off the floor and gliding across the room. Then, memories surfaced of the times that I had seen these ghosts or flyers in various public locations or around people who were possessed. I once saw a pair of them fly around a potted plant in my office and then fly out of the window and into the distance. Another time, I saw one crawl up my dresser and onto my television as I lay in bed flipping through the channels.

One of the most remarkable related events occurred at a grocery store where I was working. I was busy stocking the shelves when a mother parked her grocery cart in front of me. Her one-year old girl was sitting in the basket seat, and when she saw me I felt the Unknown move inside of her. She looked at me for a minute without any thoughts. Suddenly, her attention was caught by something that moved up over her head and to her left. She turned around and pointed to it, and made a sound like 'that.' She looked at me with her finger still pointing to it. I could feel what she was pointing to, even though I could not see it. Then I saw her attention caught again, and she swung her arm forward and to the right, and looked into the distance and said 'that' again. I knew instinctively that she was watching something in the store and was pointing it out to me.

Court was still staring at me. "Now, tell me about the fight with Lela, the one that frightened you."

"We had fights almost every other night and they were all upsetting," I replied.

"No!" he demanded forcefully. "There was one that made your skin crawl."

Before he could finish his sentence, I remembered a very dark night. Lela and I were having a terrible argument and, for the first time in our relationship, I had managed to maneuver her into a position where she was just about to recognize her fear. In the past, she had always outmaneuvered me until I was exhausted. I would finally give in just to get some rest. I had tried everything I could think of to get past her defenses, but she always turned things upside down. Now, I was pushing her with all of the power at my disposal.

I pushed again with all of my will. Just as she realized that she was about to lose her grip on this world, she jumped up and turned ruthlessly cold. I recognized this state and shot quickly out of her way. As she got to the door, however, I rallied my strength and grabbed her arm. What happened next made my blood run cold. She looked down into my eyes, and a voice that sounded like pure evil rose up from the very bottom of her throat. It spoke to me very slowly and deliberately.

"Why do you always have to know what I'm fucking afraid of?" the voice growled and spewed in its eerie tone.

I just stood there with the hair raised on the back of my neck as she tore away from me and ran towards her car. The voice had not been hers. It was too low in pitch, and I had *seen* something else in her eyes—a red glow or a burning fire surrounded by a blackness that I could only describe as being from hell.

My heart broke apart at that moment and death stood by, waiting for me. The sadness that I experienced was crushing. I knew that something dark had consumed her because of her fear. I realized then that my love for her was my love for all life. Even though she had made herself the victim of this force, I couldn't help but feel for the soul inside of her. It had reached out to me when she was strong, and I loved her dearly. I sensed that her soul was still present, but just barely. I had somehow known that since the day I met her. I had tried to help. I had almost lost my life.

"Now, do you remember what I told you about her shortly after you got together with her?" Court asked me, still in a hoarse whisper.

"You had called her an empty," I said softly. "You told me that this referred to a person whose soul had fled because it was experiencing no fulfillment or progress."

"That's right," he said. "A body without a soul is a burden to the rest of humanity."

"I remember that I was offended by your comment," I said. "I kept it tucked away in my mind, though, because I knew that you were seeing something that I was not yet ready for. Even now, it is so hard for me to completely express the utter loss that I feel for her. The punch that I had felt in my solar plexus on the first day that I met her was a cry for help from what remained of her dreaming body. It was also the challenge of the flyer—the entity inside of her. I see now that all along I was battling this entity and that I almost lost."

Court put his hand on my shoulder. "Entities of different energy can only take over in moments of absolute weakness," he said. "A person has to be ready to give up—ready to die. That's why the ghost used Lela first to seduce you, and then to wear you down. If you had ever wished for death it would've pounced on you with everything it had. We, as humans, can *never* give up or wish for death! You told me before that when you were strong she respected and feared you. But when you were weak she trampled mercilessly on you."

"Could I have helped her?" I asked despondently.

"Had you remained detached from her but connected to the Spirit she might've rejuvenated her will and forced the ghost out," he said. "It's hard to say for sure."

"Now I see why she had no volition," I said. "She could never act on her own. She could only react to a situation. She was incapable of pro-action."

"In ancient times, people referred to a woman like Lela as 'one who had sold her soul to the devil,'" Court said. "The flyer could grant that person great power over others, but only at the expense of their personal freedom. A person in that condition was incapable of experiencing guilt or remorse for their deeds. A person like that became a host, and the flyer fed off of that person's energy. If, however, the person could remain strong enough, he or she could actually command the power of the flyer. Many were not that fortunate."

"Could a flyer make a woman more beautiful?" I asked him, remembering my fierce attraction to her.

"It could make a woman bewitching to a man. There were once women who could command a flyer, bewitch a man, and then enslave his soul as well. Those were truly frightening women. They could make their slaves suffer in unbelievable ways. Lela, however, did not have the upper hand in her symbiotic relationship with the flyer."

"When I have witnessed flyers, I have noticed that their energy varies," I said. "Sometimes, I see little black shadows like cats or birds, and other times I see large and depressed amorphous blobs of energy with a kind of pale luminescence. Are they different types of entities?" I asked.

"No," Court replied. "They are simply different levels of energy. The small black animals are infant souls. Their energy is more like the energy of young wild animals that run around hysterically when they are lost or confused. The energy of old souls, however, is mellower and vibrates at a slower rate. When they are lost or cast off they are more miserable and defeated. They tend to hover in one place, bemoaning their fate."

I wondered what had become of Lela's soul. "The connection between us was so strong," I reminisced. "She even came looking for me once."

"It was her soul," Court replied. "It knew its time on earth was almost up."

My body sighed. I told him that after I had left her, I had moved back in with my parents. It was a very difficult time for me. My body was in a grave state of disrepair. I was constantly tired and listless. One afternoon late in the following summer, I decided to go for a swim in my parents' aboveground, backyard swimming pool. It was very hot, and the high clouds held in the heat and the humidity. There was no wind. Everything was still.

I climbed the ladder over the side of the pool and sat down on the top step. As I dangled my feet in the warm, thick water, I looked out over our backyard fence into the dried-out field behind our house. The last time I had been in this pool was a little over a year ago when Lela and I had been visiting my family. On that occasion, we had taken turns holding each other afloat in the water. I remembered that she had lost her favorite toe ring. We had looked all over for it.

I felt completely lost as I sat there on the ladder, staring absent-mindedly at my mother's rose vines. I slowly climbed down into the water and pulled the old inflatable raft toward me. I tried lying on it, but the breeze started to pick up and chilled my damp skin. I rolled over and placed my chest across the middle of it, my face dangling over the side. Then, I kicked my legs under the water at random as I stared at the bottom of the pool.

The water was strangely comforting. The only sound was the sound of the neighborhood air conditioning units going on and off in the heat. The breeze licked at my shoulders and wet hair as I floated aimlessly around the pool. The water was alive with memories–I had never sensed that in the past. I was reliving our experience in the pool together the year before–not just remembering it. I could see her, hear her, and feel her. All of our emotions were still in the water. I remembered that my father never drained the pool.

My face was bobbing up and down just inches above the water, the tip of my nose dipping in every so often. I closed my eyes as another breeze penetrated my body and pushed against my soul. It kept speaking to me as if it had a message. I felt the weight of the memories and of someone else, very close by.

Inside of me, something clicked and my eyes opened suddenly. I stared into the water and there, tucked halfway into a fold on the plastic bottom of the pool, was the toe ring. I just hung there, somewhere in-between the past and the present, with the breeze buffeting me more forcefully. I dove down and pulled the ring out from under the flap. I came up quickly and brushed the water out of my eyes. It was definitely hers. It was corroded in places from the chlorine. How had the automatic pool vacuum passed over this every time for the last year?

I placed the ring on my small finger. It only went down to my knuckle. I lay back across the raft and floated some more, staring at my finger. Now, I knew she was here. It wasn't just a memory–it was her dreaming body. The wind picked up more and I climbed out of the pool and wrapped a towel around myself. I stood on a hot spot in the yard to warm up. It felt as though she was caressing my back with her hands.

I walked back inside the house. It wouldn't have fazed me in the slightest if she had been sitting on the couch with my mother watching television. I walked into the kitchen and the phone rang. It was Lela.

"Hello," I said. Silence. "Hello!" I said with more inflection.

I could hear a television, very faintly in the stillness on the receiver–nothing else. I waited, but was afraid to say what I felt– that I had just found her toe ring in the pool and that I missed her. I started making lunch as I listened to the distant television, trying to figure out what show she was watching.

"I'm going to hang up now if you won't tell me who this is," I lied. I was trying to be amusing for the benefit of my mother who was sitting on the couch with a concerned look on her face. I knew that my ridiculous attempts to lighten the moment were breaking down the connection between Lela and I. I knew that she wanted me to be stronger. After about ten minutes, I quietly hung up the phone. The presence left me and I never heard from her again.

Court leaned forward in his chair. "When we don't have the courage to live a path with heart, we quietly look for death. Lela is quietly looking for death. You decided to live, and you left her to fight her own battle. That decision was the most difficult decision you have ever made."

"It was," I said. "But I thought constantly about going back. I had made some very serious promises to her, and to us. It always felt like something was incomplete–like I was still in the midst of it."

"A couple of years after leaving her, I began recapitulating," I continued. "I was determined to free myself from the burden of the past. I burned everything that I had kept from our days together. As I slowly untangled and unhinged my energy from hers, I felt my promises being lifted. I saw that it was possible for me to override them by having more energy than I did when I made them. As I continued storing energy, I could sense that she had not intended to sever her connection to me. So I did it for her. I was able to unhook her energy from me and release her completely. I felt the pressure again in my solar plexus as the fire consumed the memories. My body shook and I sweated profusely."

"When I was finished, I took a short walk outside. The rain had given way to the most beautiful sunshine. It was cool, crisp, and breezy. There was not a cloud in the sky. A solitary blue jay sang noisily in a tree just outside my window."

He looked gently at me. "Even though her motives were biased, her principles had great value—she taught you to see the true in the false. She was a complex puzzle, a fantastic riddle, and her living example helped to push you beyond your learned limitations. She was a magnificent teacher for you, an opportunity for your awareness to excel in seeing the subtle shades of perceptual distortion."

I smiled wistfully back at Court. "More than anything, Lela showed me the necessity of a powerful connection to the Unknown and an undying commitment to self-fulfillment. She taught me how to be strong in the face of fear and death. She helped me to tear down my self-image." I paused briefly. "With you, Court, as my witness, I would like to express my utmost gratitude to her."

"We wish her the highest fulfillment," he said.

SEX, POWER, AND AFFECTION

*Nowadays people are not like this.
Their passions exhaust their vital forces;
their cravings dissipate their true essence;
they do not know how to find
contentment within themselves;
they are not skilled in the control of their spirits.
They devote all their attention
to the amusement of their minds,
thus cutting themselves off from the joys of long life.*

-**The Yellow Emperor's
Classic of Internal Medicine**-

There was no denying the effervescent beauty of the southern California sun on this particular fall morning. As I lay in my bed with the window slightly opened, I relished in the fresh and lazy breeze of the foothills as it energized everything in my room. The soft glow of the sunlight sent waves of happiness through me as it danced with abandon across my blanketed body. The soft shadows of the pine trees swaying gently in the breeze outside flowed peacefully back and forth across my legs, and the sound of the wind sang of the absolute contentedness of the overflowing abundance of life.

After enjoying a very leisurely breakfast outside under the vine-covered trellis of my apartment, I made my way down the backside of the mountain with my car in neutral. Even the quiet hum of my engine did not disturb the tranquil sound of the water as it bubbled across the shade-covered rocks in the creek below. Above, the sky was a magnificent blue with large, white cumulous clouds accenting the tops of the nearby hills. The luxurious breeze continued to shimmer as it rustled serenely through the mellowed light of the trees. Everyone was smiling.

Court was on his front porch when I arrived, wearing a pair of shorts and an old, black sweatshirt. He was stooped over his kiln with his back to me as he prepared various handmade clay objects for firing. He knew that he had not been allowed to end his life twenty years earlier because of his natural talent for art and spiritual expression. He knew that the Spirit had saved him from his recklessness, and that he and his skills were needed for other tasks. He was now the happiest human being I had ever known.

He turned around briefly, smiled, and said hello. I sat down and enjoyed the silence and the sound of the neighborhood birds. He was taking his time placing and rearranging the objects in the kiln. Some of them were very thin and fragile.

"You have been thinking about relationships because your dreaming body has told you that they are interfering with your recent attempts to return to lucid dreaming," he said to me, still leaning over his kiln.

Court would do that on occasion. He would just start talking about whatever was on my mind when I arrived.

"You are experiencing internal confusion regarding relationships with women because you have not allowed your dreaming body to show you what a proper relationship is," he continued. "Your dreaming body already knows that relationships should be based on the energetic fulfillment of both people. But your physical body wants relationships based on procreation. It is interested only in the continuation of your genes and the superiority of your offspring. Your perception has twisted these natural desires and decided that your relationships should be based on power and sexuality. Because of this, your dreaming body is creating lessons for you in the hopes that you will drop your misconceptions about sexuality and power." He shook his rear at me and chuckled as he finished arranging the clay objects in the kiln.

I laughed at his clowning around. It was good to see him again.

"Does that mean that my relationships are based on one of those three things?" I asked. "They are based on the desires of my dreaming body, my physical body, or my perception?"

"That is the way that you currently respond to women," he answered.

I laughed. "That explains why my relationships never last very long, or why they always end in confusion."

Court closed the lid of the kiln and plugged it in. He placed some nuts in a bowl on the railing of the front porch, and then came and sat down next to me.

"When you were young," he said, "you were taught by your institutionalized religion to be submissive and dependent. Because of this, your second, third, and fifth energy centers, or chakras, remained underdeveloped. To me, this is evident in the underdevelopment of your physical body as well, since your physical body is a direct manifestation of your dreaming body. You have not completely matured, energetically or physically."

I pondered that for a minute. "What can I do to encourage my energy to mature?" I asked.

"The development of your energy centers and your physical body is a natural process if it is not interfered with by your thoughts and beliefs," Court said. "If left alone, your dreaming body energy will naturally develop each of your energy centers, just like your physical energy does when it works its way through the development of the different aspects of your physical body. In your physical body, there is the growing and maturation of bones, teeth, muscles, reproductive organs, pubic hair, organs, the vocal chords and the brain. The energy centers develop in a very similar fashion, but take many more years to develop, especially in our society. In our society, some people never reach maturation in certain energy centers, which is why we are experiencing such rampant irresponsibility and indulgence in sexuality."

"Your first, or root, energy center focuses on the preservation, mastery, and stability of your physical body through its connection to the earth," Court continued. "Your second energy center focuses on dreaming, reproduction, and affairs of power. Your solar plexus energy center is concerned with your ultimate success and transformation—your ultimate journey to freedom, and your heart energy center is powered by affection, joy and Truth. The expression and communication of your Truth with other people is the concern of your throat energy center, whether it is through speaking, drawing, writing, or any other medium. Your third eye energy center processes all of the insights communicated by your dreaming body to your physical body, and your crown energy center connects you to the awareness of the Unknown. Your physical and energetic weaknesses are in the areas of power, your ultimate transformation and success as a man of power, and your appropriate expression of that power."

I nodded in agreement. "I understand what you're saying, Court, but what does this have to do with my relationships with women?"

"Your relationships with women have been so confusing and volatile because you have been trying to obtain power through sex. Sexuality is power. Sexuality, personal power, and the ability to enter into lucid dreaming are all aspects of the power produced in your second energy center. Because you were taught to repress and feel guilty about your sexual drives when you were younger, you did not explore your sexuality and power without hindrance for a very long time. By the time that you began your exploration, your thoughts and beliefs were practically solidified. You have been struggling to smash through those belief structures, but in a very haphazard way."

"I remember when I used to feel affection for women because they were energetic beings like myself," I said. "My physical desires were aroused, but I was not consumed by them like I am now. Now, I feel like I'm a slave to my desires."

"That's what I am trying to point out to you," he said. "When you were young, you lived from your heart. You knew that affection was something that existed between all sentient beings–any life form or living being with awareness. You knew that all of us shared in the energy of existence. Before your perception became solidified, your energy flowed freely throughout all of your energy centers. You felt affection and arousal but knew no guilt or restriction. Later, when your belief structures solidified, the natural flow of energy was prevented from flowing into your second energy center. You experienced frustration as a result of this. You did not allow yourself to be sexual or powerful. You became soft and more feminine. Women liked to be around you because they did not have to worry about you pursuing them sexually."

"As your energy continued to grow, however, it sought release," Court continued. "You allowed some of your belief structures to crumble around the edges and a torrent of sexual energy was released. But since you had only examples of sexuality in your life, and not lucid dreaming, you focused on releasing that pent-up energy through sex. You started to feel more powerful and you began to associate the accumulation of sex with power. You became consumed by it. Your world revolved around it. But no one was around to teach you how to find that power in yourself, so you sought to acquire it by owning and possessing the sexuality of your female partners."

I stared out over the railing at the banana trees at the edge of his front yard. I had been aware for some time of my need to enter into relationships out of boredom, loneliness, frustration, or possession. I remembered a time when my feelings for women used to be light and unattached, and my affection flowed freely throughout all of my energy centers. I remembered how I used to just enjoy arousal as a feeling in and of itself, without the need to do anything about it.

But then, as I got older and more concerned with sex and

power, I began to look specifically to my partners to fulfill my needs. I had silent and implied expectations of them. I began to constantly monitor whether or not they were attentive to my unspoken needs. These silent expectations were the fuel for endless conflicts with my partners and they eventually became scapegoats for my own cowardice. I became addicted to them, and would go in search of another if the one I was with couldn't fulfill my expectations.

Court had been sitting silently as I processed my memories.

"Your intention and persistence to find fulfillment in this lifetime has given your dreaming body the energy that it needs to break through the misconceptions adopted by your perception," he said. "That's why you are so currently consumed by issues of sexuality and power. You want to be free from your attachments. You want to fill yourself up with the power of the Unknown. Through your lessons in sexuality and power, you will expand your awareness and finally succeed in *seeing* the blockages created by your belief structures. Once you become aware of these structures and blockages, you will become free of your attachments to sexuality and power. Then the source of your personal power—your dreaming body—will be free to fill you up with the power of the Unknown. Your energy centers will mature and you will not need to search for power outside of yourself."

We had been sitting on his front porch in two old vinyl chairs as we talked. The sunlight filtered through the trees and warmed our bodies. We were watching the blue jays come by to grab nuts out of the bowl that he had set on the railing. The one with the gray and black crew cut was completely unafraid. Court would hold a nut up, and the jay would fly over and grab the nut out of his fingers. Occasionally, Court would hold on tightly to the peanut shell and the jay would squawk and peck at his finger. He would laugh and tease the bird. I could tell that the jay enjoyed the challenge.

The late morning sun felt so good. Court went over to the

railing and created patterns in a small tray of sand with a miniature rake.

"Court, you said that my relationships were based on either my dreaming body, my physical body, or my perception. We've been talking about how my perception has affected my relationships, but how do my dreaming body and my physical body affect my relationships with women?"

"Your dreaming body is connected to all life. It *is* life. Regardless of whether it continues on as a soul or as energetic units when you die, it's still connected to all life. Because of this, you have an energetic history. That history has involved others. Your dreaming body wants, in this lifetime, to search out others that it has felt affection for in the past. It wants to be with them again. Or, it may want to rectify the harm that it caused in the past due to the rigid belief structures that were imposed upon it. You and I have a very long energetic history, for example. I see that we have been mother and daughter, son and father, friends, lovers and brothers in previous lifetimes. As souls, or even as energetic units, we have quite a passionate and affectionate history, and our dreaming bodies are attracted to each other as a result of that."

"Your physical body, on the other hand, focuses on the physicality of a woman in terms of procreation. How has she manifested her energy? Is it powerful and desirable? If I mate with her, will we produce genetically superior offspring?"

"It sounds like my physical desires will always conflict with the wishes of my dreaming body," I said. "How can they possibly function together, unless one dominates at the expense of the other?"

"It's very simple," Court replied. "When you finally break down your belief structures and *allow* the energy of your dreaming body to fill your physical body, you will return to the state you were in as a young boy–unified and whole. In this state, your mind was filled with the Unknown and saw the world accordingly. In this state, your dreaming body guided your physical body and led you on an adventure that knew no parallel. Your physical body all too gladly went along with your dreaming body. You had physical desires, but they coincided with your dreaming body's feelings of affection. You didn't need to fuck anybody to feel satisfied. You were already satisfied. An erection was satisfying *in itself.* You didn't require orgasm."

I recalled that feeling very vividly. It lasted until puberty. I asked Court if puberty was the time when my second energy center began developing. He said that it was. He also said that it was at this time that I discovered orgasms and guilt, and began repressing my sexuality and power.

"What is love at first sight, then?" I asked him.

He chuckled over my confusion. "The rush of energy that you feel when you experience love at first sight occurs at the precise moment when you and your partner's endless barrage of thoughts cease and energy flows freely between the two of you. That's why love at first sight feels so abrupt and overwhelming. It's the act of stopping the world."

"Look," he continued, "when you were very young your mind was quiet and empty, and so you never knew the experience of falling in love because there was already space between your thoughts. But as you got older and your mind became jammed with thoughts, you *discovered* the act of falling in love. You experienced, through an energetic connection with another, the act of stopping the world—the cessation of your endless chattering thoughts and beliefs. When the world stopped, energy flowed, and you believed that it was *because of that person* that you had experienced something transcendental. But stopping the world can also be accomplished by freeing yourself from your own imprisonment in your rigid belief structures. You can fall in love with the Unknown, if you want to."

Court said that he was hungry and went inside to make lunch. He reminded me that I still had some of my frozen beef tamales in his freezer. We prepared our food, and Court brewed another batch of coffee. We took our food to the front room and settled down in our chairs.

After we had finished our meal, I confessed to him that I had spent a good portion of my life searching for the one woman who I believed was waiting somewhere for me.

"Don't tell me that you still believe in true love?" he smacked sarcastically.

I actually blushed. I wanted to believe that true love could be a final refuge.

"I guess I'm still waiting for that one special woman who can save me by bathing me in warmth and affection," I said. "I'm waiting for someone who can make all of my problems go away."

"You're still looking for your damsel in distress, aren't you?" He laughed at me, and I gave him my best smarmy smile.

"Assuming complete responsibility for your life and actions is a subtle affair," he said. "Assuming complete responsibility for your life is an act of power. You would like to believe that love, sex, and beauty are the keys to happiness, but they are not." He poured himself a cup of coffee from his thermos and lit a clove cigarette.

"We discussed love at first sight before we ate," he said. "Romantic love, or the love between a man and a woman, is similar. Romantic love is an energetic condition brought about by your eagerness to expand your perception and learn life-altering lessons with the aid of another's energy. This is not affection."

"Then why do I only get that feeling from certain people?" I asked. "If it's simply an energetic condition, then why don't I get that feeling from any member of the opposite sex?"

"It has to do with your particular energetic configuration," he replied. "It's similar to the attraction of two magnets. If you try to press the two positive poles against each other they repel each other. But if you align the positive pole of one magnet with the negative pole of the other, they attract. Human beings are comparable. They have particular fields of attraction and repulsion. You have a specific energetic configuration that is molded by your perception and the lessons that you need to learn, and when you find a woman with a complementary lineup of energy you become attracted to each other."

"It is by *allowing* yourself to learn from another that the energetic doors open and your energy mingles with the complementary energy of your new partner," Court continued. "When you open yourself to this learning experience, you feel a rush of energy and call it love. When the lesson is over, however, you and your partner struggle to keep the romantic love alive. But it can't be kept alive. Your dreaming body knows that it is through with the lesson. It wants to move on. If you stay with that person, you will inevitably experience the usual boredom and frustration. You will become bitter towards your partner. You may cheat on her because of your frustration. You want the relationship to end—you want to release your attachment to her and her attachment to you, but you don't have the balls to say it's over. So, you try to drive her away by hurting her. It's very sad."

"Then what is affection?" I asked him. "If I have a relationship with a woman based solely on affection, won't my lessons with her eventually end, too?"

"The *intention* behind affection is what thoroughly changes the relationship," he answered. "With affection, there is no attachment. With affection, there are no expectations. Affection is the Unknown recognizing itself in another energetic being. It's the source of life flowing freely between two people. With affection, you share a common journey of fulfillment and a lifelong lesson, not just specific lessons."

"So I could enter into a relationship with someone to learn a lesson and still have genuine affection for her, couldn't I?" I asked.

"Of course," Court replied. "We can't possibly talk about every possible type of relationship, so I'm speaking in fairly general terms."

"I'm asking you this because I used to feel terrible pain during some of my breakups," I said. "It felt like I had tried to deny the affection that I felt for someone in order to move on and seek more power in another."

"You will never succeed in filling yourself up with another's power. But you also bring the pain of a breakup upon yourself because you have adopted the belief that you can only have affection for one woman. How can that be? You don't just have affection for one friend or one family member, do you? Why are you so possessive?"

"You're not suggesting that I should have multiple partners, are you?" I asked incredulously.

"Relationships don't have to involve sex!" he exclaimed as he shook his head and laughed. "I'm not talking about having sex with everyone you experience affection for because that is indulgence at the other extreme. I'm talking about not shying away from a person just because they're of the opposite sex or because you already have a partner. If you shy away from a person that you feel a connection to, then you have lost a potential lesson or life-experience because of a self-imposed limitation and fear."

"I understand that," I said. "In the past, if I have stopped myself from pursuing a friendship with another woman because I was afraid that my girlfriend might get upset, I usually wound up breaking it off with my girlfriend, anyway. I guess the trick is to learn what I need to learn from someone else without sending messages of fear, anger, or jealousy to my partner."

"Absolutely," Court replied. "Learn how to act maturely. That's what the path to freedom is about–learning to be responsible for your actions, and increasing your awareness of your deepest intentions."

I thought for a moment about how afraid I was of losing my current partner, of having her deny or cut off her affection for me. I thought about how I was constantly driven by the affairs of power and sex–how I was constantly on the lookout for women of power. Affection often took a back seat to the affairs of power. I didn't want to be a slave to any desire. Court asked me which thought I would like to talk about first.

"A few years ago, I got tired of the painful denial of affection," I said. "I decided that I no longer needed to end relationships and deny affection. I decided to break the old pattern that I had been taught and come up with something new. Now, I express what I feel towards women without allowing the fear of losing my partner to censor my words or actions."

"I like the way you phrased that," Court said. "You are no longer attached to your partners like you used to be. You've realized that relationships don't have to be exclusive–that nobody has to be hurt by you and that nothing has to end. If you express your feelings honestly to yourself and to others, then there will never be a denial of affection. Then if your partner experiences grief it will only be because she has plowed headlong into her own thoughts, beliefs, and unspoken expectations."

I pondered over these things, but was having a hard time relating them to what I had felt when I had wanted to get married. I couldn't believe that I had been so motivated by my need for power and sexuality.

"All this talking and theorizing can never substitute for the awareness gained by walking through your attachments and obsessions," Court replied. He brushed some ash from his sweatshirt and stubbed out his cigarette in a small bowl of sand on the coffee table. He leaned back and peered at me through the thinning smoke.

"Why do you think that people get married?" he asked me. "Marriage is ownership–*my* husband, *my* wife. And what is it that we own? Their privates!"

I nodded slowly as I thought about my hidden motivations. I remembered that I had wanted to keep my girlfriend from running away. I was afraid that she might hurt me, so I wanted to secure my attachment to her, and hers to me. The idea of marriage was a kind of quiet desperation.

"Marriage is usually a contract entered into out of fear of loss, not affection," he said. "Now, let's talk about the difference between your *desire* for power and sexuality, and your *resistance* to the desire for power and sexuality. They are two very different things."

"First, you have a desire," he said. "Then, your beliefs come in and say that your desire is bad. So, you try to *resist* your desire. In your case, sexuality is your desire. You try to resist it because you don't want to be a slave to it. But resisting a desire creates a division inside of yourself, between you and the desire. You have made a decision to resist your desire as if it were an entity in its own right. But the reality is that the desire is still a part of you–it *is* you. How can there be two of you? You see, it's an illusion created by thought, and what you have done is to focus very large quantities of energy into both sides of this internal battle. By obsessing over your desire, you have focused a tremendous amount of energy on the actual desire–you have fed it. And by deciding that you are also going to resist that desire, you have poured the rest of your energy into the entity who is fighting the battle. You have split yourself and your energy in two. The desire will always win."

"Then how do I disable my resistance and my desire?" I asked, truly bewildered.

"By *releasing* your energy from your desire and from your resistance to the desire," he said. "Don't resist it–*release* it. Release the buildup of energy. Focusing on a desire, worrying or obsessing over a desire, or forcing yourself to resist a desire all channel large quantities of energy into the desire. Do you see this? Allow yourself to flow gently *with* your desire and don't fight it. Walk through the desire–don't analyze or resist it. As you flow into the desire, you will begin to see why you have the desire in the first place. You don't necessarily have to act on the desire, but you must allow yourself to *feel it fully* in order to understand it. Once you uncover the root of your desire, you will be able to redirect the energy with your will, not your thoughts. In this case, you will stop your concern and worry over your sexual appetite, thereby releasing some of that energy. You will stop fighting it, thereby mending the internal division. You will allow yourself to be aroused and not fight it. You will learn to watch your desire and to see what has created it. Your beliefs will be dropped and your energy will be free to fully develop your energy centers. You will return to lucid dreaming and self-fulfillment."

"What about my need to fill myself up with power from the outside?" I asked.

"Power is a supreme challenge," Court admitted. "How do you acquire it and not be consumed by it? No one ever bothered to tell you that it was mercilessly tied to your sexuality. Our society is obsessed with it in both forms, and bombards us with it incessantly."

"So would it be the desire to own and possess sexual power that makes me want to buy pornography?" I asked.

"You don't realize how powerful those pictures are," Court declared fervently. "They are a medium for capturing sexual energy–that is their *intention*. Those pictures retain a specific portion of sexual energy designed to elicit arousal. The energy of a woman, or man, captured in such a manner becomes available to anyone. You can go to a store and buy a pornographic magazine or video and experience that sexual energy in your own home. You own a piece of that woman's energy. You can engage that energy anytime you want to."

"That's frightening," I replied. "No wonder those people begin to look so depleted at such a young age. They have put their energy up for sale." I paused. "Then would it be true that if I own some magazines I own some power?"

"You do not possess the completeness of those women," Court said as he laughed at my obsession. "Those pictures are captured fragments, moments in time, like a memory. When those fragments accumulate it becomes debilitating to the women and to you. Clinging to memories, or having your energy captured in a medium like that, stagnates the life force of those involved. A woman who has her energy captured time and time again becomes enslaved by all of those who cling to her and the sexual image that she has created. The owners of the magazines or videos carry her around in their minds and replay her energy whenever they feel like it. The people who have bought those pictures become slaves to the feeling of sexual power that they have tried to possess and fill themselves up with–they don't realize that they are more empty than before. They are not powerful in themselves, even though they may feel that way because they can make those women strip for them anytime they want."

Court stared at me with a mischievous grin. It seemed like he knew that I was thinking about a nude pose that I had seen on a magazine cover recently. "How large were her breasts?" he asked me.

"What does that have to do with anything?" I stammered defensively.

"The size of a woman's breasts is a manifestation of power," he said. "It can also demonstrate a need for attention. But attention is power. If a woman commands your attention, you are giving her energy. You probably think they indicate something like love or affection, don't you? You're still too connected to your mommy fantasies." He laughed at my blank expression.

"They really don't indicate heart center energy?" I asked.

"Having an abundance of energy in the heart energy center may contribute to their size, but the primary factor is the energy of the second energy center. Females in the animal kingdom attract men with their scent when they're in heat. Females in our society attract men with their sexuality, which includes their breasts. That's why breasts are constantly on display. When a woman is young, she sees demonstrations of this type of power from family, peers, and the media. She energetically understands how her body and the clothing that she wears help her to attract men and their energy. Her body and clothing are simply a manifestation of her intention."

"Women seek to attract sexual energy from men because it gives them power over them," Court continued. "A woman empowers herself to gather that energy by growing large breasts.

Or, if she is afraid of power she may hinder their development, or hide them if they are large. Don't pretend that you're not aware of how the physical body is a manifestation of our perception."

"I guess I never applied it to that," I said.

"You'd like to think that some things are sacred, especially the ones that you harbor unacknowledged feelings about." He looked at me with the expression of someone who knew my darkest secrets. "You still have some final issues left with sex. The issue of a woman's body and its sexuality are your last great hurdles—they are your greatest distraction from your path."

Court turned on the television. I had learned from him that the Unknown talks to us through any available medium, including the television. I had received many answers to questions by flipping through the channels when I was prompted. The results were that anyone from a cartoon character to a television evangelist could be the voice of the Unknown. He found a documentary on a famous heavyweight boxer. There were many clips of the boxer talking to various interviewers and crowds. Court was very impressed with the boxer's ability to command and entertain his audience when he spoke. He turned off the television and looked at me.

"Since you are currently involved in developing your second energy center, let's discuss aspects of power as related to sexuality so that you can see through the beliefs that have restricted your natural flow of energy," Court said to me. "The Unknown has just given us a brief glimpse of personal power in the heavyweight boxer."

"Personal power is manifested through appearance, social status, body language and posture, attitude, energy, clothes, and possessions," he said. "People think that beauty attracts beauty, but it's really power attracting power. Beauty has to be cultivated and nurtured in order to be powerful and sexual. Energy must be purposefully directed into its maintenance."

"A woman will forgive a man's imperfect beauty in exchange for his power," he continued. "In other words, a woman will be attracted to a powerful man even if he is ugly or repulsive. Sometimes his imperfections can add to her impression of his power. She gauges his power according to whether or not he is afraid of her or intimidated by her. Also, if a man is too obviously aroused by her appearance or sexuality she will interpret that as weakness and loss of control. A powerful man is detached and requires nothing. An impotent man will chase a woman around and try to attach himself to her."

"A powerful woman seeks an even more powerful man because she is subconsciously always on the lookout for the man who will lead her and her energy to freedom and fulfillment. She wants to give her energy to the man who already has his own personal power. She senses that such a man will not drain her energy, but will command and wield it with great force and authority. Conversely, weak or dependent women are attracted to weak and indulgent men because they are afraid of manifesting power in themselves."

"A man will forgive a woman's imperfections if she has large breasts or very apparent sexual energy, both of which are indicative of a woman's power. Most men, however, subconsciously seek women they can dominate. They are afraid of women who are too powerful, but they secretly lust after them. Many pornographic magazines and films are filled with such women of power. A man who is not pursuing freedom and the perfection of himself will spend his entire life lusting after, but never having, a woman of power. He will never have his own power, either."

"Why do I grow tired of a woman once she commits to me?" I asked.

He laughed. "Men who focus on power are only interested in the conquest of a woman, not the woman herself. Women who focus on power behave the same way. When men and women meet each other in the arena of power, and not affection, the rules of power apply. If one becomes weak through indulgence, the other will rise up, conquer, dominate, and then move on."

I thought for a moment. "Is the power of a woman actually

stored in her breasts? It seems like every time I see a woman with her breasts on display, I want to give up my power—I want to ejaculate."

"A woman may focus her energy in her breasts with the intention of arousing you and luring you in, but the energy is still stored below the navel in her second energy center. At the sight of a woman's chest, your available energy gathers in your sexual center and you become aroused. This creates the rush that you feel when you desire to have sex with a woman—it is the intensity of having all of your energy suddenly gathered in one place. You now want to deliver this energy into her."

"You, as a man of power, have the desire to conquer, dominate, and possess, just as any woman of power does. Part of the thrill of sex is the power of dominating or being dominated by another. But the power within you also wants to strengthen and expand itself, and so it demands procreation. The presence of a woman of power will affect you physically—you will want to impregnate her because of her physical excellence. In the human race and throughout nature, the most powerful males battle it out over the most powerful females in order to ensure the promotion and advancement of the species—the best mate with the best. In some wolf packs there are Alpha and Beta females, and they compete for the Alpha male. It's all about power. What determines who the Alpha male and female are? Power does."

I thought about what he was saying. I was keenly aware of my need to own or conquer a powerful female and her energy, even if I had no interest in her otherwise. The few times that I had almost impregnated a woman, I had been filled with a desire to do so specifically because I knew that she would then be mine—nobody else would want her after that. But through a monumental effort, I somehow managed to re-channel that energy and maintain my pursuit of the Unknown.

Court sat in his chair and watched my mental gymnastics. When I finally looked up at him, he continued.

"A man of power exacerbates the urge of women to procreate. But if he has too much sex with a woman of power he will become weak, and she will trample him and despise him for letting himself become weak. What a predicament!"

"A woman can only be around a man of power for short periods of time because the strength of his abundant energy and the spiritual frequency that he embodies penetrates the constant chatter of her thoughts and stops them," Court said. "She sees the mystery of the Unknown but thinks that it's the power of the man. She believes she is falling in love, and that energy ignites her sexual energy."

"Women want to have sex with you when they look into your eyes because you embody the Unknown," he continued. "They don't know what else to do. What can they do? How else can they express what they're feeling? There are other ways, but they don't know about them yet. The Unknown wants to burst forth from you and fill others. You only see that this can happen through sex at this point. You don't want to own women or settle down with them, you just want to fill them up. You want to create joy and life."

"You desire to have sex with a woman because in the physical world that is as close as you can get to the Unknown, but that moment can't be sustained. The only way to sustain it is by shifting that energy to your dreaming body, and that takes practice–it takes time and persistence. The energy engaged by entering a woman catapults your dreaming body into the Unknown, but can't keep it there. You have to learn to do that on your own."

"Remember to always be careful not to spill your seed inside of a woman, even if she's using birth control," he said. "Spilling your semen inside of a woman is an energetic and physical act, and will anchor your energy to this world. It will take you a year or more to recover and free that energy for other energetic endeavors if you do."

Carol walked in through the front door at that moment and asked Court if he wanted to go to the beach with her. The ocean water was still just warm enough for them to swim in, she said.

Court said that he would like to go, and they asked me to come with them. I said that I would like to go, too, but that I needed to go home first and get my swim trunks. We agreed to meet on the beach in an hour.

It was almost two o'clock when I arrived at their favorite spot on the beach, and the coastal fog had just finished burning off. It was another beautiful, sunny day on the coast.

I saw Carol sitting in her favorite spot under her umbrella, but Court was not there. I figured he was swimming. There was another man sitting with her and my old, jealous feelings were aroused. As I approached the two of them, I could tell that this man was not someone that I would normally associate with. He had straight, shoulder-length jet-black hair, and the top of it was cut short so that it stood up slightly. He was wearing mirrored sunglasses. I thought he looked like a slob. I walked up and greeted Carol. I looked at him in order to say hello but he just stared at his feet. That really irritated me. Not only was he an unwanted visitor, but he was impolite, too.

"Where's Court?" I asked Carol in my best nonchalant voice. She just stared at me, absentmindedly. The man vaguely looked at me through his silver lenses. I could see my reflection in them—it made me uncomfortable. He was fixing smashed avocados on pieces of soda crackers.

"Want some?" he mumbled.

I accepted out of my desire not to be impolite in front of Carol. Then, they both started laughing uproariously at me.

"Court's right here, silly," said Carol, still laughing. She ran off to go swimming in the ocean. I felt utterly stupid as the slob took off his wig and sunglasses. It was Court.

"Nice job, boy," he said to me. "You really need to look into that judgmental self-image of yours. Jealousy is a sign of possession, too. You cannot possess Carol, and you cannot possess me. You need to find your own power."

I felt incredibly embarrassed. I had nothing to say. He looked at me. "Other people are mirrors of ourselves if we pay attention. Otherwise, other people are a just a nuisance and something to run away from. You're here to learn from others as you make your way through life. Pay attention. Don't be so superficial."

We both sat in silence and watched the people milling around on the beach. A lady was walking her dog. The dog squatted down on his haunches about ten yards away, and excreted in the sand. The lady looked around to see if anyone was watching, and then kicked a little sand over the excrement and walked off quickly.

"Don't be so superficial," he whispered to me and laughed. "Watch what happens."

People kept milling around, and then a few minutes later a young, good-looking couple came jogging down the beach. Their energy was keenly focused on their outward appearance. Everyone was checking them out and they knew it. I was watching the well-endowed woman in her string bikini. They passed in front of us and the woman landed right in the excrement. Court struggled frantically not to laugh out loud. He started choking on the dry soda crackers and grabbed his water bottle. The woman started cursing as she hopped on one foot toward the ocean. She was trying desperately to maintain her shallow façade and composure in front of everyone while the dog poop oozed between her toes. Her boyfriend was truly distraught over the embarrassment to his self-esteem caused by his girlfriend's less than glamorous activity, but his vanity wouldn't allow him to run away. I was embarrassed to look at the woman anymore–she had lost her power. I looked at some other people sitting nearby. They were laughing at the antics of the young couple.

Court drank some more water and coughed a couple of times. He had that mischievous look in his eyes again. I quickly looked away. I didn't want him to know that I had been caught up in another sexual fantasy.

He laughed at me and sympathetically slapped my shoulder. "You have already discovered that owning a woman's sexuality is important when you haven't filled yourself up with the power of your dreaming body," he said. "But why do you think that ejaculation is so important?"

I shifted uncomfortably on my beach towel. Talking candidly about sexuality brought up old feelings of guilt.

"Orgasm is another way of stopping the world," I replied. "It helps me forget about my problems and also helps me to relax and enjoy the moment. It's a release."

"Ejaculation, like sex, can be overdone," Court said, "especially if you do it out of habit. If you're going to ejaculate, make sure that your sexual center is fully charged. Otherwise, it will weaken or injure you, and hinder your efforts to become a man of power."

"If it helps me to stop the world, how can it weaken me?" I asked, not really wanting to hear the answer.

"If you continuously ejaculate, you will weaken yourself by wasting the best of yourself," he replied. "All of your physical best is contained in your sperm. The ancients believed that one drop of semen had the same value as one hundred drops of a man's blood. Your semen contains the best of your body's proteins, minerals, and hormones. Your body works very hard to distill those elements in order to recreate itself and perpetuate its genes. When you ejaculate, you not only throw away all of the energy that your body expended in the production of that premium elixir, but you also force your body to again extract those nutrients from your blood in order to replace the semen that you just threw away. This prevents your body from utilizing those nutrients to heal and strengthen its vital organs. After constantly ejaculating like this for ten or twenty years, your glands will grow old and fatigued, and will not be capable of distilling such a high-grade fluid. Your vital organs will no longer have access to the crucial nutrients that they were once capable of producing. They will weaken quickly and substantially, which will in turn weaken the rest of your body. You will become vulnerable to all kinds of invasive energies. Old age will set in quickly."

We sat quietly for a few minutes. "What can I do when I experience the overwhelming urge to masturbate?" I asked. "Sometimes, it just comes on so strongly that I can waste hours and days trying to release the feeling. Occasionally, I can circulate the energy through my body, but I usually find myself wide awake on those nights with a bloated feeling in my head."

"Energy gets stuck in your head because you are feeding your sexual fantasies," he said. "You need to allow your sexual energy to circulate freely throughout your entire body and not accumulate in any one place. In this way, it will nourish and charge the rest of your body instead of stagnating in your groin because of your guilt, or in your head because of your thoughts. Allow the energy to circulate from your sexual organs backwards through your perineum, then up your spine, around your head, and back down to your second energy center. Let it fill your body with chills."

"I've done that many times. I still feel overcharged on some nights."

"You are feeling overcharged because there is a full moon," he said.

I stopped to consider that. I told Court that I had kept track of my sexual cycles a while back. I had noticed that I experienced a heightened sexual energy one or two days before the full moon. The heightened arousal would diminish a few days afterwards. I also remembered that during the full moon I noticed an increased presence around town of very powerful women dressed in very sexual outfits.

"Women of power intuit that men are more powerful during the full moon," Court said. "They go looking for them."

"The presence of those women makes it practically impossible to control myself," I complained. "The energy created in those situations is too powerful."

"Well, then you will fail, my friend," he replied quietly.

We looked at each other for a few moments. I did not know

what to say. The feeling that I got around that time and around those women was too electrifying. Finally, he spoke.

"You must keep yourself relaxed during this time," he said. "Don't aggravate the feeling or create more internal friction by looking at dirty magazines or by encouraging sexual fantasies. Shut off your cable television and the Internet if you can't control yourself. But be careful not to repress the feeling. If you don't let it move, it will get stuck and grow from your resistance and attachment to it." He paused and chuckled reflectively. "After retaining your semen for a while, your body will realize that your nutrients are available for feeding and nourishing other things besides your pistola."

I laughed at his usage of the Spanish slang for penis.

"You know," he whispered mischievously in my ear, "that it's OK not to think about a woman when you masturbate, don't you?"

His directness made me nervous.

"You can enjoy your sexual energy all by yourself, if you like," he continued as he chuckled at my discomfort. "It's healthier for your body if you direct your energy back at yourself, instead of outwards towards a sexual image or fantasy."

I fidgeted on my beach towel and nodded. I wasn't sure how to reply. I looked out at the magnificent ocean and thought about the things that we had been discussing. The information that he had provided me with was encouraging, and I felt a firm resolve to reduce my sexual excesses. I knew all too well what it felt like to waste my sexual energy and I did not want to continue doing that. Previously, after too much sex or masturbation, I would get a burning feeling between my anus and testicles, and my head would feel clouded and heavy for a couple of days.

I told Court what I was remembering. I told him that occasionally the burning would linger for more than a few days and cause me some alarm. I had gone to the doctors but they could never figure it out. They wanted to stick a plastic snake in my urethra. I had passed out instead. Court told me that there was a point between my anus and testicles that served as an energetic gate. This gate, he said, controlled the flow of my sexual energy, guiding it upwards in my body to mingle with the energy that I received from the Unknown through my crown energy center. This gate was also responsible for uniting my energy with energy from the earth through my base energy center.

He told me that my sexual energy was the life force energy that I had inherited from my parents, and that it would remain constant unless abused. When it had become weakened through overuse, it had caused stress and fatigue in that energetic gate. He told me that it was important to nurture my sexual energy, since it was this energy that was used to attract additional energy from the earth and from energetic forces outside of the earth. The more of that original life-force energy I conserved, the more outside energy I could attract, just like a magnet.

"I once read that the ancient Chinese considered a man's orgasm to be a form of death," I said. "I used to wonder why they thought that. Then, one night I was with this woman. She was stroking me with her hand. I suddenly felt like she was pulling my life force right out of me, almost like she was luring it out. I could feel it gathering below my navel and running out of my penis. She looked at me with this absolutely blank expression–very, very bittersweet. She seemed like a phantom, a foreign entity–very cold and detached. She was toying with my life force like it was the most natural thing in the world."

"During that orgasm, I noticed a silent feeling–something that felt like a relief. I realized that it was the feeling of being relieved of the burden of life. It was a feeling of desperation–a surrender, as though living was so difficult and death was so easy."

"An orgasm may seem like a harmless act of pleasure, but it is not," Court said. "Each one brings us a little closer to the end. In ancient lore, men who were dreamers often became the slaves of phantoms that appeared as women. These women made men into slaves by fulfilling their every sexual fantasy. You are allowed to indulge in sex or anything else only so much in your lifetime.

Beyond that point, you become hopelessly weakened and you become fair game. It's always your choice."

I sat quietly, watching the people playing in the waves.

"What makes ejaculation so addicting?" I finally asked him.

"It's an escape from the frustration of not being able to reconnect with your dreaming body and its fulfillment," he said. "The more frustrated you are, the more you will crave it. Ejaculation and the entertainment of erotic fantasies are ways of escaping from your chattering thoughts and the self-imposed boredom of not living according to your heart. If your mind were already quiet, it wouldn't crave the release of orgasm. But fortunately for you, you have been forced by the pain between your legs to find out why you are so addicted to this pleasure, to find out why you are so frustrated. You have been forced to face your habitual method of release. You must resolve this frustration, once and for all."

"If you don't resolve this," he continued, "you will continually be looking for an escape through sex, or women, or drugs, or adrenalin rushes, or self-indulgence, or drama, or whatever. You will spend your life jumping from one addiction to another in order to weaken yourself, and eventually you will succeed. Instead of it taking three days for your sexual energy to return to its maximum level, it may take a week or even longer."

"Why would I want to weaken myself?" I asked in amazement.

"In order to forget about your quest for the Unknown," he replied solemnly.

"Do women have the same problem?" I asked.

"Of course," he replied. "All frustrated people seek to forget. But women don't lose as much energy when they have an orgasm because their orgasms are independent of their reproductive processes. They lose their vital energy during menstruation, and it's even possible for them to increase the time between their periods through practice. This will slow their aging process." He chuckled. "They are better off than men because they are born with a finite quantity of eggs and cannot waste them at will like we can with our sperm."

At that point, a woman and her three young children walked by. The oldest boy pushed the middle child down in the sand. The middle child got sand in his eyes and started crying. The mother, who was carrying the youngest child, started scolding the oldest boy while she stooped over to pick up the other boy. The whole family was full of tension and none of them seemed very happy.

"Why do people have so many children?" I said out loud to Court. I disliked witnessing the self-created dramas of weak people who had no self-control or foresight. "I mean, if you haven't fulfilled yourself, why would you even think of bringing children into this world? What would you propose to teach them—the wealth of knowledge that you've so painstakingly acquired about self-fulfillment and living life to its fullest?" The kind of crying that was coming from the fallen boy was very irritating to me.

Court smiled and inhaled the cool ocean air deeply. "Children are the ultimate possession," he replied. "Parents actually believe that they can possess another living being, or that they can live out the dreams that they were afraid of pursuing through their children. In their burning quest to fill themselves up from the outside, they spawn child after child in a desperate attempt to capture a couple of years of complete dependency and unconditional love. How many times have we heard the phrase, 'I just wanted someone to love', or, 'I just wanted someone to love me back'?"

"Then they come face to face with the tremendous responsibility they've frivolously undertaken," I said angrily. "But since they've never learned to be responsible for themselves, they wind up raising confused and irresponsible children, and then they try to blame their failure on forces outside of their control."

Court laughed at my anger. "You can't change or save the world from itself, so try not to funnel your own frustration into the nearest scapegoat. We are all trying to reclaim the affection that was squashed in us by our own fear of joy, both as children and as adults. When it comes to other people, we are only here to observe and learn. The Unknown brings them into our midst so that we can see ourselves in their reflection. We are not here to judge or condemn. We are here only to perfect ourselves."

I looked at him out of the corner of my eye and grunted. We both started laughing.

"Court, what do you see as the appropriate roles for men and women in relationships?" I asked him.

"Women provide energy and men provide direction," he replied. "Those are their ideal roles. Women have a more robust energy than men. This energy comes mostly from the earth. Energy manifests as physicality, which is why a woman's center of gravity is lower than a man's—it is closer to the earth. A man's center of gravity is higher. His specialized form of energy comes from forces outside of the earth. Men are interested and consumed by the mystery of life. Women are looking for ways to invest their energy."

"Men, by themselves, have the tendency to start a hundred different projects and never finish any of them," he continued. "Women, by themselves, have the tendency to stick with things, but not initiate them. Male energy, because it is so pointed, is perfect for cutting through the stagnation of inaction and initiating movement. Female energy, because of its breadth, is perfect for nurturing and concluding the action or movement. But very powerful men and women can teach themselves to execute both roles with their abundant energy."

"This difference in male and female energy is what accounts for the confusion in the bedroom," he continued. "The man is focused on his goal, while the woman seeks to take her time and make the moment last. In a perfect male and female union, a man experiences a more sustained and steadfast energy because of the woman, and a woman experiences purpose and direction because of the man, both in and out of the bedroom. Did you know that the ancient Greeks had two separate words for love?"

"I did," I said. "They were *eros* and *agape*. Eros stood for passionate, powerful, and sexual love. Agape stood for the love of mankind–a quieter and more lasting love. It sounds more like those two words described the differences between male and female energy."

Court nodded.

"It seems like men and women mostly tolerate each other for the sake of sex and security," I said. "A union like the one you've been describing today seems almost impossible amidst the convoluted fear structures that we usually embrace. Two people would have to be on a serious path to freedom to really be partners."

Court stood up and readjusted his beach umbrella to keep the direct sun off of his skin.

"We men, today, are not as strong as we used to be," he said. "Overindulgence in sex has funneled much of our energy away from the affairs of power and awareness that we used to thrive on. Women are the ones who are remembering that there is more to life than sex because of their tremendous energetic resources. Unfortunately, they don't know exactly what they are looking for or where it can be found."

"That's why there are more women in positions of power now, isn't it?" I asked him. "They intuit that the men used to lead them, but now true leaders are nowhere to be found. So they try to do it themselves."

"Pointing is an unnatural role for women," Court replied as he sat back down, "but they won't go down without a fight. They can't allow their abundant energy to go to waste."

"Is it their abundant energy that creates such strong energetic currents during menstruation?" I asked. I remembered that he was very cautious around Carol during her menstruation, and that he would often stay physically outside of her energy field for a few days.

"Menstruation is a time when a woman experiences a very aggressive and powerful increase of energy inside of herself," he replied. "She becomes somewhat incoherent and spacey. She experiences things in slow motion. She may feel like she is in a dream because the force of her energy pushes her awareness into her dreaming body, just like it did to you when you were a child. She can enter lucid dreaming in a snap, but she may not know how to deal with this shift in perception in her daily life."

"Because she is now freed from her adopted modes of perception and belief structures," Court continued, "any repressed innermost emotions will suddenly erupt and force their way to the surface. A woman who has hardened and rigid belief structures will experience great agony during this time because she has spent the past month ignoring her true feelings. Now her rage over this repression battles it out with her belief structures and she experiences anger, cramps, and bloating. Her discomfort centers on the energy centers that deal with power and self-fulfillment, the second and third energy centers. Her anger rises up against the suppressive force of her thoughts. The more energy she has, the greater her discomfort. A woman who finds herself experiencing debilitating cramps needs to pay attention to her feelings on a daily basis–she is frustrating the expression of the Unknown."

Court excused himself to go and join Carol for a swim. He picked up his mask and fins and went down to the water. I lay down on my beach towel and stared up at the sky, feeling the energy of our conversations seep into my body.

Court returned a while later smelling of the ocean. It reminded me of my first memory with my father. He dried himself off and sat down under his umbrella. Carol came up a few minutes later and dried herself off. Then she went over to talk to some friends.

"Court, what happens when I succeed in finding my own power but my partner hasn't learned to do the same? How can I detach myself from someone who is constantly trying to get me to fill them up?"

"It's only a problem for you if you are attached to her in some way," he said. "If finding your own power has truly become your responsibility, then you need nothing from her. Her actions have no meaning for you because you are not looking to her to fill you up. You will feel sadness because the affection between the two of you is being choked off by her, but nothing else."

"Let's say that I'm not attached to my partner and I'm not looking to her for anything," I said. "I hang out with her because, in her better moments, she is a joy to be around. What do I do when she decides that I'm not taking care of her and she gets angry and sullen? What do I do then?"

"You allow her to be angry and sullen without any judgment or need to correct her," he said. "You can gently distance yourself and remain unaffected by her anger."

"How can I not be affected by her anger when it's directed at me?" I exclaimed.

"It will only affect you if you are attached to the outcome. If she yells at you and tells you that she's leaving, and you respond back in anger and say, 'Good, don't ever come back,' then you have demonstrated by your angry reaction that you are feeling rejected–that you are dependent on her emotionally. It's only when you are *expecting* some kind of energy from another that you will feel wronged when it is not given to you."

"I understand. But it's so hard to imagine being that complete."

"It's hard to imagine because you haven't yet stored enough energy to realize that possibility. Store the energy. Become complete. Then other people's actions will become impersonal and will not offend you. By becoming complete in yourself you will have the energy to find others who have done the same. These are the friends that never die."

We both looked at each other in silence and knew that we

were two such friends. I felt the presence come to us on the ocean breeze.

"What can I do to keep myself from being a slave to the sexual energy of powerful women?" I asked. "Is there something I can do to not become aroused by that energy, or is there some other way to make use of it?"

Court looked at me for a moment. "Sexual energy is just energy. It's your perception of it that makes it sexual."

"Are you saying that if I changed my perception of the sexual energy coming from a woman that it would affect me differently?" I asked him.

"Most definitely," he said. "You will still *feel* her energy, and it will excite you in some manner simply because it is a large quantity of energy. But what you *do* with it is up to you."

"But it's directed specifically at my second energy center, isn't it?" I asked. "Doesn't that matter?"

"It doesn't have to," he replied. "You are the one who decides what to do with the energy directed toward you *in any circumstance*. You can decide to place no interpretation on the energy. If a woman directs energy toward your sexual center, you can simply decide not to allow it to affect you in that way. Allow it to spread throughout your body without clamping down on it."

"You are saying that I have learned to hold sexual energy from a woman in my sexual center intentionally?" I asked.

"That's exactly what I am telling you," he said firmly. "You are a perceiver of energy. When you were growing up, someone taught you how to interpret sexual energy–how and where to hold onto it, and how to nurture it. You never questioned that. Why not?"

"I guess I never thought that there was anything wrong with it," I said.

"But now you do. When you receive sexual energy from a woman, you are the one who decides to hold onto it and feed it with your thoughts. You create energetic tension inside of yourself. You decide to become aroused. Arousal requires deliberate effort—it's not completely automatic. You decide whether or not to be attached to it or *detached* from it. You don't have to react to anyone's energy. What do you do if an ugly cow directs sexual energy at you? Do you let yourself get aroused?"

I laughed.

"You laugh, but you see the truth in it, don't you?" Court asked me.

"Yes," I replied.

"If you want to be the master of your destiny then you will never take anything for granted. Allow yourself to be released from your learned energetic attachments. Eventually, you will get to the point where you are no longer satisfied by sexuality. Your belief system will start to break down. You will want to do something else with that energy, something less transitory, something more fulfilling and permanent. As you continue to let go, that freed energy will rearrange itself and you will discover your own Truths regarding sexuality. You will no longer be ruled by it. Sexuality will take its appropriate place in the order of things. The energy that is freed when you succeed in dismantling your attachment will reawaken and reinforce other energetic aspects of your second energy center. The energy that you initially invested in sexuality and its pleasures will be redirected into the personal power of lucid dreaming. You will be free to begin your dreaming adventures again, and you will remember that real energetic mingling between partners occurs in dreaming. Your mind and body will find lasting satisfaction in the energy of the Unknown and will not crave the temporary release of orgasm. Your dreaming body will mingle with your partner's dreaming body when you are asleep and when you are awake."

Court looked out toward the ocean. There was now a beautiful, cool current of air blowing steadily inland from the water. "Your intention towards yourself is demonstrated by your unwavering persistence to remove everything that stands between you and your affection for the Unknown. You plow ahead, relentlessly. But how do you behave towards others as your belief structures crumble around you? Will you release your frustration on those with less energy or awareness? The truest indicator of your level of self-responsibility and energetic maturity is the way that you treat yourself and others as you dismantle the world of your perception."

"You are not afraid to be alone, if necessary," he continued. "You know that being alone teaches you how to find your own way in this dream. You learn how to maximize your energy, how to be proactive, how to aggressively seek your own destiny and how to think for yourself. You are willing to destroy everything in order to rebuild it according to your affection for the Unknown–according to your affection for yourself. By now you must realize that only through the perfection of yourself will you ever be capable of boundless affection for another. Only through the perfection of yourself can you work *with* another, and not against them."

"You are already capable of forging energetic partnerships–alliances based on the goal of absolute freedom and mutual fulfillment," he said. "You and your partner can experience a state in which the sum of your combined energy exceeds the value of your individual natures. The two of you become a force with a silent and unspoken understanding. You are united and have complete and utter confidence in each other. You undertake this journey together."

"Every once in a great while you will stumble upon people who are united in this fashion. They are a sight to behold! Individually, they are fierce and assertive. Together, they are unassailable and indestructible. You tremble with nervous excitement when they appear together. The energy of each member propels the others forward. The Unknown fuses them into a single unit. Energy flows through them in a completely unrestricted and staggering manner. They are cocksure and arrogant. Their precision is unmistakable. When they work together they make your hair stand on end. They never make a single mistake. You want to be exactly like them. Nobody stands in their way or questions anything that they do. Power has a face—it has a name. Every time that you witness an act of power in the future it will remind you of them. Do you hear what I'm saying to you? This is power, and this is affection."

THE LONGING

In the depths of my being lives a most terrible longing. It exists beyond the most bitter tears and finds solace only in itself. I remember the wind on a rainy day from long ago, when I was a child. Back then, after a heavy rain, when the skies were still dark and gray, and the wind blew in heavy and moist gusts, I could sense the presence of God nearby. I could smell and taste the rain in the translucent stillness of my mind, and I could watch the clouds above without being self-conscious, even though I was sitting in my neighbor's driveway. The wind consoled my spirit and mixed within, and I felt blessed by this distant and uncontainable presence. I did not need to reach out to touch God because I would have noticed that I was only touching myself.

Later, in high school, the longing lived in the belief that somewhere in this world was a person who knew me better than I knew myself. I knew that this person was out there somewhere, and that I had only to never give up my search. I remember very vividly the burst of electricity that swept through my entire body when I finally understood that this person was the Spirit–my oldest and truest friend. But still, I longed and ached in my heart for a human companion, someone to pass my years with in comfort and warmth.

I cannot even begin to describe the most unbelievable sadness and purity that I still feel at times, and over the years I have come to realize that this sadness extends beyond myself–it is the sadness of the lost dreams of family, of friends, of lovers, of children–of every human being that has ever walked this earth. We are travelers that are lost and alone, and we scour the world over looking for someone to point the way. Only once in a great while does a true inspiration come along. I've watched so many drop everything and follow someone who seems to know the way. We invest so much of ourselves in finding someone to take care of us because we know we are lost and lonely. We want to come home.

And so this chapter begins. On this particular Memorial Day, my alarm went off at nine o'clock in the morning. The announcer on the classical radio station said that he would be playing a piece of music written in remembrance of all of those who had left us behind. The Spirit told me that the sadness of this piece was for me, and that I should listen...

Court and I were sitting alone in the candlelight of his otherwise dark room. Music played quietly in the background. I felt a storm inside of me, and the heavy torrents of rain outside the window accented my mood. I was very restless, as I could feel some very old and dark memories fighting their way to the surface. I hadn't felt them for many years and I thought that they were gone. But I was about to find out that this was not true.

"What's wrong with you?" Court said. His eyes were fierce in the flickering light as they pushed their way inside of me. I was feeling a tight knot forming in my throat and I struggled to push it back down. "Don't fight it," he said. "Your body is trying to remember. Let it."

"I don't want to remember," I said. "She is gone now and so is my happiness. This horrible longing never leaves me alone."

"She is here," he replied softly. "She wants to say goodbye."

I looked at him and fought back the tears. "I tried everything I could to get through to the little girl inside of her, but she fought me until there was nothing left of me."

"She has come to thank you for trying," he said. "You took her to the desert where life was uncluttered and powerful. You showed her your strength, your affection, your sadness for her confusion, and you showed her the Spirit."

I broke down then, and I remembered in waves all of the tears I cried for her and for the others I had lost along the way.

"Why do I lose so many in my life?" I asked. "If I didn't have my connection to the Spirit, I would have died from all of this sadness. Why don't people open up to the Unknown? Don't people want to be saved from all of this?"

"They do, but they will not overcome their fear."

I wiped my eyes but they only swelled up again. "I once had a dream about a chapel that was built into the face of a towering rock. Inside, I found my entire family waiting for me. In one of the corners of the church, inside of a glass room, were all of my relatives who had already left this life. They were so present in my dream—their faces were so clear. They all wished me the best, as if they were still alive. Am I really sure that we aren't souls that live forever? Am I so sure that we're just energy that breaks apart at death?"

"I don't know that any of us will ever know that for sure in this lifetime," he replied.

"Sometimes I believe that we are souls," I continued. "This feels so much like a dream and I *see* that there is no time. I see myself moving in and out of this time and place, and I see my life stand still for a moment. I feel like I am lost in this dream and that I've been struggling all of my life to remember where I came from. I remember seeing my grandmother leave her body almost one year before she died. Her physical body lived in a nursing home in a wheelchair. The last time I saw her she had maneuvered herself face-first into a corner and was just sitting there, in a trance. She came to me later in a dream and said goodbye. She felt like a sister to me. I laid my hands over her and I felt a powerful rush of energy go through me."

"The loss is truly profound," Court said. "Even though you will be reunited with that soul or with that energy in another time and place, you will never experience her in that particular and unique intensity again. It will only exist once." He paused.

The music carried him away. "You are afraid to wake up, aren't you?"

"I can't stand to think about it," I said. "I don't want to find out after I wake up that I have left any of my loved ones behind. And yet, sometimes I think that they are already waiting for me outside of this dream. Sometimes this dream gets turned on its head and I feel that all of the people that I have affection for here in this world are really my true friends from outside of this world, and that they have come to me in my dream here in order to help me learn. I feel like they have already awakened, and that they're just helping me to learn my lessons until I wake up. Then I will see them again, but without all of this sorrow."

I went into a trance as the sadness of the music carried me further into myself. Court and I were listening to Gorecki's Symphony No. 3, the *Symphony of Sorrowful Songs*. I had purchased a copy of it after hearing it on the radio. I continued as the wind howled through the heavy, rain-soaked trees.

"I had another real dream a while back," I said. "I was at a ballroom. All I could see at first was the immaculate hardwood floor. There was a light that glowed in mellow ocher hues over the center of the floor. I was wearing white and was dancing in a ballroom style with a beautiful young woman who seemed so familiar. It felt like we had been lovers in another lifetime, or in some other place, and we were twirling around the room without touching the ground. Then, I saw another woman who appeared to be in her sixties. She was very tall and extremely elegant. Her hair was the purest white and was pulled back into a chignon. She had the most immaculate demeanor and stood very proudly. Yet she exuded absolute warmth in her strength, and I could see how power and affection existed in a perfect union. She was my mother, but not my birth mother. She was my true mother, the being that I had longed for since I could remember. She was the younger woman's mother, too. We knew her so well and she knew us. She joined us on the ballroom floor, and the three of us floated in a dance together. A profound wave of affection enveloped us as we glided in and through each other."

"As we whirled around the room," I continued, "I began to see others who were sitting in chairs at the end of the floor. They were hidden by the shadows. As I moved past them, the light would briefly illuminate their eyes. But when I strained to see their faces, they retreated silently into the darkness. I could see in their eyes that they had come with the older woman to watch us. They were my true friends, they were my home–my solace."

I had to stop talking again because my throat was so hard. Court was completely silent. I knew that he was feeling what I was feeling.

"You recognized them, didn't you?" he said very quietly.

"With all of my heart. They were the people that the two of us had left behind somewhere. They were waiting for us to finish our journey. Their eyes spoke of their affection and their longing for us to return to them. I have never felt so completely loved and missed. Here, in this world, I feel it only briefly. That's why this world feels like a dream. The love never lasts for more than a moment. But there in my longing, it lasts for as long as I can sustain it."

"You have felt it with others, too. Look deeper," he said intently.

I remembered then that I had felt it for my family, too. The feeling was buried beneath all of the debris of failed relationships and emotional baggage. I couldn't contain myself any longer. Court laid his hands softly on my head as I cried on his knees. Then he laid his head on mine. I hadn't felt like this in so long. I saw that all of them had so many lost and unfulfilled dreams. My parents, grandparents and friends–all of them were young once and filled with magnificent dreams of fulfillment. Now, they are filled with sadness. I wished that I could help them all.

"There is nothing you can do for them," Court whispered in my ear. "They have become passersby. They have made their choice and will fall along the way. They have succumbed to their fears and you cannot save them. You can't save anyone. You can only save yourself. But your affection for them will always remain."

"I don't want to let them go!" I sobbed. "I see the child in them, the one that is innocent and afraid, the one that wants to laugh and play. I see the one that runs and hides because he is confused, just like the little boy I knew in kindergarten who hid in his closet when the fire consumed his house. Why did he have to die? All of them just need someone to point the way."

"You can point, but you will die if you try to run back in and carry them out. You cannot go back to them. They must rally their strength and find their own way. It will take everything that they have, but it is never too late. It is only too late once they are gone."

"But I feel responsible for them because I *see* and they don't. I feel so much bitterness sometimes over this burden. I feel like a father to these people, a father who has failed."

"We are all simple like little children," he replied soothingly. "But at some point we have to merge our affection with responsibility. You carry a tremendous burden being able to see through this dream. But you must think of yourself as a flower on the side of the road. The scent of the Unknown passing through you fills the air, but who will take the time to stop and experience it? Who will make the commitment to embody it? Your only responsibility is to be who you are, and to not stand in the way of the Spirit as he moves through you and guides your words and deeds."

My breathing evened a little as I sat up, and my body shivered as the sadness passed through me, unhindered.

"It's one thing to be concerned with yourself," he said. "It's quite another to be concerned with yourself at the expense of others, to be self-absorbed. People want to find perfection in others before they perfect themselves. But it doesn't work that way. We cannot run and play in our neighbor's beautiful backyard and leave our own full of weeds and filth. Pretty soon our neighbor grows tired of taking care of us. He becomes worn out and his backyard falls into disrepair. He struggles to put it back together while we go and look for another one to play in. We must clean and perfect our own backyard first, and then notice the joy in our neighbor's backyard. Then we can agree to knock down the fence between the two yards. Perfect yourself first and perhaps some of those that you love will do the same. Then you will share eternal affection."

"Am I crying for myself, too?"

"You are realizing that all of us are alone on our paths. It is so hard to balance affection with sadness and longing. It takes everything that we have to pursue this path and not fall to pieces as we watch our family and loved ones give up and die. What an unbearable tragedy! The purest affection is precariously balanced by the purest sadness. We are all so frail and fragile, ultimately. We struggle constantly against seen and unseen forces that would consume us in any moment of weakness. Who can we turn to? Where can we run? And yet, out of all of this sadness comes an unfathomable silence—a feeling more powerful than the undercurrent of a bottomless ocean. As you swim deeper into your dark sadness, you will discover a great source of strength that lies hidden in the silent depths. It is this strength that sets you apart and helps you and others to stand alone. This silence will show you that this dream is about your affection for the Spirit and for life. Affection exists independently of people. Affection is life. It sets you free."

"If your life centers on people or things then you will lose them as your world collapses," Court continued quietly. "But if your life centers on the Spirit, then your world will remain unshakable. As you persist along this path the Spirit will bring others to you who have had similar experiences. You, and they, will find comfort in each other and will guide others who have the courage to be helped—those who long silently for the Spirit—those who are not satisfied with mediocrity."

"When I am face-to-face with this sadness, I wonder how

any single moment of pettiness or fear can survive," I said. "I see death sitting quietly nearby, watching all of us with its dark eyes, waiting for us to give up. How can anything ever be more important than opening the doors to affection and ridding ourselves of anger?"

He nodded. "When two people talk with each other through affection, the conversation–the words–are not important. It's the feeling, the honesty, the intention behind the words that is significant. What do you see in their eyes? What do you feel coming from their hearts? Are they bursting with joy to be sharing this brief dream with you?"

"Why do we constantly frustrate each other and ourselves?" I asked. "Aren't we all involved in a common struggle to find our way home–to deliver ourselves safely to those who are waiting for us on the other side of this dream? Affection *must* come before fear."

"Fear creates division, separation, and loneliness," Court said. "A life full of fear is a life spent in the most dismal isolation and living death. The people that live this way are committed to punishing themselves, and for what? They cling to their scraps of memories and shallow moments of happiness or pleasure, and reaffirm their misery daily by feeding their fear. They are prisoners of their own thoughts and beliefs. They don't allow themselves to feel, or to trust their intuition. The only way that they know that they're alive is through the sting of pain. When will they wake up? They don't understand that they don't have to wait until they die to see God or find lasting happiness. The same energy that is devoted to creating this hell can be used to create heaven–right here, right now. What can they possibly lose by trying?"

As I sat there permeated with grief, I remembered a feeling. It was a fear from long ago–a fear of joy. I recalled how I had learned it from my parents. It was the fear of having happiness stripped away. I had learned as a young boy that whenever my parents allowed themselves to feel and express joy it had always been accompanied by a remote fear of loss. This made them cling to the moment of joy even more, as if it would be the last one they would ever experience. I learned to keep my joy hidden within me–to never let on that I was deeply moved by anything until it was safe. That way, I would never be disappointed.

Court looked at me through the shimmering candlelight. "Their fear of losing joy was what took it from them. They couldn't see past their fear enough to realize that there would be more joy, if they wanted it."

I remembered how their fears had manifested so forcefully. "One time, Court, my father got a new job in another city with a big promotion. The whole family was very excited. The job was to start in three months, so my parents went and found a piece of land in the new town and had a house built. But somewhere in the midst of this I could sense their apprehension. They were afraid of getting what they wanted. A short time before we were supposed to move, my father got a phone call. Everyone held their breath. The company's budget was smaller than expected and they couldn't afford to hire him. They were very sorry. My parent's fear had quietly manifested. We lost the house and our new future."

Court looked past me into the darkness at the edge of the room. For some reason, I automatically turned around. "There are unseen forces that live off of our fear and sadness," he said. "We have talked about this before."

"Are you referring to the flyers?" I asked.

"Yes, I am. These entities sense fear and the accompanying worry. They simply hook themselves to it, since it is energy. It lures them closer to us, like bait. By feeding off of this energy, and because fear creates a weakness within us, they are able to help us manifest our fear."

"It's another self-fulfilling prophecy," I said.

"Of course it is. There is nothing mysterious about it. Animals attack humans when they sense fear. Why should it be any different for other energetic entities?"

Without warning, I felt something grip my heart. My body tensed and I saw something that I had never seen before. "I experienced the same fear of joy with Lela," I said with surprise. "Whenever I was happy or strong, she would do something to try to make me afraid–to try to weaken me. I remember now how I constantly shut down my heart in order to remain with her. I could actually feel myself clamp down on my heart internally. I remember even turning my eyes away from beautiful sunsets after I left her. I did not want to be happy, ever again. I could never understand why I did that. Even now I still struggle with that reaction."

"The flyers had a powerful grip on you," Court replied. "They lured you in, and then slowly began to wear you down."

"I guess I used to think that the flyers only made their presence known in more catastrophic ways."

"That is exactly why they continue to succeed," he replied. "They operate on a daily and mundane basis. They chip away at us constantly, feeding themselves on our everyday fears and worries. That's why it is so very important to pay attention to the smallest details in your life. It is only through the constant preservation of seemingly insignificant bits of energy that you will attain what you seek in life. As these insignificant bits of energy accumulate they will create an avalanche effect, and you will begin to succeed in leaps and bounds. At first, though, the accumulation is practically undetectable."

"So our suspicion that we should keep joy hidden was based on a premonition–a bodily knowledge that there was something out there attempting to take away our happiness," I said.

"It's part of a vicious cycle," Court replied. "You feel joy. You are afraid of losing it, so you cling to it. It is mysteriously taken from you and you feel sad. You worry about it happening again. So, the next time around you suppress your joy and also cling more tightly to it. Now the loss is greater. Eventually, you prefer to feel miserable because happiness has always disappointed you. At least your misery is reliable and constant. You complain about it, but you never take action. Even if you wanted to do something about your despair you wouldn't have the energy. You are now a prisoner, and you define your life through your misery."

He put his hand on my shoulder and said, "Real joy is experienced when the energy of the Spirit passes through you unhindered. Nothing and nobody can ever touch it. Put your energy and your affection there."

We hugged each other and then sat in silence as the soprano sang her haunting melody. The candles danced on the gusts of wind that came in through the barely open window. Court lit a fire in his fireplace and the presence filled the room. The smaller logs began to crack and pop, and I knew that there was no place else I would rather be.

"If this dream is the illusion," I said, "then my wish is to bring the magic from the real world into this dream and to manifest affection here and now—to make this dream and our time together feel more like home."

"As you wish," Court said as he smiled warmly back at me. "Don't allow anyone or anything to distract you from your love or passion. Paint the world that you've always dreamed of. Set yourself free and don't ever give up. Rise above it all and create a tapestry rich in feeling and understanding. Breathe life into yourself and others. This is your life. You only have yourself to answer to."

The faces of people who had died in my life were coming and going as we sat in silence. I saw my aunt, the firstborn of my father's family, who had experienced so much frustration and anger in her life. She had died within a few days after having been diagnosed with cancer. My father said that she had been resentful up until her last breath. I could see how powerful she had been. Even her death was potent and filled with rage.

I saw my grandfather and felt his anguish over having died so suddenly, leaving my grief-stricken grandmother feeling completely forsaken. Had they said goodbye to each other? Then I felt the presence of a friend, a fellow man of power whom I had left behind a few years back when my journey took an unexpected turn. This man had been responsible for showing me my path with heart. I had left him, however, to learn the lessons that he could not teach me. Much later, the Spirit brought me back to California as if it had been planned all along. I was to see him once more before he died. I was just in time for what turned out to be his final public appearance.

As he lectured on the podium, I was caught up in his gift. His words were like a salve to me, a balm. He set my heart on fire and revived my despondent dreaming body. A friend later informed me that his health was poor and that his vision was failing him. There had been people stationed around his podium to make sure that he didn't fall off. I remembered how he had tried to make light of the fact that he had lost his favorite shirt, saying that it was an omen for him. Perhaps his time on earth was up.

I broke the silence. "Why did he die like that, Court? I still feel a tremendous sadness when I think of the loss. When he died, it felt like I had lost a brother. I felt his failure almost as if I had experienced it myself. A few weeks after the news of his death leaked out to the newspapers, I got a call at six o'clock in the morning. It was a man from Russia who had found my name and number on a website. He asked me in halting English if it was true: Did my friend die like a man, or had he succeeded in leaving this world on his own terms and under his own power? I told him that my friend had died of liver cancer, and the man on the phone was suddenly very quiet. He mumbled something in Russian to someone in the background, and then very quietly said thank you, and goodbye. I could hear that faraway sound in the silence of the disconnected line."

"Liver problems indicate anger and frustration," Court said. "I sense that your friend was angry with himself for his inability to overcome his fear of losing the things that he was attached to. His more recent writings were less joyful, less passionate. They also expressed a longing for the past–a melancholy that was never resolved as his life neared the end. He had lost his way and was frustrated that he could not help those who believed in him. I sense, too, that he may have injured his body with drugs."

"I feel that, too. A friend of mine who remained with him after I left said that they were given something to drink at one of their gatherings. She thought that it may have had a hallucinogen in it."

Court stared at me in the flickering firelight. "The truly sad part is that we know nothing of his last days, firsthand," he said. "Knowledge of his mistakes and failures as a man of power could help so many people avoid or recover from similar experiences. That is the kind of information that has been lost and hidden throughout history. It would be invaluable to all who seek freedom. But now we must find these things out on our own and hope that we have enough time."

I watched the fire dancing, now. I did not want this night to ever end. I did not want to go back to the cold heartlessness of my daily life in the morning. Then I remembered an artist that I had known when I worked for the record company.

"Court, did I ever tell you about Anthony?"

"No, I don't think so."

"He was a very charismatic man, bold and fearless," I said. "He was in touch with the Spirit in a very compelling way. Anthony never approached a problem by submersing himself in the problem. His joy and fervor dispelled problems and darkness instantaneously. How could any problem exist when joy was present? All pettiness and bickering crumbled in the face of that ultimate love and passion. I have never seen anything like it."

"Anthony never came down off of his mountain," I continued. "If someone approached his mountain, he would lower his message down in his hand and pull that person up to where he was. He was never infected by the reality of others. He was solid. He was pure fire, and everyone responded to it. He believed that God wanted him and his band to start a revolution through their music. He wanted to save the children of the world. His plan was to get on a bus with his band and travel the country, stopping at every elementary school. He was going to use his power to help the children to see past the mindset that told them that joy and originality were not acceptable. If something did not come from the heart, it did not exist in his world."

"Everything had a double meaning for Anthony," I continued. "At that time, I was using my bicycle to get to work and even to the nightclubs where he was playing. One night, he delivered a message to me in a dream. He said, 'Instead of using your bicycle to get home, why don't you try using your wings?' Anthony was talking about getting home to God."

The logs from the fire hissed in the stillness. There was a purple glow above the tips of the flames. Anthony's presence was in the room.

"He and his band went everywhere barefoot," I said slowly in a faraway voice as I remembered my feelings for him. "He had the most uncanny ability to walk into a room full of business executives, sing a song, and start talking to them as if they were his children. I could feel the energetic struggle in the room as the executives fought to maintain their dominance and control. But Anthony's conviction was more powerful than anything they tried to hold on to. Anthony would succeed, and affection would flow through everyone. I could feel everyone in the room unite under a common purpose–the purpose of spreading that feeling throughout the world. It was beautiful. I watched him bring roomfuls of people at Los Angeles nightclubs to this place of affection, and the rooms would be transformed from cliques of trendsetters into playgrounds full of children. People would actually look into each other's eyes and smile. He broke down all of the walls and barriers. I felt a lot of affection for him. I guess that's why I'm remembering him right now."

"He was not afraid of joy," Court said. "That was his power. He had found his path with heart and poured everything he had into it. People respond instantly to the energy of the heart, but are immediately afraid of power without affection. What happened to him? Did he succeed?"

"No," I said, feeling the weight of that loss. "Somehow, he lost his footing. When he got his recording contract, the balance of power shifted inside of him and affection was lost. He struggled against the enemy of power–the flyers in another form. The record company cancelled everything. The last time I heard from him he was living on the streets of Denmark. He had lost the thread–his connection to the Spirit, and was a broken man. It was unbelievably sad to see my friend fall."

Court paused, reflecting on the message of Anthony's life. We were both keenly aware that the same fate was always waiting for us, too. Finally, he spoke.

"I sense that you were afraid of Anthony, too. He pushed you beyond your limits, didn't he?"

"One morning, we were driving down Melrose Boulevard in Los Angeles," I said. "He saw an adult video store on his right. In the window was a giant penis-shaped dildo. He pulled over and asked me if I was with him. I was afraid, but I followed him inside anyway. He went in, found the owner of the store and preached God to him. Anthony opened the owner's eyes to the fact that this object was in a window where children could see it. Did he really want to be responsible for putting an image like that into the mind of a four-year old child? The owner immediately took it out of the window."

"You were afraid the owner might become angry," Court said.

"I was very afraid of anger in those days, and afraid to stand up for what I believed in."

"But that's not the case anymore, is it?" he asked.

"I have learned to stand up for affection in the face of rage," I replied. "I have learned to be vulnerable in the face of hatred, and how to bare my heart and feelings while being trampled upon. I have learned that arrogance and fear will destroy my connection to the Spirit and destroy my life. I now know that affection melts away the barriers, that power balanced by affection is the Spirit."

"Nothing can stand in its way," Court said. We smiled at each other. Then he spoke.

"There is so little kindness, so little politeness left in this world. We have lost our integrity and tenderness. We have become nothing more than predators looking for energy. But if we can rise to the challenge and find that energy in ourselves, then we will have no need to take power from another–no need to complicate their journey. We will experience the sadness of the world while overflowing with joy."

"We will become happy and content in ourselves," I said. "We will truly enjoy other people and their predicaments, as well as our own."

"We will experience an affinity for life and all of its mysteries," Court said. "We will see that affection is constant. We will not be attached to anyone or anything. We will be free to embrace the Unknown and make the ultimate journey."

THE PREDILECTION TO DREAM

*When you see your likeness, you are happy.
But when you see your images
that came into being before you
and that neither die nor become visible,
how much you will have to bear!"*

-The Gospel of Thomas, verse 84-

For six years after my near-fatal bout with the flyer, I had been unable to get myself to start lucid dreaming again. Something was obstructing me. There was now a darkness around me–perhaps a heaviness. It felt like I was under a thick black woolen blanket. For the first three years of this period, I would wake up suddenly in the middle of the night, frantically gasping for air. In my dreams, I had been yelling and screaming at different people, trying to get them to listen to me. I felt that these dreams were therapeutic because I could feel the trapped energy moving out of me as I yelled. Later, after the screaming episodes subsided, I had dreams where my energy would mingle with incoming energy, and then explode out of the top of my head and rush upwards into the Unknown.

I hadn't seen Court in several months. The last few times that I had gone to see him, I had mostly indulged in whining and complaining about my pitiful condition: I didn't feel well; I felt lost and drained. I told him that I felt like I was getting old. He had looked scornfully at me, almost with contempt, as he shook his head very slowly from side to side. He told me that it wasn't old age that was my problem–it was old habits. I knew right then that even though it was comforting to have him around, I had work to do. He could not help me with that. It was up to me.

I had taken the time to clear some emotional baggage, rest, eat, pay off a few bills, clean out my closet, and do some hiking and exploring. In essence, I had tightened up my life and regained some of my strength. Now, it felt like spending time with him would be productive and beneficial.

I drove to his house on this mildly cold morning, enjoying the new lightness of my being. I parked across the street and made my way into his front yard. Even from outside I could smell the sweet and rich aroma of his clove cigarettes. I felt his warmth before I knocked on the front door.

He opened the door and stared past me. He coughed.

"Ghosts," he mumbled. I stood there patiently while he discharged them. Then he smiled at me and we embraced. We laughed as we walked with our arms around each other into the living room. Our affinity for each other never ceased to amaze me.

As we settled down into our chairs, I noticed that Carol had been out shopping again. The furniture was covered with new throws, and there was a new, plush rug on the hardwood floor. The heater was blowing warm air up from the floor vent and I relaxed into the pleasantness of the room.

"Thirty seven from your entity," he said. "You got the ghosts from your twin soul–someone from work."

I thought for a minute, and then remembered that one of the managers had unexpectedly attached himself to my girlfriend a couple of weeks back. When my girlfriend came home one night, I thought that she had started a love affair with him. I kept seeing his face and feeling his presence. A few days later while she was at work, I opened her bedroom door to turn on her heater. I practically jumped out of my pants as an enormous flyer darted past me and flew down the stairs. I stood there in the doorway, completely frozen. My whole body was shaking. I wasn't frightened, but the rush of energy as the flyer flew by had jolted my dreaming body. I immediately made sure that the flyer had left the apartment. After that, I stopped seeing the manager's face and feeling his presence in my girlfriend.

I told Court about this episode. "Yes, that's him," he said. "You've felt a connection to him since the first day you met him."

"Whenever I looked at him," I said, "I felt like I was looking at myself. I knew that he was from my entity."

"Unconsciously, he knew that, too," Court replied. "Energetically, he tied himself to you through your girlfriend in order to cast off his ghosts. They came from his mother." He smiled at me.

"Do you see flyers or ghosts the same way that I do?" I asked Court.

"No," he replied. "I *smell* them!"

I thought he was joking, so I started to laugh. He chuckled, too, but looked back at me with a serious expression.

"You're not kidding, are you?" I asked.

"No, I'm not. If the ghosts are infant souls, I smell something resembling diapers."

I burst out laughing. I couldn't even begin to imagine how unsettling that would be.

"Whenever I'm out in public," he continued, "I get various smells coming at me from all directions, just like you see darkness or shadows. It's simply my predilection to smell them, just as it is yours to see them. I still get bombarded, just through a different sensory avenue. Other people hear them."

My jaw dropped open. "That's why some people say that they hear voices," I said emphatically.

"Of course," he said. "However, there's a difference between hearing voices and hearing someone talking to you. Hearing voices is a way of saying that you hear many voices at once, like in a restaurant, just as I may smell many smells or you may see many dark shapes. Hearing ghosts in public places is another form of seeing. Hearing one voice, though, usually means that that person is under the control of a flyer. These two things are dramatically different than the hearing that comes from intuition, or from direct knowledge. The hearing that comes from direct knowledge may be interpreted as someone talking to you but is, in reality, just a way of describing the feeling of suddenly knowing something for sure. Don't get them confused."

"I won't," I said. "I know that the voice of intuition isn't really a voice. It's more of a feeling–a surety, a *knowing*."

I smelled some coffee brewing, and Court got up and went into the kitchen. He poured the fresh, hot coffee into a thermos and placed it in the front room by the coffee table. He sat down and poured the coffee from the thermos into his mug. He took a couple of sips. I knew that he would continue to do so during the course of the day in order to aid his continued rejuvenation process. I wondered if he smelled coffee whenever there were old soul ghosts around.

I had come to see him this morning because I wanted to ask him about my inability to return to lucid dreaming. I wanted to get back to it more than anything–nothing else was as pleasing or constant. I intuited that there were vast secrets and mysteries waiting for me there.

"Let's go back a ways," he said as he took another sip. "You've already told me about your dreaming experiences as a small child. What kind of experiences have you had as an adult?"

"My lucid dreaming began again after college," I said.

I proceeded to tell him how so many of my experiences on the path to awareness and dreaming had come from listening to my body. The most difficult part of listening to my body was not questioning what I heard. My body told me that it needed to rest, and so for eight months I found myself back at home with my parents, completely taking advantage of their generosity. The only thing that kept my guilt in check was my body's desire to rest and not be stressed in any way.

After six months of sleeping, eating, resting and reading, I began to feel very peaceful. My bed was in the front room near a window that I always kept opened at night. I had the most unreasonable fascination with the air at my parents' house. It always brought back such strong memories—memories that never fully materialized. They were always just beyond my reach and contained vague shadows of faces and moods that I could never place.

It was springtime, and I could feel the pressure of my renewed vitality increasing. I knew that I was waiting for something. On this particular night, I fell asleep like I had done every other night for the past six months. My parents were asleep in their room with the door closed. The house was completely dark. My mind and body were relaxed and completely still. I didn't have a care in the world.

A few hours later, I was deep within my sleep. It was utterly quiet. Then, I felt somebody tap me on the shoulder—or maybe they softly called my name—I wasn't sure. Whichever it was, it felt completely natural, like I had been expecting it. I was not alarmed.

I had been sleeping on my stomach with my face pointed to my right, towards the wall. My right arm had been under my pillow. But somehow, I suddenly found myself propped up on my elbows while I turned to my left to look behind me. It wasn't like I had been suddenly awakened and had looked around the room to see who had called me—I already knew exactly where to turn and look, and I was completely awake even though I felt like there was a fog surrounding me. As I looked behind me, I saw a white luminous being the size of a man. It looked like a white ghost, and it had me completely riveted. I struggled to formulate a thought, but something was preventing me from doing so. My eyes were wall-eyed and I struggled to focus them, but something was preventing that as well. I realized then that my struggle was distorting the image, so I relaxed and let my body do what it knew was right, even though what it was doing was completely foreign to my mind.

As I relaxed into my seeing, I discovered that I was looking at an amorphous blob of whitish light, not especially bright, but almost with a hint of blue. Somehow, I knew that I wasn't seeing this image with my eyes even though I saw it superimposed on the closet doors in the entryway. Some other part of me perceived it, and was translating it into an image that my brain could interpret. That was why my eyes had to remain out of focus. As a matter of fact, they were so out of focus that it felt as though each eye was pointed as far away from my nose as possible.

As I watched the visitor, I noticed that he was not rigid, but seemed to be breathing or pulsing in a very gentle way. He was vaguely shaped like a human, but was a little taller and wider. I sensed some kind of affection for him, though the affection was somehow impersonal and unattached.

After a couple of minutes, I felt my mind struggling again to interpret the image. Slowly, my eyes straightened out and my thoughts reappeared. The image faded, and I found myself alone in the darkness of the living room. My whole body was alive with sensation and was glowing with happiness. I felt unbelievably content.

For almost six years afterwards, I thought that I had seen an apparition of some kind and wondered why I had seen it. Finally, after storing enough energy, I realized that I had seen my dreaming body. That was how I knew when and where to look that night. The energy that I had stored by resting and relaxing had created that moment. It was thrilling beyond belief.

Court listened intently to my story. He was looking directly at me. "Having a still mind and a relaxed body are of supreme importance for dreaming," he said. "Your life at that time was simplicity itself, although you were behaving irresponsibly toward your parents."

I nodded. "When I wasn't reading, I was flying kites with my brother and sister, and the neighborhood kids. I was completely focused on the present moment. I put my all into each thing that I did, no matter how trivial, and enjoyed it completely."

"That's very appropriate," he said. "Your body and mind are designed to focus on one thing at a time. The idea of multitasking is a horrible misconception. Why would you split yourself in two? What will that accomplish? The truth is that doing more than one thing at a time fragments and disturbs your natural, tranquil condition. Many believe that they can get more done when they do two things at once, but they fail to realize that they are not doing two things *simultaneously*—they are really alternating back and forth very rapidly between two separate tasks. That kind of rapid alternation is what creates internal stress. After a full day of that kind of activity the brain is mush and is filled with all kinds of images that have not been properly digested by the body."

"Any form of energy that you don't pay complete attention to will remain in your mind and body until you finally focus on it and release it," Court continued. "It happens at the office and at home. If you don't pay attention to your feelings *at the moment that they occur*, there will be a residue left in your system. It's all just energy. And if someone directs energy at you, it will remain with you until you do something about it. That's why it's so very important to be completely present and focused on the moment."

He poured himself another cup of coffee. "Recapitulation isn't just about recollection," he said, "it's about the assimilation of energy. You, like the rest of us, move about so quickly and are so bombarded by constant input that you don't have the time or space to sort through the energy that has been sent to you throughout any given day. If you don't sort through the energy, your sleep will be disturbed causing further stress in your body. You need space, downtime, or quiet time, where the rapid sequences of events are allowed to unfold in a manner more befitting the energetic speed of your body and organs. Then, the day and its events can be laid to rest, and you can go to sleep fresh and unencumbered. Your brain will be silent because there is nothing left to think about. Life becomes simple. Only then will your dreams be about freedom and not about regurgitation."

I started laughing. Court asked me what was so funny.

"I have truly had some bizarre dreams brought about by bodily imbalances," I chuckled. "One time, I dreamed that I had to fart very badly. There were all of these people in my room–I could wait no longer. I threw back the covers and unleashed an enormous, out-of-control tornado. As the wind came blasting out, I saw huge objects being ejected out of my rear end. Each one made a sound, like a basketball being shot out of a tube. First, there was a baby grand piano, then a couple of chairs, and maybe even a chicken. It was a colossal relief."

Court laughed uproariously and shook his head. Tears welled up in his eyes. "Did you crap your pants?" he stammered. He could barely get the words out amidst his uncontrollable laughter.

I doubled over. "No, but I sure woke up in a hurry and checked everything out."

"Maybe you just had ta goat da bafroom." His poking fun at the jargon of a famous friend of ours was too much. I slapped him on the leg and he pushed me. We both had to go stand outside for a few minutes.

After we had calmed down, we came back inside and sat down. Court was still wiping his eyes. I continued, chuckling.

"During those months at my parent's home, I noticed another bizarre detoxification taking place. At any random moment an old memory, or an old song, or an old jingle from a television commercial would surface and repeat itself over and over in my head. Once, I got a musical commercial slogan stuck in my head for two weeks until it finally played itself out. It was maddening."

Court chuckled. "Your brain looks for patterns. That's its function. Thought is a pattern, music is a series of patterns, and language is a pattern. If you are full of fear, watch out! Fear and frustration are what drive you to seek patterns. The more afraid you are, the more patterns you will try to fill your head with. Patterns create an almost seamless cycle of mental noise in your brain. If there are no holes in this repetitive cycle, you will never have to worry about facing the fears and repressed emotions that are lurking just beneath the surface."

I nodded. "I've had many friends," I said, "who could not be by themselves without the radio or the television on. They have very fragile beliefs about what sanity is. They're terrified of the thought that they might lose their minds. When I suggested that they might turn off the radio or television once in a while and enjoy silence, they became very angry."

"People pay good money to be distracted," Court replied. "Their anger manifests in direct proportion to their fear. They expend large quantities of energy to forget and cover up their frustration, fear and sorrow. Money is energy! If you are full of frustration, fear and sorrow, you will have a hard time being silent by yourself. People like that create their own distractions by making messes that they will have to clean up later. That's why meditation is not something that can be practiced–it's something that must be lived. It's a complete state of being. It's something that *happens to you* as a direct result of ridding yourself of your past and emotional baggage. You can't forcefully quiet your mind if it is motivated and driven by fear. You can only distract it or fill it up with nonsense. Or, you can gather your courage and face the past."

He paused for a moment. "Our world will continue to get more complex and sensational," he finally said. "Technology is a bottomless pit of thought. You will discover infinitely more useful knowledge through silence. The bottom line is that an empty mind is the only way to reconnect with dreaming and the Unknown. A solid intention comes from a unified and unfragmented mind."

"You said that thought was a pattern," I said. "What do you mean by that?"

"Thought is a repetitive pattern of symbols and images in

the mind. Haven't you ever seen the images of speech in your mind?" he asked.

When I thought about it, I recalled that I had indeed witnessed that phenomenon. I remembered that, in some very quiet moments and also in some very sickly moments, I had seen how my thoughts were attached to very swift images or pictures. The quieter I became, the longer those images remained viewable. I saw that there were images attached to language and also to feelings. Each of these images created a preprogrammed reaction in my body.

"As your mind becomes still and empty you will possess the speed necessary to become consciously aware of these pictures *as they form*," Court said. "You will have sufficient energy and velocity to disable the thoughts, beliefs, and fears that create those pictures and trigger the corresponding bodily responses. Then you will become even quieter, and your body will enter a state of unparalleled rest and repair."

I told Court that I recently had noticed something else that I had never noticed before. In order for my brain to hold onto memories, ideas, or beliefs, I saw that I had to tighten certain tissues in the center of my brain, just like I might tighten my hand in order to hold onto an object. I also noticed that the same was true with emotions, except that they were stored by tightening my various internal organs. Each organ held onto specific emotions or fears. He reminded me that if I were to hold onto an object with my hand for an extended period of time that my hand would cramp up—the flow of blood and oxygen would be decreased, and my hand would eventually deteriorate. Disease would inevitably follow.

"Then the same would be true for my brain and internal organs," I stated. "That's why my dreaming gets disrupted. Recapitulation can release that tension and allow my energy to flow again."

"Energy is what directed your brain and organs to tighten in the first place," Court said. "Energy is what will release them. In order for your body to hold onto a thought or fear, an initial effort–an expenditure of energy–was required. Do you understand? You had to decide on some level to tighten up and hold onto the thought or fear in the first place. There was a beginning."

"At some point in your past," he continued, "you decided to embrace a belief structure, a fear, a memory, or an expectation. You were cajoled or threatened into learning by rote while in school. So, you taught yourself to memorize facts, melodies, beliefs, fears, and other patterns and symbols. You learned to clench the appropriate cells, tissues, and organs in your body until you succeeded. You *learned* retention. You taught your brain to retain pictures and your organs to retain emotions. If you hadn't forced yourself to learn in this manner, the patterns would've passed right through you leaving your brain and organs fresh and untouched. You would never have become so narrow-minded and rigid."

He laughed at me while I sat there, allowing it all to sink in.

"Don't you remember a time when you were younger when it was impossible for you to recall a favorite song or melody at will?" he asked. "All that you could remember after a song finished playing was the *mood* that the song conveyed."

I nodded.

"Melodies, memories, facts, and feelings are nothing more than permanent contractions of your brain or other organs," he continued. "Thoughts are contractions of your brain. Why do you think so many men go bald at the crown? They have pinched off the incoming energy of the Unknown with their incessant thoughts."

I chuckled, remembering how my hair had started falling out during a period of heavy thinking and worrying.

"Your brain and internal organs can learn to be relaxed again, allowing your thoughts, beliefs, and past to go free," Court said. "You may need some help from a masseuse or chiropractor, however, in order to help loosen some of your frozen joints or knotted muscles. I can see that the muscles and joints that surround your various organs have already cramped up from being frozen for so long. After your brain, organs, muscles and joints have begun to relax and repair themselves, you will enter a condition of acute sensitivity. You will become maddeningly aware of the sounds of the world."

"What 'sounds of the world' are you talking about?" I asked.

"You will be bombarded by the noise of people and their machines, even more than you are now," he stated. "As your organs become more sensitive, you will become aware of the energetic pulses generated by the contractions of other peoples' organs and tissues."

"Do you mean that I will be able to sense their thoughts and intentions?" I asked in amazement.

"You will become more aware of their energy at all levels," he said. "At first, you will be practically terrorized by the amount of input because you will not be completely free from your self-image and your own frustration. You will spend hours talking to yourself about how inconsiderate people are. But you will also become aware of the magnificent sounds of the earth: the wind, the animals and birds, the insects, and the moods of the earth itself. Once your detachment is complete and you have succeeded in manifesting your path, you will rise above it all and rejoice."

We sat together in the warmth of the room, feeling an affinity for our mutual path. Court lit a clove cigarette. I pulled out my pipe and some of the tobacco that I still bought on occasion from Alaska. I filled my pipe and lit it, and the combined aroma of our different fragrances spun about the room.

"Joy is another necessary condition for lucid dreaming," he said as he looked reflectively at the swirling smoke. "Thinking requires an expenditure of energy. Feeling requires a letting go. Thinking is active; feeling is passive. One requires motion; the other, rest. Thinking is something that you do; feeling is something that you don't do—a not-doing. Thinking impedes feeling, and takes you away from yourself and from the present moment. Feeling is listening, watching, and, therefore, knowing. It is honesty and joy. It is your link to the mystery."

"The mystery is not outside of you–it is not something to be acquired," Court said firmly. "It is within you, and is something to be remembered. To know this is to choose the hardest path: the path of self-fulfillment through self-responsibility. This is where you will find joy."

"Awareness is joy," I replied. "It's a force that I feel that is independent of thought. It only operates fully when I get out of the way–when my brain is silent. That's when I become something more than myself. I become the Unknown."

"Becoming the Unknown is Truth," Court asserted. He paused for a few minutes. I could see that he was feeling his way through the labyrinth of consciousness with a silent intensity.

"Thoughts are from the past–they are the known," he said. "If you try to interpret the present with those thoughts then you have brought the past into the present. How can you go forward and explore new horizons if you are constantly re-circulating and reinforcing the past, the known? That's absurd. You are looking for a *new* way of life, a new answer. Wait, instead. Sit with the feeling and allow the energy to come up from within. Hold onto the thread that connects you to silent knowledge and don't let it get away."

"Your awareness struggles to emerge amidst the endless chattering of thought," he continued. "Your thoughts and fears are amplified by the thoughts and fears of others. They constantly thwart the joy of awareness. Modes of perception restrict and shut down your dreaming body. You were able to see your dreaming body because you listened to your body and followed its intuition. You did what you felt like doing in the moment without ever asking why. You didn't think about anything. You trusted the voice of awareness."

"There is no resistance in the midst of pure joy," he said with a full voice, "and because there is no resistance, there is no residue, no memory of the moment. There is only a lingering."

He put his finished cigarette in the ashtray. "Now, let's talk about your more recent attempts to set up dreaming."

I told him that I still remembered very vividly the day that I was sitting outside at my parent's house with my feet in the sun, reading another of Carlos Castaneda's books. I was sure that he was my ticket to dreaming and to a new way of life. My will was burning inside of me. I knew that it was connecting itself to him. *I could feel it.* My brain was struggling with the details of how I would find him, but I let it be. My body knew that it was only a matter of time. My will had found the thread of energy that was the link to the man, and I poured all of my available energy into feeding and nourishing that thread. It grew and grew, and one morning I just picked up the phone and called his publisher. They referred me to his management company. I couldn't dial the numbers fast enough.

"Hello, this is Toltec Artists. How may I help you?"

"Hi, I'm wondering when Carlos Castaneda will be publishing his next book, and if he has any plans to give any lectures or workshops?"

"He has no plans to do anything," the woman replied. "He is currently somewhere in Mexico. We have not heard from him in a long time."

"OK," I said. "Thank you."

I was disappointed, but something in me already knew how to wait. Six months later, I moved to Burbank and got a job as an apprentice in a custom furniture shop. I had just returned from Alaska. I was feeling stronger everyday. My muscles were swelling and my dreams were becoming more and more vivid. I would wake up in the middle of the night to go to the bathroom, and wonder where I was and how I had gotten there. I was beginning to sense that I might be able to manipulate this dream. The nights started to all seem the same, as if I hadn't gone forward in time but was just repeating the same night over and over in an attempt to see through the illusion and wake up. On one of these nights, the thread suddenly got thicker. I got up the following morning and pulled out my phone book.

"Hello, this is Toltec Artists. How may I help you?"

It was a different woman this time. "Hi, I'm wondering if Carlos Castaneda will be publishing any new books soon, and if he will be giving any lectures?"

"Yes," she answered. "His new book will be out next month. Did you know that two of his female associates have books already in print?"

"No, I didn't know that. I called a few months ago and was told that he had disappeared in Mexico."

"That's not true. He's been here the whole time. His associates will be giving a workshop in Payson, Arizona in about three months. Would you like the information?"

I was shaking with nervous energy. My timing was impeccable. I hadn't *done* anything except wait and hold onto the thread. I took down all of the information and went out and bought the books. I put in extra hours at the woodshop and bought my plane ticket to Arizona. One week before the workshop, Carlos' new book was in my hands. I read it in three days. I was recapitulating twice a day and sleeping every chance I got. I had even joined a Castaneda discussion group. Nothing mattered except my connection to this energy.

After much nervous anticipation, I found myself in Payson. I could hardly keep myself from shivering with excitement. I knew that they would discover me, that they would recognize me. I was filled with pride. That first night, one of Carlos' female associates spoke to us.

"...And there will not be a new party of seers. Don Juan's lineage ends with us. We are not looking for apprentices. If you want to succeed on this path, you must do it yourself. We will provide you with as much information as we can, but it is still up to you. No one is going to help you."

Her words struck a chord in me. For the first time in my life I understood that it was completely up to me. I wasn't going to have someone taking care of me, or spoon-feeding me silent knowledge. If I wanted to be a man of power, then I would have to make it happen. I had come hoping to see Carlos, but I had only seen myself.

On Monday, after returning to Burbank, I felt a very strong compulsion. I knew that if I wanted this path to become more than an idle wish that I would have to take action. I drove to the management company's office in Los Angeles and walked up the stairs. I paused outside of the door, my heart pounding furiously. I was starting to have second thoughts about the abruptness of my visit, and I wanted to think of something pleasant to say when I opened the door. But before I could formulate a thought, I allowed my will to take over. I knew that my dreaming body was already inside the office–I knew that it was opening the door for me. My vision narrowed and I saw my hand reach out for the doorknob.

The next thing I knew, I was saying hello to one of the female associates of Carlos. She was already halfway to where I was before I could say three words. Out of the corner of my eye, I detected a startled group of people standing in a back doorway staring at me. They had been talking to each other and my sudden appearance had interrupted their conversation. I recognized them as the women who had led the workshop in Payson. They were surrounding a short, brown-skinned man with gray hair. They quickly maneuvered him into a back office.

"I'm sorry, but you're not allowed in here," said the woman as she firmly escorted me out of the office and down the hallway to the stairs. "How did you find us?" She was definitely vexed and somewhat alarmed by my sudden entrance. I could feel myself starting to clam up, so I allowed my will to become active again. I wanted to make sure that she was clearly aware of my intention and determination.

"I didn't mean to intrude, but I wanted to take this opportunity to thank you and the rest of the group for the workshop in Arizona. I also wanted to let you know that I want to be a part of this group and its path, even if you just need me to work in the office. I have excellent computer skills."

She paused as we reached the bottom of the stairs and I could see an energetic opening.

"Perhaps we will be in touch with you. What is your name again?"

I told her. "I have left my phone number with you before," I said.

"Yes. Yes, you have. Please do not tell anyone else about this office. Good bye."

She walked back up the stairs and I drove home, trembling the entire way.

One month later, I received a call from the woman informing me that Carlos was intending to set up a small, private group that would meet on a weekly basis. He wasn't sure what the format would be yet, but we should wear loose, comfortable clothes for some movements that we might be doing. He also wasn't sure that he would be involved in these groups. His involvement would be decided by the energy of intent. We would be meeting at a small dance studio in Santa Monica, and had only to contribute twelve dollars each per month to cover the cost of the studio rental. I was not to tell anyone of my involvement in this group.

On the night of our first meeting, the woman called to inform me that Carlos would not be attending. Still, I was excited that I was getting closer to meeting him. I arrived at the studio and waited for the women to arrive. When they walked in the door, they were surrounding a small brown man. It was Carlos. I felt a hot rush. I had succeeded in following the thread. I had entered his world.

The format for our two-hour sessions consisted of mini lectures from Carlos, followed by some new movements that he was experimenting with. He told us that ancient seers had discovered these movements in their lucid dreaming. The movements were energetically designed to optimize the health and vitality of the physical body and the dreaming body. He had decided to call these movements, *Tensegrity*. Each week we tried out new movements. It seemed like he wanted to see what kind of energy each movement produced when performed by a group. Later on, these individual movements were combined and made into longer sequences of movements. These were called energetic passes.

One night after Tensegrity, I felt a very strong desire to meet the man face-to-face, to know the man behind the scenes. I wanted to stand inside of his energy field and feel what it was like–I wanted to know if he was the real thing or just another author full of pretty ideas. I had no idea what I would say to him. I thought that we might not even speak. I waited outside of the front door of the dance studio for him, but ten other people were, too. I decided to move farther away. The thread was very active. I looked back and noticed that he seemed to be involved in a very lengthy discussion, so I decided to try again the following week and I crossed the street to my car.

Then, I felt the thread suddenly thicken and get hotter, and I turned my head and saw him coming towards me with the women. Their van was parked a short distance behind my car. I turned to face him in the complete darkness and I knew that we were locked–I could feel the thread become solid. As the group approached, he stepped away from them and came towards me. I could sense the alarm of the women since they didn't seem to recognize me. He walked right up to me and clasped my hand.

"What is your name?" he asked me.

I told him. I could barely make out his face. Everything around us was black and the rest of the world had ceased to exist. In that moment, I felt as though I was standing alone in a vacuum with a disembodied voice. It was more like a dream than any dream I could remember. He put his other hand on my shoulder and whispered in my ear with a foreign raspiness.

"I saw you at my lecture last week. Your energy stuck out like a sore thumb. What do you do for a living?"

"I'm an apprentice at a custom furniture shop," I nervously replied. I noticed that the women had loosely meandered over to their van, but were still watching warily.

"Excellent!" he exclaimed. I knew right then that what I had felt about my job was accurate. I had discovered that the only way to work without making any mistakes around dangerous saws and other tools was to have an incredibly quiet mind.

"Are you practicing the movements at home?"

I said that I was. He then said some things to me that I still, to this day, cannot remember. I can't even remember how I felt when he said them. Then he walked away.

During the few months that I was a member of this group, my dreaming attention increased dramatically. At the time, I thought that it was due to the Tensegrity, but I later understood that it was due to the intention that I poured into my Tensegrity and my daily life. I continued recapitulating, and reduced my activities to eating, working, and sleeping. I barely talked. I thought about nothing. Everything I did was spontaneous. I didn't even talk to Court or Carol during this time. I had succeeded in bringing a large quantity of my energy into the present moment.

As I continued to rest, relax, and recapitulate, I noticed that my brain and body began to release their grip on my fears, emotions, and limiting modes of perception. I stopped reading books, and discarded all belief structures and preconceived ideas. I eliminated syntax and complexity. I threw everything out the window.

I walked with abandon wherever I pleased and allowed my dreaming body to direct my movements, even if they made no sense. There, I found a path untainted by thought. Quite unexpectedly, I could feel my body again. It responded to the change instantaneously and rejoiced. I was whole. I was absolutely free. My determination to live my life to its fullest extent was unconditionally reinforced. A world of wonder and awe stood by waiting expectantly for me to touch it. I was detached and at ease.

I finished my narration and Court excused himself for a few minutes. My body was alive with the memories. For some reason, a phrase popped into my head: "Dying is not hard–living is." Court returned just then. He straightened out the throw on his chair and turned around. Just before he sat down, he placed his hand lightly on my shoulder. He removed it as he sat back in his chair.

"You manifested your dream through the sheer force of intent," he said to me. "Your will was focused and you persisted. Your will became more powerful because you allowed it to act. How were you living during this time?" he asked me.

"I was renting a room in Burbank from my sister and her husband," I said. "I worked from nine in the morning to three in the afternoon, five days per week. I went to bed at ten o'clock and got up in the morning at eight o'clock. I was working at the woodshop with my boss and one other apprentice. The job was physical, but not too strenuous. I was not in a relationship at the time and was not in contact with any people besides those that I was living and working with. I had debts, but was not worried about them. I had recently sold the majority of my possessions, and I had stopped listening to music. I took naps constantly"

"What about your eating habits?"

"I ate very lightly, mostly fresh juice, turkey, and beef jerky. I ate dinner at about five o'clock and would brush my teeth immediately afterwards so that my body knew that it could start shutting down for the night. I never ate just before bed. If anything, I would go to bed slightly hungry."

"Dreaming can only occur when your physical body is optimized," Court said. "If you go to bed less than three hours after eating, your digestive organs will still be active and their energy will not be available for dreaming. Your organs require some time to rest and rejuvenate before being called upon to perform their secondary function–that of providing energy for dreaming. The type of food you eat is also important, but each body has different energetic preferences. Eating only enough to satisfy your body, but not overtax it, ensures that your digestive organs are not exhausted or fatigued."

"All of these factors contributed to my lucid dreaming," I said. "I would get into bed when I felt relaxed and mildly tired. I slipped easily into the seam between being awake and being asleep. My daily awareness slid, fully active, into my dreams. I watched myself fall asleep."

I told him how my dreams became more vivid. I began to remember them every morning without effort. I began to notice a presence in the night, something that seemed to stand next to me whenever I woke up to go to the bathroom. This presence pushed relentlessly on me. Every night without fail, as I stood silently at the toilet, the voice of the presence would ask me how I knew that this world was real. It was more like an absence than a presence—the absence of *anything*. It was so thorough that I would wonder how I got to where I was, and then I would wonder where I came from and how to get back there. It was not a frightening feeling, but an incredibly exciting one. It was so impersonal that it became more personal than anything or anyone that I knew. It was more lucid than my most intense emotion or moment of clarity. I knew, without any doubt, that I was in-between the two worlds, and that I was somehow standing outside of the force of time. I seriously could not tell which world was real and which was the dream.

Court bobbed his head up and down in a rhythmical agreement. I noticed that he was in a trance. I waited for him to come around.

"You accept what you see because you expect to wake up at any moment," he finally said. "Both worlds seem real and both worlds seem like a dream; they are now equal. Your dreaming body was becoming *aware of itself* in this world. Normally, you are aware of your existence only through self-reflection—by reflecting on things that have happened to you *in the past*. You have never been aware of your existence *in the moment*. Awareness in the moment requires you to step outside of your perception, which is what your dreaming body was doing. It was seeing itself without the mirror of self-reflection, without being hindered by your thoughts or beliefs. It saw the dream *as it was being dreamed.* Things must have changed drastically for you in your daily life when this began to happen."

"They did, but it was the most natural thing that could've happened to me," I said. "I felt like I had simply remembered something that I had once forgotten. And, even though my life changed abruptly, it did not bother me in the least. It was seamless."

"What event heralded the change?"

"What do you mean?" I asked.

"In order to begin dreaming, you pursued joy. Joy and the elimination of your rigid perception brought your dreaming body back into your physical body. The connection between the two was reinforced and strengthened. When this happened, your dreaming body and physical body became one. The awareness of your dreaming body merged with the awareness of your physical body. They were united. That is why it became difficult for you to distinguish between waking and dreaming. Listen to the Gospel of Thomas." He thumbed quickly through the pages of his favorite book.

> *When you make the two into one, and when you make the inner like the outer and the outer like the inner, and the upper like the lower...then you will enter the Kingdom.*

Court was beaming at me. "You've discovered a great secret! Dreaming becomes waking and waking becomes dreaming. When your dreaming body and your physical body become one, the gap between the two worlds is bridged and awareness flows freely between them." He paused. "Now, there was an event in your life that heralded the emergence of your dreaming ability in your waking state. What was it?"

I suddenly knew exactly what he was talking about. One day at the woodshop when the other apprentice was out sick, my boss was busy reprimanding me because I had not clamped some wood trim down firmly enough after gluing it onto some drawers. I was watching his agitation increase as he noticed that I wasn't reflecting his concern or his fear. I saw that he was having to work very hard at increasing his anger because I was not providing him with the energetic blockage that he usually relied on to intensify his anger. I was drifting further and further away. My dreaming body was watching him intently as he got more and more irritated.

I was very calm and detached. I could see that his anger was petty and useless. Then, it happened. The bottom dropped out, the world stopped, and I saw the dream as I was dreaming it. I was looking directly into his eyes when this happened. The energy that it produced was so forceful that I felt it burst out of me and shoot into his eyes.

He stopped talking in mid-sentence and just stood there, staring blankly at me with his mouth half open. I saw that his world had been stopped, too. I watched indifferently as his mind struggled to put the pieces back together—to make sense out of what was happening. When it couldn't, he got flustered and tried to fidget. He was stupefied by the energy of the Unknown. His body trembled slightly, and then he very rapidly picked up where he left off. He was now terribly frantic and nervous, and ended his explanation abruptly. He quickly sent me back to work.

Court laughed in spurts. "The constructs of our perception are ultimately very flimsy, especially if we desperately hold onto them. If your boss had been working to quiet his mind, he might have recognized this moment in his life as a momentous leap forward. The Unknown used you to punch a hole in his perception." He chuckled some more. "What else do you remember about your attempts to set up dreaming at this time?"

"I began waking up before my alarm went off in the morning," I said. "That was highly unusual for me. Because my awareness was learning how to remain operational both in, and out of slumber, I could see the space that existed before my thoughts became active. It was like the reverse of entering into dreaming. Only, instead of entering that quiet place *before* going to sleep, I would enter that quiet place *before assembling the world.*"

I told Court that I could literally watch my perception start to function. I could even make the silence last for a few minutes as I stored more energy. I would remain calm and not allow my mind to engage. It was the purest space, with no thoughts or emotions. I would see things, like shapes, starting to gather. It resembled floating in a colorful vacuum where emotions took on visual qualities. And then, as the world started to assemble, these qualities would start to get corners on them. I could feel a subtle pain in my head as deep interior tissues contracted in order to engage my daily belief system. It hurt my head to see this calm turn into brashness and linear coldness.

I saw that the emotion of the space that existed before the assembling of my world was pure and not funneled or segregated into any one particular emotion. In other words, it was the place where all of my emotions lived together simultaneously, as a complete whole. I saw that the belief that enlightenment is devoid of emotion was incorrect. Enlightenment is, rather, a place where all feelings reside and all emotions exist as one—they are unified. In our world, we single out or separate emotions because we lack the energy to unify them. This singling out of emotions makes them harsh, brittle, and incomplete. Our linear perception robs us of our completeness and vast emotional fulfillment.

"We are capable of so very much," Court replied. "We limit ourselves uselessly. You didn't have sex during this time, did you?"

"No. I hadn't had intercourse in almost three-and-a-half years. If I masturbated, my dreaming would be suspended for two or three days. When I woke up in the middle of the night to go to the bathroom, I would be unable to remember having ever had sex at all. It was, incredibly, a most energizing and awesome feeling. I couldn't remember anything about *any* sexual act—not even how it felt or what it looked like. It seemed to me that I had *dreamt* all of my sexual experiences. It felt like I had never had those experiences at all."

"More than anything, this lack of sexual partners helped to secure your energetic freedom," he said. "You said that when you woke up in the middle of the night it felt like you had slipped through time. This is what happens when your attachments to others, and their attachments to you, cease to exist. Without the assistance of others helping to hold your perception of time steady, you start to shift erratically back and forth in time and space—between waking and dreaming. You start to see that time and space are only constructs, not realities. Dreaming is a release of, or a seeing through, your perception. It is a letting go of the known." Some of Court's friends arrived then, and our conversation ended.

A few days later, Court and I went hiking on one of my favorite trails off of the Pacific Coast Highway. I quietly admired the condition of his body amidst its process of rejuvenation. The muscles of his body had grown very limber. They had a quality of strength that was new to my eyes, a quality that was a mixture of strength and pliancy. They had a peculiar state of vigor without being rigid or tense. They were completely relaxed, but with an overriding sense of vitality. Everything flowed as he moved, and his skin was radiant with feeling and color. He breathed easily and moved gracefully, but with a definite purpose. And, most importantly, he was enjoying every step that he took.

He reminded me of the importance of pleasurable and moderate physical exercise in order to optimize my body and motivate my lymphatic system, provided that my brain and mouth remained quiet. He told me that the Tensegrity that I had practiced had done just that, since I had not been attached to the accompanying belief structure. The health of my physical body was crucial to the success of my attempts to begin dreaming again.

It was a beautiful, sunny, fall afternoon. We had been hiking for a couple of hours. It was getting late, but that meant that there were fewer people around. We were sitting at the top of a hill that overlooked the Pacific Ocean. Hills and mountains always evoked a strange feeling of plenitude and well being in me. They attracted me deeply. An hour earlier, we had fallen asleep in the sun on this hill. I asked Court about my feelings.

"It's a power spot," he replied. "Hills and mountains are places where energy has been compressed and the earth has risen up in response to that compression. A mountain is power."

I quietly reflected on his words. Then, it hit me. All of my instances of lucid dreaming had occurred on elevated land! How could I have missed that before?

"Not all elevations are powerful enough to enhance your dreaming," Court replied. "But, to answer your question, those places where dreaming occurred for you were power spots. What were their elevations above sea level?"

I thought for a few minutes. "The spots were all about two hundred and fifty feet, or higher."

"Selecting the appropriate power spot is necessary for dreaming," he said. "Certain locations have very powerful geomagnetic forces and will enhance your energetic capacities. Major cities can be very powerful places. Why else would millions of people be living and touring there? However, the quality of the energy varies. Each power spot attracts a certain type of person with a certain energetic intention. Remember, too, that sometimes your body needs to rest and repair itself, and will choose a location to live where the confluence of energies is more conducive to healing and undisturbed tranquility, a place where it is fully embraced by the energy of the earth. Those places are more introverted than others."

"Are women affected in the same way by the elevation?" I asked.

"Yes, but not as completely as men. Women have a more natural ability to dream in practically any location because the earth is their ally and source of energy. The energy that manifests just prior to their menstruation will launch them into dreaming no matter where they are. Men need to be closer to the energy from the universe and require elevation to achieve this. But power spots will enhance the dreaming abilities of both men and women, and push them even further into the Unknown."

"Are there other factors that influence dreaming?" I asked.

"Aren't you aware of how the seasons affect your dreaming?" he asked me.

"All seasons except summer have a positive influence on my dreaming," I said. "I know that the moon affects my dreaming, too, but I can't remember if its influence is helpful or not."

"Let me know when you figure it out," Court replied.

We stood up and hiked back into the mountains. Just around a bend there emerged a shallow, flat valley–something resembling a small prairie. We walked down into it and settled in a sunny patch of light brown grass. The sun was still warm enough to make it very comfortable.

"So, your recent dreaming experiences occurred because you experienced a period of quiet and relaxation that lasted almost two years," Court said. "Repairing your body and setting up dreaming are very gradual processes. You need unlimited patience and persistence. In addition, there was a three-and-a-half year period where you mysteriously refrained from sexual intercourse and the accompanying emotional baggage. Since you were alone for most of this period, you talked very little. This allowed your mind to rest. Talking is one of the fiercest anchors that we have to the world of time."

"On some days," I said, "I would not talk to anyone. There were periods where I would not talk for a couple of days. I noticed that my energy remained concentrated in the lower half of my body when I did not talk or think. As soon as I started talking or thinking, the energy would rise up into my head. I remember how I eventually discovered that I could use my dreaming body instead of my brain to lead me in all of my activities, even in my work at the woodshop. It was as if my dreaming body already knew how to cut wood or build cabinets. Because of this, my brain felt fresh and hardly touched when I went to sleep at night."

"Your first adult experiences with lucid dreaming were conducted on borrowed time and energy," Court said. "In other words, you were not in charge of your life and your world. You found your dreaming body almost by accident. You relied on family and friends to take care of you. Now, your challenge is to return to dreaming on your own time and energy, and with the full and conscious awareness of your intention. But be aware of the pitfall of thinking your way back by reconstructing the events that led you there the first time. You are not the same person that you were, then."

"How should I approach it, then?" I asked.

"Allow joy and spontaneity to lead you again," he replied. "Circumvent your thoughts and memories. Don't allow them to trip you up. Your awareness will hook you to the feeling, and then you must let go and allow it to pull you back without trying to guide or direct it."

The sun had disappeared behind the mountains and so we retraced our steps back to the place on the hill where we had slept earlier, and sat down. The sun was starting to set over the ocean. We both stared at the orange-red glow and felt it fill us with its penetrating and melodious fire. We sat in silence, absorbing the life-giving energy. I watched the breaking waves down below as they reflected the various colors of the sunset. There were so many colors that it seemed like the waves were coated with a fine layer of clear oil. My heart swelled inside of me.

We watched the untiring display of the impersonal affection of the earth until the sun finished setting. Then the fog rolled in and the sky turned gray. The wind picked up in gusts and we covered our heads with our hoods. We were both keenly aware of the power of the twilight wind and did not want to be disturbed by it.

"When we were talking the other day, Court, you mentioned that other people help us to hold our perception of time steady," I said. "How does that work?"

"Through attachment," he replied.

"What exactly is attachment?" I asked. "I'm so sick of that word. People use it all the time, but no one really knows what it means."

"Attachment is an energetic condition in which a person hooks a band of their energy to another in order to generate thoughts or feelings about themselves in that person," he said.

"Then, I could hook one of my bands of energy to you and that would cause you to have thoughts or feelings about me?" I asked.

"Yes," he replied. "Then, you would have succeeded in getting me to direct my attention toward you, even when you were not present. And every time that I thought about you, you would receive a small current of energy from me."

"Can that occur over great distances, too?" I asked.

"Absolutely. But you have to be very strong energetically in order for your band of energy to remain functional over great distances."

"Can people that I don't know attach bands of energy to me?" I asked. I had been thinking about people who seemed to leave their energy lying around in order for others to trip over it.

"People like to leave their energy spread around in various places and in other peoples' way in order to draw energy to themselves," he said. "It's a way of making themselves known, even when they're not present." Court chuckled. "They resemble animals that run around pissing on things in order to mark their territory. Loud talking in public, the lingering odor of perfume and cologne, carefully misplaced personal belongings, and the energetic residue of emotional dramas all draw attention to the perpetrator."

"But that means that anyone who gets a band of energy attached to them becomes a victim if they have no volitional control over other peoples' attempts to gather energy from them," I said questioningly.

"They still have a choice," Court replied. "Once a person becomes aware that this kind of energetic attachment exists, he or she can *choose* to no longer be a part of it."

"How exactly do they do that?"

"By not thinking about, or being engaged by, that person," he replied. "It's no different than somebody coming to your house and knocking on your door. You don't have to open it, and you can pretend not to be home, either. It's just a matter of awareness. You can teach yourself to be aware of energetic attachment by saying something like, 'Closed to incoming energy,' before you go to bed at night. This will teach you to pay attention to your thoughts and feelings, and the energetic messages and psychic turmoil that you get from others. It will teach you to retract your own energetic web when you don't want to have others think or feel things about you. It will keep you from spending entire nights checking up energetically on the feelings of your friends or family towards you."

"What if their energy is stronger than mine and tries to dominate me?" I asked.

"If that's the case, then you may have to sever your ties with that person," he responded.

"So, there may be times when we have to give up certain people in our lives if they can't respect our energetic boundaries?" I asked.

"If you aren't strong enough to break their energetic fixation on you, then yes," Court said. "You can't allow people into your life who form opinions or judgments about you because those opinions and judgments will limit you. You must be extra vigilant not to do that to your friends or partners, as well. We, as energetic beings, have a right and an obligation to pursue fulfillment. We simply cannot allow anyone or anything to jeopardize that. And anyone or anything that can't respect that needs to be left behind so that we may be free."

"One of the hardest fears for me to overcome was the fear of leaving others behind," I said.

"Sometimes you have to go away so that you can come back–you have to go away to find yourself," he said. "You have to break their hold on you so that you can see yourself clearly. Once you embark on this path, you can't surround yourself with those who will not rise to the challenge of overcoming their fears. The energy of their fear projected onto you will affect you in a negative manner and will darken your world. You will cease to laugh. They will unmercifully hold onto you with their fear. It is a drain and a detriment to your path and your awareness."

"It sounds like you don't care about them," I complained.

"It's not about not caring," he said. "It's about taking care of yourself and not letting others get in the way of that. If that person is aware of what it means to take care of him or herself, then he or she will understand if you don't have the energy to deal with them at that moment. They will come back when you have more time and energy, and will not be offended by your need to care for yourself. If you want to dream, your energy must be free and untangled."

I sat quietly for some time. I saw the faces of the people who had chosen to stay behind. "Court," I said, "I've felt from some people that, while they want me to succeed in finding freedom, they also want me to fail. Is that because they don't want to realize that they have failed to find it?"

"Deep inside of every human being is something like a homing device," he replied. "We are all born with the ability and desire to find our way home to freedom. We want to succeed and we want others to succeed. Fear, however, stands immediately in the way. Fearful people absolutely cannot allow you to succeed. Your success will only amplify, and bring unwanted attention to, the fact that they have failed. They are cowards. They are the ones who want to hold you back with their fear. If they can keep you with them then they will feel safe and secure, knowing that a man of power is one of them."

"Even though I've grown used to it, sometimes being alone is depressing," I said.

"The trick is to like yourself," Court said. He looked at me in the twilight. His eyes sparkled. "If you clear out the debris that keeps you from being one with your dreaming body and one with the Spirit, then it won't matter whether you're alone or with others. You will overflow with affection."

"Don't they feel guilty if they try to hold me or others back?" I asked.

"Their energy turns sour within them," he replied. "They feel even more unworthy of life. Their end is hastened. But you become more solid."

He stood up. There was only a little bit of light left. We headed back down the trail. I could see just fine but I knew that it wasn't because I could see in the dark. It was because my mind was empty and my thoughts were not interfering with the delicate energy of the night. We reached the bottom of the trail as the blackness consumed the hills. The air was filled with the smell of sycamore and wild oak trees. I had spent many nights here by myself. I always felt soothed by this place. Court picked a spot on a log by a campground and we sat down.

"Let's finish your recounting of your dreaming adventures," he said.

"What does it mean when I start to fall asleep and I suddenly feel like I'm falling off a curb?" I asked. We both laughed at the thought. "My body always jerks at that moment as it tries to brace itself for the fall."

"Falling off of a curb, or something more life-threatening, is the exact moment when your thoughts shut off," Court laughed. "It's the sudden release of the energy that your brain has trapped in order to hold onto your perception. You can see by the intensity of the spasm in your body just how much energy is needed to sustain the thoughts that create your daily world."

"Sometimes I fall asleep on my back and then hear a hissing sound, like someone is letting the air out of a tire. What is that?"

"Are you making the hissing sound?" he asked me.

"No, it's coming from outside of me. But as soon as I hear it, I wake up. Sometimes it's very forceful."

"What you're 'hearing' is the sound that your physical body makes when your dreaming body exits for its nightly adventures," he replied.

"How can my dreaming body hear my physical body sighing?" I asked incredulously.

Court laughed. "Much stranger things will happen to you as you progress."

That reminded me of an instance when I had suddenly slammed back into my body in the middle of the night. That night, in particular, had a very lasting impact on me.

I was renting a room from a couple in southern California. They had gone away for a couple of weeks on vacation. I was alone in the house and my bedroom door was locked. I was sound asleep on my back. Without warning, I heard a very loud and violent sound. It woke me up so quickly that I almost vomited. It sounded like someone had propelled a three hundred pound body into the wall just below the ceiling, directly outside my bedroom door. I thought somebody was trying to break into my room. I sat up so quickly that I almost fainted. My body was absolutely alarmed. I was trembling. I lay there thoroughly frozen, propped up on my arms for five minutes while I listened and waited for someone to burst in. Somehow, I had *seen* a black shape just before awakening, and had felt the intrusion of something foreign into my room. I was sure that somebody had been watching me. I had almost gotten sick because the 'sound' that I had heard had been produced by a forceful spasm in my lower abdomen. My terror seemed completely out of proportion.

I told Court that it felt like something had attacked me as I slept. I thought that it might have been a flyer, even though I couldn't completely remember seeing it.

"That's exactly what it was," he exclaimed. He was agitated. He stood up and paced back and forth in front of me a few times to release the energy. "It was a very powerful one, judging by your violent reaction to it. It tried to penetrate your physical body while your dreaming body was away. But your dreaming body returned with a vengeance and ejected the flyer. That's why you experienced a concentrated and furious impact." He paused. "Didn't you tell me once that you thought one of your landlords was possessed?"

"Yes," I said. "I always knew that there was something else driving her on. There was something very frightening about her."

"The flyer must've come looking for her every night while she was away. When it couldn't find her, it made a bid for you."

Talking about this episode outside in the dark made me nervous. I abruptly remembered that this had happened one other time, many years before.

"I had a similar experience on one of the first nights that Lela and I slept together," I said. "I suddenly 'slammed' back into my body and could not move a muscle. I was forced to wait a few minutes until I was 'back together.'"

"Her flyer made a bid for your body early on," Court said. "It quickly realized that it would have to wear you down first. So it waited, slowly chipping away at you. You need to be more careful about the company you keep." He suddenly burst out laughing, and then sat down next to me.

"Do you remember any other waking moments that were impacted by your dual awareness?" Court finally asked me.

I told him about the night that I was driving home on the freeway outside of Los Angeles. My heightened awareness and the resulting increase in energy kept me from falling into my usual pattern of falling asleep at the wheel. A welcomed lack of conversation over the past few days left my mind in a very pleasant state of emptiness and unparalleled clarity. I was enjoying the drive.

As I rounded a bend in the road, I felt something give inside of me. It felt similar to falling asleep, but my head did not bob and my eyes were still wide open. I felt something in my umbilical region connect to another place. I wasn't sure where I was. I looked and I was still on the freeway. But for some reason I was not on the freeway in southern California!

My perception scrambled for a minute and then I realized that I was at some kind of an energetic crossroad. My dreaming body told me that I could choose to be on a different freeway several hundred miles from where I currently was–the one directly outside my parents' hometown. It showed me with absolute clarity the green freeway road sign that hung from a bridge one mile from their off-ramp. It asked me where I wanted to be.

Time vanished. I was thoroughly thrilled by the option to choose my reality. I had no doubt that it was real. What frightened me, however, was the sudden resurgence of my daily perception and its reminder that I was driving a solid metal vehicle at sixty-five miles-per-hour. Immediately, I was back on the southern California freeway.

Court asked me if this had happened while I was living in Burbank. I said that it had. I told him that the majority of my dreaming adventures had occurred while I was living in a two-story condominium on a hill in the city. I recalled that every time I walked up the stairs to the second floor bedrooms that the third step from the ground was colder than the others. It wasn't that the step felt colder to my feet as I walked across it; it was that the air immediately above the step was colder than the air above the other steps. It occurred to me that an entity lived there, but it was not the lurking darkness of a flyer. It felt detached and almost amicable.

I told Court that my dreaming continued to become stronger by large degrees while I lived there. It began with very vivid and lucid dreams that would go on for hours. I remembered that one night I was dreaming of a force that kept swooning around me, almost like a light or a cloud. It was very ominous and foreboding. I was afraid of its power but also very excited. I watched with tremendous agitation as it got closer and closer. Then I said, "Here it comes!" and it swept into me and I began to scream. I kept screaming for what seemed like hours. My scream was one of ecstasy and pain–the ecstasy of freedom and eternal life, and the pain of too much beauty–of something too powerful or too clean.

A few weeks later, I dreamt that I was outside of an apartment complex. It had a grassy hill along the side of the corner apartment. I could see a light on in the living room. I looked down at the grass in the darkness and it was covered with droplets of water. I had some trouble getting up the hill because the dew made it slippery.

I walked up to the front door and paused. Then I opened it. I felt that somebody had just left the room very quickly. I walked slowly into the room. The light in the room was dreary and yellow. It was lit by a single floor lamp with a low-wattage bulb. There was a drab, light brown couch against the wall to my left, and a brown coffee table with an opened newspaper on top of it. The walls were bare and painted in an off-white or cream color. The carpet was a dull, rust-brown and very worn. The newspaper had been dropped on the table in a hurry and had fallen in a crooked fashion. The room reminded me of a very low budget hotel room. It seemed too real.

I could still feel the presence of whoever had left the room so quickly. I knew that the person who had left the room was aware of my presence and was very *awake*. I had either frightened the person out of the room, or they had left in order to lure me further into the dream. I turned to my left and noticed a bedroom door. I knew that it had just been closed and that the person was waiting anxiously behind the door. I walked toward the door and grabbed the knob. It was cold and metallic. As I turned the knob, I felt a tingling sensation in my head and then in the rest of my body. There was a rush of energy as the air around me started hissing, and I felt like I was going to pass out. I felt an alarm going off inside of me. A voice was telling me that if I opened that door, *I would wake up in that dream.*

I stood there, motionless. I had never been face-to-face with the possibility of discovering another conscious life form in a dream. It was as real and tangible as if I had walked into a stranger's house in Burbank and chased them into the bedroom, except that *this was supposed to be a dream.* I knew that if I opened the door I would be confronted with the energetic entity behind the door. My fear became so powerful and terrifying that I woke up.

Court patted me on the back. "We can't continue our conversation about dreaming until you open the door," he said as he looked at me in the darkness. "Your beliefs come from outside of yourself. You have allowed them to flow inward and obstruct your dreaming body. Direct knowledge comes from your dreaming body. It flows outward through your physical body and into this world. Joy is the act of allowing that direct knowledge to blast through your beliefs and manifest itself in this life until it is perfect. This is how you become whole. This is how you return to dreaming."

He stood up and indicated that it was time to leave. We got into my car, and I drove him home.

THE MANY FACES OF POWER

*Hence the sages did not treat those
who were already ill;
they instructed those who were not yet ill.
To administer medicines to diseases
which have already developed
and to suppress revolts which have already developed
is comparable to the behavior of those persons
who begin to dig a well
after they have become thirsty.
Would these actions not be too late?*

-The Yellow Emperor's Classic of Internal Medicine-

I had just finished another dusty day of work at the woodshop. I was standing at the bus stop, sweating sluggishly on the ninety-degree pavement and getting all puffed up about the heat. The summer heat had always been a source of great discomfort for me, especially if I was clothed in anything more than a pair of shorts.

As I stood there waiting, a memory surfaced of a bus ride I had taken a few years before, traveling from the Fairfax district of Los Angeles into Burbank. There was a young man sitting in the front seat directly across from the bus driver. He was sandwiched in-between an elderly woman and a middle-aged businessman in a suit. The young man had his headphones on and was listening to very belligerent and aggressive music. It was turned on full-blast. As the music became more intense, his body became more rigid. He was sitting straight up on the edge of the seat, and his muscles were bulging and quivering under his restrained aggression. He was perspiring because of the tension.

He suddenly turned his head toward the businessman. He just stared right at him, his eyes barely twelve inches from the businessman's, while his whole body continued to shake in silent fury and the music blared on. I had never witnessed so much rage in a single man. The businessman struggled to maintain his composure, but quickly realized that he was no match for the man with the headphones. He quietly got up and moved to the rear of the bus.

The bus stopped at a red light. Nobody made a sound. Nobody wanted to call any attention to themselves. I quietly watched the angry man through the corner of my eye. The angry man stood up very quickly and ran to the front door. The driver quickly and gladly opened the front door, and the angry man ran off. Everyone sighed and then laughed nervously as they looked at each other, very much relieved that he was gone. The businessman slowly moved back up to the front of the bus.

I remembered that I had seen this young man before. I had seen him in a park across the street from a house that I once lived in. Even the homeless people were terrified of him. One pleasant afternoon, a young woman had gone to the park with the seven children that she was babysitting. She had laid out a blanket on the lawn, and they had all sat down and helped themselves to the food that she had brought along. Without a whisper, the man with the headphones was suddenly standing next to her. She was visibly shaken by his unexpected and angry arrival. She bent over to protect the food that she was sure he was going to steal. But he didn't move a muscle. He just stood there, staring down at her. His rage was like a laser beam, and I was simultaneously repulsed and fascinated by it. She, like the businessman, instantly realized that she was no match for him. She prepared a plate full of food and cowered as she handed it up to him. She did not want to be the first one to witness the violent discharge of this man's broiling wrath.

After she had tremblingly placed the plate of food in his hand, he continued to stand there and glare down at her, fully consumed by his own hostility. He didn't even take a bite from his plate. It finally dawned on her that she had not given him anything to drink. She hurriedly poured him a cup full of punch and held it straight up without even daring to look up at him again. He snatched it forcefully from her hand, spilling some of it on her arm, then walked backwards about twenty feet and squatted rigidly in front of a tree. He ate greedily, staring at her the entire time. I wondered how he had learned to direct his will so perfectly.

I was breathing calmly in the heat back at the bus stop, slowly unwinding the tension that I felt in my solar plexus as a result of those memories. I had been training myself to recapitulate on the fly. It was very effective, since memories would spontaneously rise up inside of me when something triggered them. I knew that the most effective form of recapitulation was energetic recapitulation. It really had nothing to do with the pictures stored in my brain, but dealt specifically with the energy that was still locked in various parts of my body. It was a more natural and thorough form of recapitulation in which my body proceeded to flush certain memories according to its needs. Sometimes, I would have to review the same memory on many different occasions until my resistance to the trapped energy was overcome and its secrets were finally revealed. In this particular case, it was fear that was stored in my third energy center–my solar plexus. I focused on the feeling, allowing myself to become completely aware of the tension that it created on that spot, and also its constricting effect on my breathing and heart as it radiated upward. Then, I let it go free. It flowed outward in all directions and was instantly released.

I looked across the street into the city park where there was very little activity in the late afternoon heat. A homeless person was asleep under a tree in a rough patch of dirty, dry grass. He had a newspaper covering his face and was snoring now and then. Some high cirrus clouds moved overhead and brought a moment of relief. I watched a patch of leaves scuttle across the street toward a trashcan. They swirled around, picked up some more debris, and then turned into a little twister. I watched as the twister gathered street dust from the gutter along with some plastic cigarette package wrappers and other various dried-out junk. I felt a twitch below my navel and knew that the twister had connected itself to me. I was calmly spellbound, even though I was secretly dreading being dusted by garbage. It picked up momentum and meandered across the street toward me in a very haphazard way. There was another person waiting at the bus stop a few feet away, but I paid no attention to him.

A moment later, I was completely surrounded by the dirt devil. It pummeled me with little grains of sand and bits of debris from head to toe, but the underlying feeling I had was one of peace. I closed my mouth tightly to keep the sand out of my teeth. The twister stayed with me for a few seconds and then died on the spot. I smiled inwardly, and then got on the bus.

As the bus rocked and pitched its way down the street, I found myself back in my recapitulation. I disliked riding the bus because the derelicts would always try to attach themselves to my energy. A few years ago, it would've happened by now. Predators could always sense my fear and vulnerability, even though they weren't cognizant of it. I remembered the time that an older man tried to rub his hand over my buttocks while we were waiting for a bus in downtown Los Angeles. He sensed a young and naïve college student with lots of underdeveloped awareness. I had since changed all of that.

After I arrived home and had showered and eaten, I sat down

to do some more recapitulating. I allowed my mind to wander without interfering and did not engage any trains of thought. Within a few minutes, I had found another energetic blockage.

Six years before, I had immersed myself in the works of J. Krishnamurti. I would sit in my apartment in the Fairfax district for hours and days on end, absorbed in his silence and simplicity. I would read, fall asleep, wake up, and read some more. He had the most tremendous sense of peace and conveyed it so well. The awareness that he talked about I had experienced, firsthand. I couldn't believe that I had been so close in proximity to him and that our paths had never crossed. I could only imagine how peaceful it would've been to be around a man like that. The fact that I had discovered his work just a couple of years after his death was thoroughly perplexing to me.

I made many trips to bask in what was left of his presence at his home and library in Ojai. I could still feel his energy in his house, and I felt a penetrating stillness when I sat in his living room or outside on the grounds. He had said in one of his writings that there was a presence in Ojai that he hadn't found anywhere else. I decided that I would go in search of that power in the hills nearby.

I left Los Angeles early one morning and began the short trip to Ojai. When I arrived in town, I stopped at a ranger station and bought a map that showed the hiking trails in the area. It was a hot day with just enough cloud cover to give it that uncomfortable, slightly muggy feeling, and a dull fear began to pursue me.

I drove down the highway looking for a sign or feeling that would guide me to one of the trailheads listed on my map. I had a nervous feeling in my abdomen and the oppressive quality of the heat was exacerbating my discomfort. As I rounded a turn in the highway, a bee flew into my windshield and startled me. It was followed by another and then another, and then I saw a swarm of them right in front of me. A sickening feeling enveloped me as I heard the sound of bees bouncing off of my windshield. I was overcome by an irrational fear, as if there was a presence nearby that did not like me. The heat in my intestines intensified and then I heard the buzzing of a bee inside the back window of my car. I pulled off the road, got out, opened the hatch and let the bee out. I was panting lightly. As I stood there trying to understand my agitation, I noticed that I had stopped by a trailhead. I had decided to try it out when I heard a shotgun blast. The sticky hair on the back of my neck almost managed to rise. I left immediately.

I drove a few more miles around a winding road and then spotted a dried up riverbed down below. Remembering that entities lived near water, I doubled back and parked in a turnout. The sun was past the apex now and was lightly camouflaged by the high clouds. I took off my shirt, put on my pack and headed down the trail. I was still feeling upset and pensive. The tall weeds stuck to my damp skin as I tried to shake off my irritability. An abnormally large horsefly buzzed around my head, and landed on various parts of my naked shoulders and face.

I arrived at a small wooden gate. I was just about to hop over it when I suddenly heard something that made my skin crawl. It sounded like a growl from an animal, and yet I knew that I hadn't heard it with my ears. It was a vibration that had come from the bushes just past the gate. It had entered my body through my abdomen and had then been translated by my senses into a very dark growl. I thought I saw something and froze on the spot. I looked into the bush ahead of me to my left, and listened intently. I kept thinking that I saw a dark mass behind a bush ten feet away, but I wasn't completely sure.

My nervousness and agitation mounted steadily as I waited. Then, quite automatically, I turned around and headed straight for my car. The horsefly was still following me and it landed on my back between my shoulder blades. I could sense that it was angry. My fear increased. I knew I was becoming more vulnerable. Then, it bit me. I cursed. I couldn't figure out how a fly could create so much pain. I knew that something did not want me in that area at all.

Finally, my eyes opened and I saw it. It was my self-image that was not wanted—I did not have the proper intention to be there. I quickly got back into my car and headed back to Los Angeles. As I drove away from the area, the pressure in my abdomen mysteriously vanished. I was completely exhausted.

Back in my room, I calmed my breathing and silently reflected on my recapitulation. My body registered the conflict of my self-image against the power of the entity. My body saw instinctively that my desire to possess power in order to be admired by others had weakened me and left me vulnerable in the face of foreign energy. The cultivation of my self-image at the expense of my dreaming body was an immature and impotent attempt at creating the illusion of power for others to fear. I understood that the cultivation of power and strength was a lifelong investment, and should be guided by a sense of awe and wonder in the Unknown, not self-aggrandizement.

I mused wordlessly over how my ability to relive the past through recapitulation had grown substantially over the years, and how it had become so exciting and rewarding. I thoroughly enjoyed being able to play with the element of time and my growing ability to slip in and out of this world. I reveled in the chance to take another step forward in my journey by systematically eliminating my past. I felt another memory surface, and I let go.

After ten years of living in Los Angeles, I had my intentions set on the vast expanses of Alaska. I moved out of Los Angeles and back in with my parents to prepare for my journey. In order to be alone and still, I decided to go snow camping in my truck in the mountains. I drove up one night and was overjoyed to see a few feet of snow already on the ground. There was only one other vehicle around, and that was good enough.

The sun was just about to set behind the mountains when I arrived, and so I wandered into the tourist center to pass some time. I had been thinking about joining the Forest Service as a way to earn a living without having to resort to computer work. I looked at some of the pamphlets and photographs on the wall, and then went back out to my old enormous truck as the sun finished setting.

I prepared some dinner on my propane stove and relaxed into the quiet and solitude. The mountains were ominous in the last of the blue-black light, and the thin, cold air licked at my neck. After I finished eating, I lit a small fire in the fire pit by my truck. I tried to sit next to the fire for warmth, but it was too cold. I climbed into my truck and closed the doors, and stared out the window at the silent flames. The power of the mountains pushed me deep inside of myself. I entered my favorite state, and everything slowed to a standstill.

I watched calmly as a mountain lion emerged from the shadows and stealthily approached my campfire. His bronze fur glimmered and shook in the firelight. I had no idea where he came from. A blackness abruptly followed, and I suddenly found myself sitting on a rock ledge. It was round and just large enough for me to sit on. It dropped off into the darkness of infinity on all sides. About five hundred feet away was another ledge that led back to the rest of the world. There was a campfire there, and its dancing red-orange glow illuminated a cave and some rock formations behind it.

As I sat on this rock spire in the middle of infinity, a voice told me that this little island was my perception. The island was myself–it was everything that I knew or had allowed myself to know. The infinity around me was the Unknown. It was an indefinable black vortex without beginning or end. I felt completely awed. I saw how unimportant all of my thoughts and worries were when measured against that unlimited expanse. The ledge on the other side of the void represented a perfect blending of the known and Unknown. It was a powerful tapestry. All of the elements were perfectly balanced. It had the right amount of control and the right amount of abandon. I saw, in the glowing light of the fire, the face of the mountain lion. Its energy existed there. That world felt like home, but somehow I would have to cross the chasm that separated us.

Just then, a cold wind blew up from the chasm. It didn't chill me to the bone, but refreshed me in a most disturbing manner. It was immense and boundless. I stared down precariously into the endless void and saw the whirling white edges of the wind as it rose up toward me again. I felt it expand as it buffeted me, and it filled the darkness with power. The detached and impersonal nature of the current made me feel strangely comfortable. It was ruthless, yet aware. It told me how to cross the void. It was a feeling, a knowing very deep down inside of me. It came from a place that I knew so well, but hadn't yet experienced in this life. It was a riddle with an answer that my body understood but when my mind tried to grab it, it vanished like the cold air that it rode on–I could only cross the chasm if I became the Unknown.

I found myself back in my truck. I was tired and decided to go to bed. I crawled under the blanket and tried to sleep, but something was preventing me from relaxing. An hour later, I was freezing. I quickly got up and put on every last piece of clothing I had. I sat waiting for the warmth to come, but it didn't. What I perceived as cold was a force that I was not prepared to meet. All through the night it attacked me, and I experienced an endless barrage of nightmares and uncontrollable shivering. I knew that it was more than physical cold that I was experiencing. It sought relentlessly to move me outside of my known world. I knew intuitively that I did not have the energy to embrace that impersonal force at this time. I barely had enough energy to last the night there without being seriously injured. The next morning I tried to go for a hike, but was completely exhausted. I headed home shortly thereafter.

I slowly returned to the quiet comfort of my room. I was tired from my recapitulating, but also refreshed. As my energetic connection to the past was severed, so was my desire to return to those outdated modes of behavior. By severing my connection to the perception that had led me further from my true path, I was freeing up the energy necessary to engage new options, and I knew that these options would lead to the Unknown. I crawled into bed and slipped peacefully into sleep.

A few weeks later, I went to Court's house. Just as I arrived, his phone rang. He went into the other room to answer it. I settled down into the old, comfortable chair and opened the window behind my head a little. The sun had set and the tall trees surrounding the living room kept the room very cool and dark. The ocean air blew in through the open window along with the smell of dusk. I heard a coyote cry out in the foothills nearby. A few others joined him. I had decided to come and see him this evening because my recapitulating was exhausting my physical body. I was feeling a lot of heat in my liver and solar plexus, and a mild fever kept coming and going.

Court came back into the room and examined me. He said that the energy of my solar plexus and liver were stagnant. He said that undoubtedly my recapitulations were bringing up feelings of anger and frustration from that area of my body. He asked me why I was not letting the feelings flow.

"I think it's just too much at once," I said.

"I agree," he replied. "Sometimes, it's necessary to temporarily stop the recapitulative flow to allow the energy to move and sort itself out. Your body needs time to process the garbage that it's releasing. As you continue to recapitulate and your energy increases, you will suddenly remember things that happened to you in the past when you had more energy. These dormant memories will be awakened when your current level of energy matches the level of energy that you had at that time. Physically, however, recapitulation releases toxins and sludge from your organs, muscles, and tissues. Give your lymphatic system a chance to process and release that debris."

"Dead and damaged cells pass through your lymphatic system," Court continued. "Sometimes the lymphatic system becomes sluggish or irritated when it's driven too hard. Tobacco and niacin in small doses help dilate the system. A teaspoon of lemon juice in a glass of water first thing in the morning electrifies the thyroid, the master gland, and turns the system on. Ice cream, eggs, and chocolate in small doses help create and introduce more lymphatic fluid into the system, which helps to force the old fluid out. Drinking plenty of water allows your cells to flush toxins regularly. Deep breathing displaces the carbon monoxide in your cells. Physical activity is responsible for the movement of the lymphatic fluid, not the pumping of the heart. Have you been enjoying playful exercise?"

"Not much," I said. "I've been too tired and listless. I did walk to the movie theater last week…"

I had barely finished the sentence when I found myself driving back from the movies with my sister in Century City, eight years before. I was at the wheel. We had just pulled up behind one other car at a red light. It was late at night and there was hardly any traffic. I was looking ahead at the light and my sister was facing me, talking. Then everything went black. Eventually, I heard the sound of someone tapping on my car window. There was a man standing there and he was saying something. I couldn't seem to wake up. My vision was blurry and I kept slipping in and out of consciousness.

I managed to regain some control and I looked up at the man. He was trying to hand me a piece of paper. I realized then that my engine had stopped and that I had run into the car in front of me. With great effort, I reached forward from my slumped position and opened the window slightly.

"I'm OK and my car is fine, too," said the man, calmly. He was trying to push the piece of paper through the small slit at the top of my window. "Here's my name and phone number. Call me if you need a witness or if you have any other problems. I'm leaving now." The piece of paper fell onto my lap.

I looked over at my sister. She was grimacing and holding her neck. My neck was sore, too, and I saw in my rearview mirror that my rear windshield was shattered. But then I noticed that the gallon water jug that I kept in the rear of the car for my radiator had blown open and sprayed water all over the inside of the window. I watched in a daze as the car in front of me slowly drove away.

"We got rear-ended," my sister finally said. She was completely conscious. I stiffly turned around and noticed that a large sedan had hit us. Two police cars appeared at that moment. One of the officers came over to my window and said, "You need to move this over to the side of the road. You're blocking traffic." He seemed a little put out.

I slowly brought his face back into focus.

"I would like to file a report," I mumbled.

"No report needs to be filed because there are no injuries," he said in an irritating manner.

"I'm in a lot of pain!" yelled my sister.

I could tell that the police officer was not pleased with that response, and he went back to the other car to see if anyone was injured. He came back very quickly and said, "Don't move a thing. We've got a probable D.U.I. here."

I was becoming more lucid now, and the officer came over to have me answer questions for the accident report. "You've been hit by a car of four drunk men." I could see the other officers pulling them out, one-by-one, and leading them to the side of the road. The four, young Hispanic males were being tested for drunkenness.

"Make sure that you get an attorney," the officer said. "I don't think their insurance is valid."

The officers arrested the driver and then let the rest of us go. I drove away, but couldn't shake the feeling that something strange had just happened.

The next day I found myself on the phone with my sister's attorney who told me to take my car to a body shop and have it inspected for damage. When I arrived, the inspector came out and looked at the rear end of my compact car with its insubstantial rubber bumper.

"Where'd they hit you?" he asked.

"Right here in the bumper, I guess." I wasn't sure where the pointed, chrome-plated steel bumper of the sedan had hit. He looked at me sideways with obvious doubt, and then crawled under my car. He inspected the bottom and then jumped up and opened the glass hatch window. He checked the inside of the trunk and the tire well.

He shook his head and looked at me. "Are you sure this is where you got hit?"

"Yes. I was even knocked unconscious. My sister's at the chiropractor right now."

"There's not a scratch anywhere on your car. There are not even any signs of distressed metal. Your bumper is perfect." He kept looking at me, waiting for me to tell him that I was joking. I just shrugged my shoulders. "This isn't going to help you much with your claim," he mumbled as he walked off.

After I got home, the attorney called me. "What's going on?" he practically yelled at me. "How am I supposed to get a settlement out of this if there's no damage to your car? I'm sending you to another body shop." He paused. "How fast were they going when they hit you?"

"I don't know. I don't remember anything."

I went to two more body shops after that and no damage was ever found. The insurance company settled out of court with my attorney.

I looked at Court after I finished narrating the story. "What happened?"

"I'm really not sure," he said. "Maybe the event had nothing to do with the men who hit you. Maybe it had to do with the guy who handed you the piece of paper. Did you ever call him?"

"I did, but it was about four years later. He had moved. The whole event would have made perfect sense if I had felt the crash or if there was some kind of damage to my car. But there was only blackness."

"That indicates the presence of foreign energy," Court said. "You will have to wait until you have stored more energy to know the whole story. But now I think you'd better go home and get some rest. Sit in front of the fireplace and burn some dense logs. The energy of a fire can help to energize and rebalance your system. The benefits cannot be overemphasized."

One week later, the Christmas holiday season began. I had two weeks off from work, so I went to visit my parents. When I arrived, they informed me that they both had the flu and nasty coughs. I steadied my energy, but the emotional issues that afflicted them were also still afflicting me.

My body had been struggling under the weight of my unprocessed memories and a suppressed fear of failure. It was not operating smoothly. I had tried various herbs and diets, but my condition had only worsened. My parents were dealing with their own fear of failure and were struggling with the onset of old age. I knew that I was going to have to deal with some things very quickly.

A few days later, I returned to southern California. I quickly came down with a high fever and diarrhea. The next day my throat swelled up like a balloon and I developed an excruciating cough. Carol came by that morning to check up on me and bring me lemons and soup. I was a mess.

"Matthew, it's over a hundred degrees in here!" she exclaimed. "Why don't you open the windows?"

I could only stare at her and smile weakly. She laughed at me in a caring and friendly way.

"Look at your hair! It's sticking straight up. And what on earth are you doing sitting on your skateboard?" She was beside herself with laughter.

I could barely talk because my throat was so swollen, but I managed to speak in an agonizingly hoarse whisper. "It was too tiring to crawl across the floor so I used my skateboard. The heater's on because I'm cold."

She couldn't stop laughing at me. "It's sunny and seventy-five degrees outside and you have your heater turned on? Aren't you warm enough in your bathrobe and sweats?" She looked at me incredulously.

I thanked her for the groceries and told her I would pay her back as soon as I got better. She told me not to worry about it, and said that she would be checking up on me.

Two days passed. It was nighttime. I was lying on my bed, still wracked with fever and relentless coughing fits. My throat was numb from all of the insults, so I finally took an anti-inflammatory medicine. I soon fell fast asleep.

At two o'clock in the morning, I woke up. I got out of bed to use the bathroom and my body temperature suddenly plunged. I ran back to bed and threw on all of my blankets and shivered until my body couldn't control the spasms any longer. When I finally calmed down, I fell asleep again. An hour later, I woke up. This time I was drenched in sweat.

Carol called me later that morning and I told her that I thought that I was doing better. She threatened to bring me to Court if I didn't snap out of it. I laughed weakly.

I honestly couldn't tell if I was getting better or worse. All I knew was that the symptoms kept changing. Carol told me that Court said my body was still cleansing itself, and that it had waited for my vacation when it could do so, undisturbed. I never took my temperature because I knew that an abnormal reading would only reinforce my perceptual belief in my sickness. I wanted to see *through* the sickness—I wanted to see it energetically. I wanted to know the emotional issues that were behind it. I stayed away from drugs and painkillers in order to keep my brain and body alert and aware as that knowledge surfaced. I stayed away from drugs and painkillers so that my body's immune system would not be compromised. I allowed the pain to push me outside of the limits of my perception.

I intuitively recognized that the terms that were used to label various diseases were loaded with the fear of millions of people who had poured their fearful energy into them. These people had attached themselves energetically to those terms, and by doing so had unconsciously tapped into the fear of all others who had done the same. These people became bound to each other and to that pool of fearful energy that they had all created. By immersing themselves in this energetic network, they had unconscionably aggravated and intensified their own illnesses. I understood this because I knew that the only way that those people ever got well was by disconnecting themselves from that term or label and by deciding that they *would not*, and *did not*, have that disease. The ones who got permanently well were the ones who stopped believing in their sickness. The ones who got well were the ones who believed in their own power.

Later that evening, the fever intensified and my ears started ringing. I went to sit on the toilet and the room started spinning. I laid my head down on my knees and everything went black.

I woke up on the floor. I had no idea how long I had been there. I had apparently slumped forward off of the toilet onto my face and then rolled onto my side. My pants were still down. I had vomited on myself. My legs, buttocks, and abdomen were coated with enormous beads of sweat. But I felt unbelievably calm. I chuckled to myself and enjoyed the peace of the moment.

After I cleaned myself up, I noticed that the fever was gone. I called Carol to tell her what had happened.

"Alright, Matthew, that's it! I'm coming to get you."

"But I feel better now. It's not necessary."

"Get your toothbrush and some clothes. You're coming to our house where I can keep an eye on you," she demanded. "And that's final. Good bye."

A short while later, she arrived and helped me up to her car. When we got to her place, she took me in to see Court. He looked at me from the smoky haze of his drawing room and exclaimed, "Put him to bed!" She escorted me upstairs, and I slept like a baby until the following morning.

When I awoke, I felt thoroughly refreshed. I went downstairs and washed my face. I went out to the front room where I found Court sitting in his favorite chair. He stood up and offered me his chair with a sweeping gesture of his hand, and then he moved over and sat down in my usual chair. It was another beautiful, sunny and cool winter's day in southern California. He looked at me with hard eyes, and then his face relaxed into a soothing smile.

"I think you're all better now," he said.

"I do feel a lot better–and relieved," I said. "When I was throwing up it felt as though something was releasing inside of me. It felt like other peoples' energy became dislodged and was catapulted out of the depths of me along with old emotional sludge. It was very difficult to let go, but I wanted to get it done."

"Your body, if it wants to stay vibrant and fluid, has to cast off emotional residue and the scars of the past," Court said. "Your brain is a part of this process as well. When you went to see your family, your body was energetically reminded of the residue that was hidden away. Because of your persistent desire to intend yourself forward, your body knew that it had to get rid of that crud. From what Carol told me, you must've let go of an awful lot all at once."

Carol walked in and ruffled my greasy hair. She handed me a small glass of hot water with some fresh lemon juice and ginger squeezed into it. I thanked her, and did my best not to drink it too quickly. I was extremely thirsty.

"I'm glad you're feeling better," she said with a warm smile. "You looked pretty bad this past week." She excused herself to go to her class, and she left.

"What exactly is disease?" I asked Court as I slowly swallowed the hot, sour water. It felt good on my throat.

"What you call disease is nothing more than a predetermined sequence or group of symptoms," he replied. "It's a generalized method of diagnosing abnormal physical conditions according to the symptoms displayed. Not only is this system highly inaccurate, but many have also died as a result of this carelessness. Everything is energy, even *disease*."

"What about the pathogens that the medical researchers have isolated and classified?" I asked. "These pathogens have been seen to invade and destroy healthy cells in our bodies. Bacteria, viruses, and germs are living, malignant forces."

"There are forces that live with us in our world," Court replied, "but what science has truthfully discovered is energy. They don't realize it yet, but what they're viewing in the microscope is the energetic imprint of a preconceived belief manifested in our physical world—they see the energy of perception manifested in a microscopic physical form. Everything that manifests in our physical world is energy, *first and foremost*. There is no such thing as disease."

"How can you believe that?" I yelled weakly.

"How can you *not*?" he retorted. "You retain within your cognitive system—your perception—imprints of energetic blockages and fears that have been taught to you by your family and peers. These people have even gone so far as to teach you to sterilize everyone and everything before you touch them. How crazy is that? These energetic imprints have been pounded into you from the beginning of your existence and from even before this lifetime. You retain the imprints of these manifestations energetically, at the cellular level. When you experience a similar energetic condition brought about by fear, sadness, anger, repression, etcetera, your body responds by producing the memorized and preprogrammed cellular imprint and manifests the appropriate 'symptoms' of a disease."

"Stress, however, is the primary cause of the majority of our modern diseases," Court continued forcibly. "Stress is both energetic and physical. Energetic stress is created by *indulgence* in fear, and physical stress is the *result* of that indulgence. Just as there are hundreds of different types of fear, there are also hundreds of different types of resulting stress. Stress is produced as the result of too much thinking or mental activity, or from getting up too early in the morning or going to bed too late at night. Stress is produced in the organs of your body when you eat too much or not enough food, or when you eat the wrong foods for your body's needs. There is stress from emotional upheaval or drama, stress from too much exercise, stress from too much talking, too much sex, too much noise, too much hurrying, or too much to do. There is stress on your body when you live next to high-voltage power lines, chemical dumps, radar towers, or when you're surrounded by polluted air. There is stress from overcrowding and lack of personal space as your body is constantly bombarded by the energetic disturbances of those living in apartments above and below you. There is stress caused when your body and mind don't get the stillness and rest that they need. There is stress when you don't follow your path with heart."

"Stress keeps your body from getting the rest that it needs," he said. "Stress, along with the toxic residue of past memories still stored in your body, overloads, weakens, and eventually suppresses your immune system. When your body gets fatigued, it only has enough energy to repair your vital organs–it doesn't have any extra energy to maintain, or let alone revitalize, your immune system. Your bones become weak and your muscles, flaccid. Your mind becomes sluggish and cloudy, and your body becomes insensitive to itself. Toxic waste continues to accumulate. This makes you more vulnerable to the 'pathogens' that you and others have created. It also makes it difficult for your body to properly digest food. This creates food intolerances and allergies. Your immune system is poisoned and exhausted, and therefore, compromised. Your energy, as well, is weakened and susceptible to invasion."

"If you're saying that I have control over my energetic blockages, perceptions, and the resulting manifestations, then why would I want to be sick?" I asked in confusion.

"Sickness forces you to stop, rest, and reflect," he answered. "Illness is one tool that your body uses to bring you back to the present moment. It forces you to pay attention to the mess that you have created. It's your body's response to your refusal to live in the present or follow your path with heart. Sickness is a challenge—what is it saying to you?"

I grinned thinly. "I've always been afraid of sickness. I always think I'm never going to recover."

"You're afraid of sickness because you were conditioned to believe that sickness is a sign of being weak, of being a failure," he said. "But sickness is not a sign of weakness, it's a sign of blocked energy and blocked energy is a sign of attachment to the past. If you release your grip on the past it will feel like death, and your mind is truly afraid of that because the past is what anchors you to your thoughts, beliefs, and expectations. To your mind, the past is what you *are*. Without it, your mind would experience nothingness—it would experience death and the *Unknown*! But it wouldn't know what to do with that vastness or how to contain it, and would feel the tongue of insanity licking at it. It doesn't understand that insanity is nothing more than a condition in which it is faced with the vastness of the Unknown while holding on too tightly to its beliefs and fears—its *past*. It's a condition wherein it struggles to interpret the boundless energy of the Unknown within the frail and limited framework of the known. It can't be done."

I stared at him as the weight of his words hit me. "I remember when you were really sick, Court," I said. "It was the time when your kidneys were rejuvenating themselves, casting off the scars of so much fear and abuse. You were excreting black stools and I was very worried about you. I almost took you to the hospital."

"You hadn't learned yet about the unbelievable capacity of the body to heal itself," he said. "The only things that ever obstruct that miraculous process are our preconceived ideas about health and sickness—our thoughts and beliefs. The body knows how to take care of itself if left alone. All cells have the capacity to regenerate and many internal organs can be completely replaced by the body. The body has its own consciousness, independent of our dreaming bodies. You think that your body is stupid and needs help because of your old beliefs that you are stupid and need help. But now you know that that is not true. You're not a victim and you don't need anybody's help, and neither does your body. Trust it to know and dictate what it needs. Remember the time that your beliefs sent you to the hospital?"

"How could I forget that?" I exclaimed hoarsely. It was one of the most embarrassing moments of my life. It was the year before, and I was trying out new diets according to my fears. I did not know that cooking with fear would inject that fear into my food. I had stopped eating meat because I was afraid of getting colon cancer and I was trying to be a vegetarian. At dinner one night, I tried eggplant even though my body absolutely hated it and told me not to eat it. I proceeded to force myself to eat practically the whole thing. I did not know that an eggplant could be poisonous.

I woke up in the early hours of the morning feeling very dizzy and ill. When I lay down and closed my eyes, I felt like I was going to pass out. Court and Carol were out of town, so I could not call them. I panicked and called a friend who took me to the emergency room. There, they ran all kinds of invasive tests. My fear was so high that it flustered everyone. The phlebotomist couldn't find my vein and made holes all over my arm when he panicked. The doctor got confused and gave me too much of the wrong solution because the machine that analyzed my blood wasn't calibrated properly. He even got his finger stuck in my rectum because I refused to relax and let go of it. When they finally released me twelve hours later, I walked outside and barfed in the parking lot. And, to top it all off, I wound up with one thousand dollars in hospital bills because I had no insurance.

Court laughed at my story. "When you let go of your belief in sickness and start seeing the energy behind it, then it will become something that you have control over. The entire syntax of sickness presumes that you are a helpless person who has been victimized by some powerful force, except that it was *your* force to begin with!" He started laughing very loudly, and I joined in, weakly.

"Once you are in that predicament," he continued, "you have no choice but to further relinquish your individual power to a doctor so that he can 'magically cure you' of your own stupidity and lack of awareness by energetically invading you. Your belief in sickness gives him that power over you."

"I tried listening to my body, but nothing helped," I complained. "No matter what I ate or what I did, it did not feel better."

"You were struggling with your beliefs," he replied. "When they ran up against a situation that challenged their existence, you caved in and let your fear decide how to proceed. What you should've done was drop your beliefs and let energy determine the proper course of action. The time to change beliefs is when you find yourself in the midst of a situation where your beliefs suddenly fail you. It's not something for you to change later, when you're comfortable."

He looked at me with a cold and mischievous gleam in his eye.

"Do you honestly believe that you have the luxury of waiting to become a man of power until you *feel* like it–until you are no longer sick or tired?" he said icily. "Your life can be taken from you at any moment. Don't imagine for one second that the forces of fear and foreign energy that work against you will be gracious enough to allow you to have your last battle on this earth when you are at your prime. They will snuff you out when you are defenseless, vulnerable, disoriented, weak, tired, and indulging in self-pity."

"The only way out of fear is *through* fear," he continued. "When you are tired is when you must push harder. When you are down is when you must rise up–how quickly can you do it?

You need to increase your tolerance to pain, not because you want to injure your body but because you want to smash the forces that compel you to settle for mediocrity and irresponsibility, the forces that make you want to give up and fail. In order to possess victory, you must ignore the odds and take the risk. The difficulty of your battles will determine your level of excellence. Be in your prime while everyone tramples upon you. How do you know that you will ever recover?"

He leaned forward, peered deeply into my eyes and whispered very forcefully, "People die when they are *sick*, not when they are well."

In my weakened state, I could only just stare at him with my stale and pasty mouth half open. I thought that he was making fun of me. That look in his eyes, however, told me that he was challenging me to let go of my self-importance, to stop indulging in my self-pity, and to laugh with him. Deep within me, his words were stirring an energy reserve that I did not know I possessed. He was rallying that strength for me. The stupid look on my face turned into laughter.

He smiled and leaned back into his chair. Then he picked up his copy of the *Tao Te Ching* and read to me:

> *He who is skillful in managing the life entrusted to him for a time travels on the land without having to shun rhinoceros or tiger, and enters [an army] without having to avoid sharp weapon. The rhinoceros finds no place in him into which to thrust its horn, nor the tiger a place in which to fix its claws, nor the weapon a place to admit its point. And for what reason? Because there is in him no place of death.*

Court sat silently in his chair. I excused myself and went to the bathroom. After that, I went to the kitchen and found some leftover pancakes that Carol had made that morning. I took one and put it on a plate with a few drops of honey. I went back out to the front room and sat down.

"What is the energetic difference between the sickness that I just experienced and a chronic disease?" I asked as I slowly chewed on my pancake. I was famished.

"The sickness that you just experienced was a purging, energetically and physically. It was a release. Chronic conditions, such as cancer and other deficiency diseases, are brought about by a continued and prolonged refusal to let go of the past. These conditions are further complicated by stress. Haven't you ever noticed that a disease doesn't release until you fully accept and surrender to it?"

"I have," I said. "I've also noticed that I can't do that if I'm busy analyzing the disease or trying to mask the symptoms with pain-killers."

"Surrendering is a condition in which your thoughts and judgments are turned off and your body's awareness is left alone to do what it needs to do," Court said. "If you sit quietly with the sickness, your body will discover the source and will provide you with that knowledge. But if you search outside of yourself for answers, then your energy will become diffused and your ability to understand will be reduced."

"Then the physical body and the dreaming body each possess their own, unique awareness," I stated with enthusiasm.

"Your perception is a tool whose only function is to provide the parameters necessary to survive and communicate in this world," he said. "That perception should never interfere with your physical body's awareness or with your dreaming body's awareness. That is the rule."

"How can I develop my perception so that it doesn't interfere?" I asked him.

"Re-train your perception to follow the awareness of your dreaming body," he replied. "In the past, your perception was trained by society to be fearful and ignore the intimations of your dreaming body—it was trained to be myopic. Now, teach your perception to *listen*."

Shortly after this, I met a woman who convinced me to try out the healing power of a local Chinese herbalist. I felt a strange resistance to her insistent suggestions, but I eventually allowed myself to go. My physical body responded immediately to the non-invasive form of treatment. I liked the fact that I had to invest more of my own energy in my recovery than the herbalist did. Within three weeks, I felt my strength begin to return. The six months that I spent drinking the tea of the bulk herbs could not have been any more successful. The detoxification cleared out enough sludge that my body was able to remember what it needed to do to heal itself. I understood, because of this process, how my body was able to assimilate the energy of the plants in order to correct the energetic problem that I had created in the first place. I saw how the complete energy of the plants was complementary to the energy of my body, and how these plants did not help one organ at the expense of another like the manmade chemicals did.

Using his own process of rejuvenation as an example, Court told me one day that the physical body heals very slowly, sometimes taking many years to rebuild itself.

"Since the moment of your birth, you have been creating the stagnation that now plagues you," he said. "Now, your task is to undo that process. And, believe me, it's worth it."

As a result of my newfound energetic awareness, I noticed a very strange transformation in the way that my body manifested illness. In the past, my usual pattern of illness began with a sore throat that would quickly erupt into my sinuses and head. Then, the illness would proceed to invade my chest and lungs, producing a cough. Next, my body would be racked with fever and chills. I would inevitably wind up flat on my back in bed for three or four days.

Now, however, I recognized the energetic blockage at the

back of my throat *before* it became a sore throat. It felt like a tingling, a localized heat. I realized that I had the ability to release that blocked energy and let it flow. I noticed that the energy would then make its way up and over the top of my head, and down into my sinuses. If I released it again, it would flow down through my chest, solar plexus, abdomen, and eventually out through my first energy center. If I allowed that energy to stagnate in one of the energy centers, it would flare up and cause a localized fever in that energy center. It seemed that the earth provided a grounding point that I could discharge this energy into once I got it down to my first energy center.

I also discovered, as my body continued to relax, that I had somehow created tension in my bowels and lower organs. I felt that the years of unreleased stress and anxiety had created such a fear of death in my body and first energy center that I had tried, literally, to hold on for dear life by clenching my base energy center continually. I slowly gained control over my bowels and lower organs, and learned how to relax them when I felt them tense up or when I felt pain. When I relaxed them, I could feel the energy circulate. The pain would intensify briefly as the energy dislodged, but then would dissolve as it circulated throughout my body and out into the earth. I immediately experienced better digestion and elimination, and the heat and fear in those areas dissipated. My organs and bowels began a natural cleansing and healing process since the toxic waste in my intestines was no longer being held inside and reabsorbed. The lower half of my body, including my legs, regained their feeling and connection to the earth.

I was very excited by these discoveries. I told Court about them the first chance that I got. He told me that my decision to try an alternative form of healing had helped to disable my beliefs in 'disease' and had allowed the awareness of my physical body and my dreaming body to teach my perception about the energetic causes of 'disease.' Without the interference of my perception, I had become more sensitive to the subtle nuances of the energy flow within my own body.

In response to my discovery about sore throats, Court said that I had initially experienced a constriction of energy in my throat energy center as a result of not expressing, or acting on, my Truth–my path with heart. This energy had built up in the back of my throat like a static charge of electricity. I had discovered that my body could not reabsorb this ball of energy, but that it had to be released back into the earth. I did this by releasing my grip on the ball of energy and allowing it to continue its natural movement along my energetic meridians. This natural movement followed my governing meridian up and over my head, then down my central or conception meridian, and out through my first energy center.

He said that when I was younger and unaware of this, blocked joyful energy had festered and accumulated in my throat until my physical body became so weakened and incapacitated by it that it was forced to shut itself down. Then, while flat on my back in bed, that large ball of 'diseased' energy exploded into the rest of my body, causing fever and sickness throughout. It took three to four days for my body to expel that energy and repair itself.

Court told me that my decision to free myself from my own fear of sickness had provided me with a learning opportunity. He said that without fear, pain and sickness became opportunities for me to see other aspects of myself–they became further opportunities for me to enhance my awareness.

"Pain brings reflection, then insight," he said to me. "It takes time to completely rearrange your energy, just as it took time to build your old modes of perception. Be patient with the process–it could take some time. You must store enough energy to overcome the level of energy invested by your perception in creating the 'disease.' In other words, you have to store at least as much energy as is harnessed in the 'disease' to break through it. That's why it gets harder as you get older and weaker, and the illnesses become more severe and terminal. Breaking through terminal illness requires major life and perception-altering changes. Making these changes releases vast reservoirs of repressed energy, energy that was repressed by your limiting beliefs."

He paused for a moment. "Only when you realize that you alone have the power to permanently block or unblock your own energy will you have conquered 'disease.' An energy worker, healer, or doctor can only provide you with temporary relief from your own creation. Until you discover how to permanently remove the block, the symptoms will keep reappearing, sometimes in different forms or in different locations. Being responsible for who and what you are is an all-encompassing energetic fact. Storing energy will increase your instantaneous insights into these matters, but only the deliberate persistence of sustained action will successfully solidify your new awareness."

I discovered that the best way to solidify my new awareness was to fully submerse myself in it–to apply it to my life and to live it. I went to lectures and workshops conducted by people who lived according to that energetic awareness, and studied many ancient texts. I had many sessions with various energy workers. In one session with a very powerful energy worker, the room immediately filled with green fog as soon as he waved his hands over my head. I noticed that when he talked his speech was slurred, almost as if he were drunk. I remembered that I had felt the same way whenever I ventured far away from my perception. In that state, I did not want to talk or think.

At long last, my latent knowledge in the power of energy and my dreaming body was becoming a reality. I could feel a forgotten part of myself coming to life. I began expressing and demonstrating my new awareness to friends and family, and I experienced their fear and resistance–the same fear and resistance that I had once displayed. I realized that they wouldn't change until their belief systems failed them and that, even then, they might just alter one facet of that structure in order to patch things up. They might not allow the energy of that failure to show them that the *entire concept of beliefs* is what keeps them from fulfillment. Beliefs are only necessary when there is not direct knowledge. I saw that my knowledge had become power. I decided that I wanted to help others with this power, even though I knew that they might not want to be helped. I laughed to myself about this seeming paradox, and realized that my laughter came from my lack of attachment to the outcome.

I moved from California to Oregon in order to be free of the limiting thoughts of those that wanted me to remain like them. I wanted to intend myself forward, to actualize my dreams–to become what I had always wanted to become. I realized that by knowing myself I knew the world. I began working on other peoples' energy. I found out that this was possible only when I detached myself from my perception and allowed my dreaming body and the Unknown to take command. I *intended* wholeness and the possibility of fulfillment–the feeling of life without limit. By living my Truth, I provided others with the opportunity to have their intimations about the existence of energy validated in this dream. And by working on others, I realized that I was also working on myself.

A few months later, I flew to Los Angeles for a workshop. On the night before my return flight, I drove to Court's house. He was sitting in his front room reading when I arrived. The soothing darkness of the room pushed against the frail light emanating from his reading lamp. We greeted each other and then sat down. The walls were alive with the presence.

I told him about my adventures while working with energy. I relayed to him how baffling it was that there were people in this world who had nurtured substantial awareness, but then refused to direct it back at themselves for their own development. Instead, these people distorted their perception and became professional whiners who channeled their energy into the propagation and promotion of self-indulgence and victimization. Then there were other people who were direct creations of their surroundings. They had accepted and internalized the belief systems of their family and peers without ever questioning them. Everything that they were was a direct product and reflection of their perception and limitations. They were thoroughly predictable.

"They are afraid of their fear," Court chuckled quietly. I could tell that he did not want to disturb the presence in the room. "They complain and blame, instead."

"Did you know, Court, that a person's past is stored in the back of their body?" I asked.

"It's stored behind the body because those people are trying to hide those memories," he replied. "They are trying to run away from their past. They think that the past is gone because they can't see it anymore."

"I've noticed that many of my clients don't really want to get well," I said. "They come to me so that I can alleviate their misery, and then they return again the following week with the same complaints. They cling to their diseases as an excuse to be less than what they are. They are afraid to go forward and prefer to stay where they are, stuck in their self-imposed energetic blockage. They like the attention that they get as a result of their sickness, and the fact that they can come to others or myself for support instead of supporting themselves. I don't enjoy working on them—they are a burden and a drain."

"Sick people are not looking to get well," he said. "They are looking to be taken care of. Their intention is to stay sick. People on a path with heart, however, learn lessons from their sickness and from your example as a man of power, and they move forward, never looking back. They elevate themselves through their sickness. Their bodies rise up because of the challenge. They are the ones who lust after the Unknown. That is the difference between a man of power and a victim. A victim gives up in the middle of the fight and lies down, sobbing, exposing his vulnerability. He tries to cling to others for support. A man of power fights until he wins, or until he unabashedly dies."

"In older times," Court continued, "people had to face their creations on their own—no one else was in control of their lives.

A healer could clear the energetic blockage temporarily, but the person had to deal with the complications that they had already produced within their bodies. They were forced to battle their sickness alone, and to come to a decision about whether or not they wanted to continue living if the illness became terminal. They weren't rushed to the emergency room and given life support. In those days, weak and unaware people tended to die."

I told him how I had observed that people who were related or who lived together experienced common ailments that were nothing more than shared energetic configurations. All of the people in the household or family adopted the energetic beliefs of the stronger person, good or bad. I also noticed that there were people with tremendous energy linked simultaneously to tremendous fear. They had the ability to focus their energy on a particular location of their body according to their latest fear, and create a 'disease.'

"Life is only as accurate as you make it," he said. "Now you see for yourself how important it is to apply your awareness to the entirety of your life, not just to one portion. The people that you are talking about might be very powerful and successful in their careers, but they have not applied that intelligence to discovering other distortions in their perception. They have misconceptions about their physical bodies. Big chunks of their energy are jammed in confusion and misalignment. You can determine where people have not fully applied their awareness by talking to them about different topics. In one example, they are completely clear and lucid. In another, they are full of opinions and judgments. They have not allowed instantaneous intelligence and comprehension to burn through their sacred indulgences and thrust them into high, solitary existence. They haven't listened to the voice of direct knowledge."

He paused, allowing that voice to fill him up.

"Do you know what power is?" he finally asked me.

"Power is not having the need to believe in any side," I said. "It is a belief in your own definitiveness."

Court laughed freely. I could tell that he liked my answer.

"Power is joy!" he exploded forcefully. The dark room shuddered. "Fear-based power is dark and malicious, and seeks to dominate. Power based on joy is clear, translucent, and unattached. Fearful people demand that others be like them. Joyful people could care less. When there is fear, the bowels are heavy and full of heat. When there is joy, your life force reaches down through your feet into the earth and lifts you up. This is how you became an energy worker."

His eyes shone in the dim light. The unseen presence smiled at me. I felt joy and richness bursting inside of my chest. We broke out simultaneously in laughter.

"Living your path comes about by strengthening your connection to the Unknown, bit by bit," he said. "It's like sifting through the sand along the bottom of a river to find gold nuggets. Each nugget is a small fortune, but comes with the price of many hours of hard work. At first, it seems like you have nothing, like all of your hard work is in vain. Your energy gathers imperceptibly. Then, one day, you start to feel something. You become more secure, more confident. You start to follow your own advice. Finally, you wake up one morning and everything is new, fresh, and lavish. You no longer need to search outside of yourself for the Truth. Your teachers have become your students. You look back at your past and wonder how you could have ever possibly been such an imbecile."

"You've seen power manifest itself through your work," he said. "You've realized that the miracle of healing is a two-way street. First, there is the energy worker and his or her connection to the Unknown. Then, there is the person who wants to overcome the hurdle that they have placed in front of themselves. The two people open themselves up to the power of the Unknown and remove their doubts, their *perception*. Then, the energy of the Unknown is funneled through the energy worker and into the patient. Both are strengthened and the blockages are cleared. That is why Jesus could not work miracles in his home town—everyone perceived him as a carpenter, not a healer, and they could not get past their own jealousy of the power that flowed through him. They resisted his efforts."

I nodded. "I saw just how true that is," I said. "My youthful appearance was a tremendous hurdle for the older patients. But, at the same time, they could not deny the force of the Truth that I spoke about with them. One woman, who had children almost my age, listened to me only slightly more than she would've listened to her own children. Occasionally, she would open up and see past my appearance, and the Unknown would fill her and she would understand. She kept vacillating back and forth. When she was lying face down on the table and I was working on energetic blockages in her back, though, she felt the heat and tingling from my hands over certain areas. When I saw her again the next day, she treated me with a mixture of respect and doubt, as if she shouldn't have allowed herself to open up to me the day before."

"But the clients that were younger were a completely different story," I continued. "They saw my youthful appearance as a sign of power and accomplishment. One man in his twenties completely opened up, and the force of the Unknown moving through the two of us was shocking."

I told Court that this young man had called me one month earlier and told me that his body was confused—he could not find food that was satisfying. I told him that his body was full of sludge and that he would see more lasting results from the energy work if he first flushed out his body. I sent him to a Chinese herbalist.

Six weeks later, he came in for his initial appointment. I talked with him, as I did with all of my clients, about his perception first. The Unknown showed him how his thoughts and beliefs were hindering him. I then had him lie down on his back on the table, and I opened myself up to the Unknown and directed it through him. The room started vibrating more slowly, and his breathing became heavy. After working on the front side of his body for about ten minutes, I left the room to allow the energy to seep into his body. I knew that people were more apt to allow themselves to relax if I wasn't present. I went out and sat on the couch in the lobby of the office that I worked in. The sunlight was streaming in through the window behind the couch. I kept chuckling. I felt so good, like I was intoxicated. My speech was slurred. A man who also worked out of the same office kept staring at me. He said that it looked like the Unknown had zapped me, too.

Ten minutes later, I walked quietly back into the room. It was completely still. I could tell that his thoughts were absent. I quietly asked him to turn over, very slowly. He stretched, and slowly sat up. He was completely groggy. He asked me what all the colors meant. I asked him what he had seen. He told me that a very bright red had blasted him when I started, and that it had later turned into different primary colors. The colors had begun swirling. I said that they were his body's perception of the energy as it flowed through him, unhindered.

He rolled over onto his stomach and I finished working over his back. I thought he was going to start snoring, but he remained in-between waking and sleeping. When I finished, he sat up on the edge of the table for a long time, consumed by the stillness. I brought him some water and we sat down in the chairs again. He said that the last time he had felt that way was the last time that he had smoked pot, many months before. I told him that the power of the Unknown was available to him at all times, if he could get out of his own way. I asked him to remain in the office until he felt a little more lucid and in control, and then he left.

While I had been telling Court this story, the presence in the room had started pulsing and moving. It had affected both of us, just as if I had been working on Court's energy. We sat for a long time, breathing deeply and slowly. The darkness pushed the light of the lamp into a small sphere, and the encroaching darkness turned almost a violet color. I sat, watching Court's face. It turned black and the room vanished. I felt something emerge from my stomach area. It was a slightly uncomfortable feeling, as if I was trying to keep it from coming out. Suddenly, Court's head turned into a green fog. It was practically fluorescent. It was sizzling with energy and moving, yet it remained perfectly in tact. He stared back at me and I felt my stomach area clamp down. The blackness vanished, and the light of the small lamp pushed its way back into my eyes.

"I think he's starting to believe," Court said with mock surprise. I laughed at his preposterous sense of humor, and enjoyed the chills that were sweeping up and down my body. I allowed them to penetrate every hidden crack and crevice.

"There comes a time in the life of a man of power when he must finally lay claim to that which is rightfully his," Court said. "You have risen up and seized your power, your birthright. It finally became clear to you that no one was going to hand it to you on a silver platter. Power and Truth must be silently wished for, *intended,* until you arrange your life to accommodate them. Then you must rise up and command them."

"I realized, Court, that the only way to be in charge of my life was to *take* charge of my life. I asked myself, 'Who's in charge?' The answer came back, 'I am.'"

"Was that the first time that you had worked on other peoples' energy?" he asked me.

"I had only tried it out a couple of times on my girlfriend," I replied. "The first time, I was in another room and my girlfriend was half-asleep on my bed. I quieted my mind and raised my hands up and felt the power flow through me and into her in the other room. When I went back into the bedroom, she asked me if I had been working on her. She said that she had felt as though I was standing right next to her with my hands just over her body. That's when I knew that I had the ability."

"I understand," he said. "But what made you *try it for real?* When did you decide that you might actually be capable of energy work?"

"It just kept building inside of me," I said. "I wanted to see if it was real, but I was chicken to try it out. I was afraid that nothing would happen and that my dreams would be shattered. Finally, I just *knew*. I let go, and it happened."

"Exactly," he replied. "You intended it perfectly. You finally understood that there is no way out of the box if you always think inside of the box. You allowed your thoughts to leap outside of the box—to follow the awareness of your dreaming body instead of the other way around. You saw that your dreaming body was connected to all life and that it could communicate its findings about others to you in the spaces between your thoughts. This is how you became aware of the blockages of others and the way to unplug them."

"You also saw that there is never a perfect time to begin as an energy worker," he continued. "You will never be a perfect healer. You will always be a work in progress. Every person that comes to you will be a new energetic frontier for you, an opportunity for you to learn and grow. You have to trust the Unknown to take care of your clients. You are only a conduit. But even as an imperfect conduit, you will not worsen anyone's condition. It is only the degree to which they are helped that you can improve upon."

"I finally understood those things," I said. "I learned that I had to take chances. I saw that by taking chances I was steadily overcoming my fear. By pushing myself constantly and maintaining a kind of internal tension, I was able to propel myself out of my old habits. I taught myself precision, just as I was once taught to be sloppy by others. I learned how to ask the right questions because I knew *who* I was and *where* I was. It was action, and not thought, that gave me this awareness."

I laughed as I remembered something. "The force of the Unknown has also been very direct with me," I said. "Another time, my girlfriend was asleep and I started working on her energy. Without warning, someone in another apartment screamed, 'Knock it off!' I knew instantly that the Unknown wanted my girlfriend to do her own work, to learn for herself. It didn't want me to interfere."

"That's a lesson that I've reminded you about consistently," Court said. "Touch people lightly and do not interfere. Let them do their own work. Show them the door and then step away."

"How come I don't always feel something when I work on other peoples' energy?" I asked. "Sometimes, I don't feel a thing."

"You don't always have to feel the undercurrent," he said. "It's still active, as long as you're not blocking it."

"I remember another lady that I worked on," I said. "I hardly felt anything when I worked on her, but every time I placed my hand over her abdomen her bowels started rumbling. She asked me what she should do about her fear and discomfort. I told her to rest and recapitulate as much as she possibly could. I told her that the lower half of her body, especially her feet, was cold energetically. I suggested that she spend more time in her garden and cut herself off from the people who kept trying to impose their fears and twisted logic upon her. She said that I was the only person who had told her to rest more. Everyone else had told her that she needed to get out of the house and get a job. I said that her extreme fatigue was inciting her fear and that working would only increase her fear by making her more tired."

Court and I sat quietly. The owl that lived nearby began hooting softly. The sound of its voice was very pure. A few minutes later, another joined it. The hooting of the second owl did not seem to be a response to the hooting of the first because it followed its own, unique pattern. The two owls, though next to each other, were completely independent of each other in their song. As they continued on according to their own independent rhythms, their voices would sometimes mirror each other exactly, as if answering the other, and sometimes join in perfect unison and harmony. We listened to them for quite a while.

"All awareness intuitively recognizes the power of silence," Court finally said. "That silence and detachment are a sign of self-confidence and self-knowing. The solidity of your energy solidifies the energy of others and makes them more confident. That's why people are attracted to you. You don't talk or think about the Unknown, you *are* the Unknown. But before you knew yourself, people were attracted to you because of your energy and then repelled, disgusted, and angered by you because of your fear. Your fear and lack of confidence inspired the same in them. Nobody wants to be unconfident, especially those who seek fulfillment. They wanted you to propel them forward."

"You have learned how to pool your energy," he continued. "You know that you must let it accumulate like water behind a dam if you want to be forceful when you act. Silence is what allows this pooling to occur. If you release it too early, it will drizzle out and will have no effect whatsoever. It may even incite others to attack you. But if you store it until you are ready to burst–until you *know* it's time to release it–then it will explode from within you and obliterate every obstacle in its way."

"You have pooled your energy and released it on the Unknown–you are thoroughly obsessed with it," he said. "Your singlemindedness and sense of purpose have made you into a beacon for others like yourself. Others are drawn to the strength of your conviction and your ability to lead yourself. The abundance of the Unknown within you pushes them hard and redirects the course of their energy. They feel doors opening inside and they can sense their own potential. It propels them forward. Now, they want to join you and add fuel to the fire. Your new friends challenge you and reflect the image of the Unknown in your eyes. Things have started to just happen to you."

He paused for a minute. "You have intended to become a man of power–that was your decision," he said. But you cannot decide *how* you will become a man of power. The Unknown will decide that for you."

"The Unknown decides what challenges I will face?" I asked.

"Your dreaming body, the Unknown, is keenly aware of your fears and will draw challenges into your life as opportunities for you to face in order to overcome those fears. You will continue to grow as a man of power until the moment that you shy away from a challenge. In this manner, you learn to accept whatever comes your way and be completely detached."

"Understand that awareness is a tool," he continued. "You must sharpen it and become skilled in its usage. Your challenges in awareness will pit you against the forces of awareness from our world and from outside. You must acquire insight into the awareness of light *and* the dark awareness of distortion. You must understand them both because they *exist*. And because they exist, they can act on you. You won't be able to protect yourself if you don't understand *life* in all of its forms. It is truly an act of war to maintain the sensitivity necessary to see energy, but not be adversely affected by it. Your intention must be impeccable."

"Once you fully realize that your life is yours to master, both in this world and in others, you will cease to be afraid of death. You will know your destiny. Those who do not master their lives will always be afraid of death–they will die with no awareness. They will die with no power. Their eyes will glass over in horror and disbelief when death comes for them. They will reach out for their trinkets–their crutches–that they have accumulated in a cowardly attempt to grasp meaning during their empty lives. But their ornaments will not help them. A man of power knows that there is nothing left over from his adventures. The only thing left over from his adventures is silence, and that is what he carries with him into the Unknown."

NEW UNITS OF AWARENESS

In medieval times there existed the Sapients;
their virtue was preserved
and they upheld Tao, the Right Way.
They lived in accord with Yin and Yang,
and in harmony with the four seasons.
They departed from this world
and retired from mundane affairs;
they saved their energies,
and preserved their spirits completely.
They roamed and traveled all over the universe
and could see and hear
beyond the eight distant places.
By all these means they increased their life
and strengthened it;
and at last they attained the position
of the Spiritual Man.

-The Yellow Emperor's Classic of Internal Medicine-

I sat on the floor, staring out my bedroom window on this darkened fall day. The clouds were thick and gray, and very low. The lazy heaviness of the vaporous fog hung limply in the still air and blanketed the rich, green grass with a delicate fleecing of exquisite pearls. It had been drizzling on and off for the last hour, and I could feel the cold air leaking in through my windows. I gazed across the courtyard and watched the mist dripping thoughtlessly from the golden leaves of the slumbering birch trees. In the distance, the maple trees were aflame in their transitory display of orange and red, as if the leaves had ruptured with unrestrained passion over their imminent fate. The dull glow of the sun cast a balmy serenity over the sleepy scene, and I felt a smile slowly play upon my lips.

The birds called only briefly on this tranquil morning. I inhaled deeply as the rich fragrance of the hickory smoke from a nearby chimney slipped unseen through my window. The mood of the earth had pierced the most recondite depths within me, and had imbued all life with a lasting sense of awe and respect. Amidst the absolute peace, the leaves fell continually, and I felt the energy within me quicken. I knew that my time of year had arrived, and that for the next nine months I would accomplish whatever I set my intention on.

I stood up and moved effortlessly down the steps to the living room. I opened the blinds and slid them aside, and settled into the couch across from the window. Outside of the large window was an old sycamore tree, by now almost bare. The thick, yellowed trunk rose up four feet out of the ground and then branched. From where I sat, two of those solid branches curved to the left, one above the other. They crossed each other again about three feet later, framing the distant sky in an oblong sphere. This sphere seemed like a portal, a window into another time. More than once this portal had served as an energetic gateway to other worlds and had pushed me deeper into the Unknown. Messages from the Unknown rode through this gateway on the fog.

Court was on his way over to my house. It was highly unusual for him to visit me. He never wanted the strength of his energy to influence my space. He said that my space was there for me to fill and adjust according to my needs and lessons. He implied, however, that there would come a time when I was as empty as he, and then my space would be filled with the Unknown. Then we would share the same space, whether or not we were in the same room.

He arrived a few minutes later. We embraced each other and stood there silently. He inhaled deeply and pressed his stomach into mine. I felt a rich surge of energy go through me. I smiled silently as he held the back of my head.

After a couple of minutes, we let go and went to the kitchen. I prepared some fresh apple and cranberry juice in the juicer, and added a touch of sparkling water. He helped me cook up a batch of pecan pancakes, some potatoes, and a small portion of meat. We took our brunch to the front room and settled into the couch. It was somewhat dark, but we left the lights off so as not to disturb the delicate mood that had filled the room. We did not want to impose our mood upon the earth, but wanted instead to merge with its mood in order to reinforce our seeing.

We ate in silence, as two old friends. I remembered the same feeling from my childhood, when I would sit quietly next to my father under the shade of a tree in the summertime, or on the morning that my mother first spoke to me without the interference of her perception. It was my tenth birthday, and she and I were alone in the front room of our apartment when she was suddenly overcome with emotion. She said that she couldn't believe that it had already been ten years, and that it seemed like only yesterday that she had given birth to me. Even though her words were simple, I knew that their meaning was not.

Court lit a clove cigarette and inhaled deeply. I handed him an ashtray that used to belong to my aunt. He turned to me and spoke slowly. There was great feeling in his voice.

"For many years now, you and I have discussed the trials and difficulties of becoming a man of power. But today, it is appropriate for us to begin talking about the beauty and endless possibilities that await you as you accept your birthright and begin to live as a man of power. We will talk about these things with the intention of opening your eyes and inspiring you. I offer them up for your consideration." He paused for a moment, feeling.

"Even though you will become aware of these possibilities through our conversation, you will still have to establish your own link to them in order to make them a reality in your life, in order to *live* them." He inhaled the smoke slowly and the end of his cigarette glowed brightly. He pointed out the window with it.

"This portal has already been speaking to you, silently filling you with unheard of things, possibilities that have been long forgotten in our modern culture. Men and women of power are the last of the great adventurers, explorers with a lust for the unseen and the unspeakable. Now, the possibility for you and I to become partners and journey together as friends exists. Where would you like to go first?" He smiled broadly at me.

I was beaming, too. My body started to tremble—I was filled with a nervous excitement. I turned and stared out of the portal into the Unknown. I started shaking more and my teeth started chattering. Court chuckled at me. I let the energy flow, and waves of chills went up and down my body. I slowly settled down.

"I want to go everywhere," I said. "I want to see it all. My need to explore is insatiable."

He peered at me over his cigarette as he inhaled.

"Awareness is the key," he said. "The Unknown is *here*." He held out his cupped hand as if someone had just filled it with water. "Your dreaming body can already see this. Have you ever watched a colony of ants?"

I turned my head in a questioning manner.

"Follow me," he said. We stood up and he led me out the front door. We walked over to the sycamore tree. There was a thick trail of ants going up and down the trunk. He said, "Look at the ants. Do they know that you are watching them?"

"No," I said.

"Put your finger in the middle of their path." I did, and they marched around it. One crawled up my finger.

"Do they see you now?" he asked.

"They only see an obstacle," I said. "Only this one on my finger seems to be aware that the obstacle might be something worth exploring."

"That one ant is aware of something more," Court said. "The rest continue on with their mundane chores, silently moving around the obstacle. But this one ant still does not *see* you. Has he stopped and turned his head towards you? Has he looked into your eyes? No. This is all that he is capable of. This is the limit of his awareness."

I put my knuckle against the tree and the ant crawled back onto the trunk. He wandered around and eventually rejoined the others.

"You and I are like this one ant," Court said. "We are aware of other levels of awareness. We sense their presence, and sometimes we even see them. But have we ever stared into their eyes? Can we?"

He paused, looking around the hills nearby. "Look up into the sky," he commanded me. "Do you see the eyes of the Unknown?"

I looked up. I did not see them, but I shuddered involuntarily. He laughed at me.

"The Unknown is watching you," he said eerily.

He walked back inside and I followed. We sat down again on the couch.

"Your dreaming body is capable of more," he said. "Though it may never see the eyes of the Unknown, it can hear the sound of its voice."

A blue jay landed on a branch of the sycamore tree, right above the portal. Another one landed nearby. I told Court of the time that I had witnessed something unusual while I walked through a park one summer day. As I was walking down a dirt path between some bushes, I heard a rustling to my left. I looked, and saw three blue jays on the ground between a large bush and an old stone wall. Two of the jays were watching the third one.

They had not seen me and I was very aware of this. I stopped immediately and watched. The third jay, which felt like a female, began rustling around in the leaves with her feet and beak. She cleared a small area, and then slowly spread out her wings to their fullest extent. I looked, but saw nothing on the ground beneath her. There were no babies and no unhatched eggs. I recalled seeing birds spread their wings in the past, but only to preen them or shake them out. This blue jay stretched out her wings and left them out. She then slowly leaned forward over the cleared patch of earth, and lay down on her belly with her wings flat against the ground. For some reason, I felt like I was intruding and that what they were doing was somehow private and ultra-personal. I noiselessly moved away.

Court looked back at me as if to ask me what my question was. I realized that I didn't have one. I had witnessed something that was for my eyes only. It would always be a mystery. I turned and looked back out at the jays on the sycamore. They squawked a few times and then flew away. I suddenly remembered a question that had remained with me for over fifteen years.

"Court," I asked, "Where do all of the dead birds go?"

He smiled slowly, as if I had finally uncovered the greatest secret known to man. His eyes were electric. "Why do you ask?" he said.

"Wherever I go, I always see many birds. They are in the trees, on the power lines, on the rooftops, and in the air. I hear them day and night. If there are so many of them, how come I never see any dead and on the ground? How come I don't see half-eaten carcasses on the sidewalk? When I cut down a tree, why don't a few corpses fall out? The only dead birds that I ever see are those that are caught by a cat, run over by a car, or those that have died in captivity. The only dead birds I ever see are the ones who have had their lives interfered with in some way. Where do the hundreds of others go?"

"There lies the mystery of awareness," he replied. "If you focus your awareness only on the obvious or on the things that you can see with your eyes, then you will never be aware of the things that are hidden from you. But you have learned to listen with your eyes, and so you have learned to see the *absence of things*. The birds, and other wild animals, have stepped out of this dream, unseen. You and I have the same option."

I sat there, reflecting on his words and staring out of the window. I felt my thoughts shut down as I relaxed the tissues in my head. Gradually, the voice of the Unknown pooled inside of me, filling me with a pleasant tension. It pushed outward from inside of my belly and radiated upward. My perineum pushed downward into the couch. I shivered slightly, feeling as though I was being stretched to make room for more. My eyes glazed over, and I sniggered against my will. Suddenly, I heard a voice, but it wasn't really a voice. It was a bubble of perception, a unit of awareness that soundlessly burst inside of me, filling me instantaneously with an otherworldly intelligence and comprehension.

As I came back to the living room, I noticed that things seemed to be in slow motion. They were a little bit out of focus. I looked around the room and at Court. I had a very strange feeling, as if I had lived this moment in time already. I searched my memory, but knew that he and I had never been together in this room before. He started talking to me and I already knew what he was going to say. Somehow, I answered him, and I knew before I spoke that I had already uttered my answer. I moved my arm and *recognized the movement*—I had already seen myself make that movement. I suddenly got very hot and felt dizzy. My fear thrust me back into the present moment. I felt whole again, but disturbed by the incident. This was more intense than any déjà vu I had experienced in the past.

I asked Court what was going on with me. He chuckled at my concern.

"Normally, when your dreaming body is outside of your physical body, you experience this world *as you dream it*," Court said. "You watch it as it occurs. You are not caught up in it, or attached to it. You are not buried under the weight of your thoughts, beliefs, expectations, fears, or emotions. You are disconnected from your physical senses. You are not judging yourself or others. You are simply observing, completely in the moment."

"When your energy grows and your perception shuts down completely, however, the chance for you to experience this world *before you dream it* increases," he continued. "This is what you call a déjà vu, or the feeling that you've seen or lived this situation already. It is the act of witnessing your dreaming body spin this dream, *before* you actually live it. For that brief moment in time, the awareness of your dreaming body is completely in command while you are awake."

"It feels like I'm *remembering* the future, just before it occurs," I said, thoroughly confused by my own words.

He laughed heartily. "Someday, you might just scare yourself to death and remember your entire life before it occurs." He broke down laughing at this point and excused himself. He went to the small bathroom just off of the living room. I could hear him giggling in spurts as he urinated. He emerged a few minutes later.

"Court," I asked as he sat down, "what is the future then? If I can see the future, does that mean that it's cast in stone, that it's already predetermined?"

"No," he replied. "Your dreaming body is spontaneous. It dreams this dream according to your successes and mistakes. If you learn from a lesson that it has drawn to you, then it moves ahead with other lessons. If you botch the lesson, then it creates more of the same kind. Your future is not cast in stone. It is only as predictable as your tendency to cling to your thoughts and beliefs. In other words, if you cling to your thoughts and beliefs then your future is completely predictable, and it will be based on those thoughts and beliefs. You will act according to those fear-based patterns and will not try anything new."

"You see," he continued, "you create belief structures in order to create points of reference. You can look at these points of reference and see if you have grown or stagnated. If you have grown, then you can cast aside those beliefs and adopt new ones that allow a safety zone in which you can grow further. At some point, though, you must completely abandon all structures in order to face the ultimate challenge of the Unknown. The future is nothing more than the lessons you do not face today. If you want to wake up from this dream, then stop running away from yourself."

I reflected on the various beliefs that I had adopted during my life, from religion to philosophy, true love to sex, fear and abstinence to indulgence, and humility to pride. I saw how I had been uncomfortable being original or spontaneous for most of my life, and so I had adopted beliefs that were already in existence—the beliefs of my peers. I had attached myself to pre-existing energetic patterns in order to feel safe so that I wouldn't be singled out in a crowd and asked to stand on my own. Adopting those beliefs created a feeling of safety where I was perfectly aware of what was expected of me—the parameters of my beliefs dictated what I could and could not do, and what I could and could not be. I could become perfect within those parameters and be admired by those beneath me. I could become a master of those beliefs and then grow old and die. I was an expert at wasting time.

Court looked at me curiously. "Each person has his or her own limited vision of this dream," he said. "Don't allow your awareness to be twisted or influenced by their lack of awareness. What you call the future is the projection of your current energetic state forward in time. Your life force will continue in this form or another until it becomes aware of itself. Then the future will cease to exist. You will have learned your lessons. You will have come home."

A car alarm went off just then in a nearby parking lot. We both laughed at its perfect timing.

"Trust your inner feelings more than any outward sign or

omen," Court said. "Your direct knowledge will always be more reliable than signals that come from outside of yourself."

I nodded absent-mindedly in agreement. I was still thinking about what he had said about stepping out of this dream, unseen.

"How is it possible, Court, that we can intend alternative ways of leaving this earth, this life?" I asked. "I mean, sometimes I can sense very powerful possibilities within myself and I have already seen things that some others will never believe are true. But death seems so final. How can I escape that?"

"The same way that you have allowed yourself to witness things that you didn't believe were possible in the past," he replied. "Instead of doubting or completely dismissing the notion, and instead of trying to force yourself to believe in the possibility, just suspend your judgment and look. You've already noticed something about wild animals that raises a question in your mind and kindles energy that has been hidden away. You can feel a possibility arising, a door opening within. You have an intuitive premonition that there is something more, that maybe your dreaming body is capable of unfathomable, yet absolutely pragmatic things. That question inside of you is your dreaming body testing the water to see if you are open to lessons that will clarify and solidify these new possibilities. If it sees that you are open to these possibilities, then you will suddenly find yourself in the midst of perception-altering lessons and you will have all of the proof that you need."

"Your daily awareness–your perception–is a unique product of the union of your dreaming body with your physical body," he said. "It contains the known–all of the visual memories of your life. It will not last beyond this lifetime. If you invest all of your energy into it, then all of that energy will be lost at death. If, however, you invest all of your energy into the Unknown, then you will discover your dreaming body in this lifetime and you will effortlessly flow with it into worlds with greater awareness. This is what our ancient ancestors did. They were intensely aware of this fact, and they pursued it relentlessly."

"Where did all of that knowledge go?" I asked.

"They took it with them," he said. "The knowledge left with the ones who succeeded. Knowledge used to be handed down orally, within a culture. When a person, or group of people, discovered how to leave this world, who was left behind?"

"The ones with less energy, the ones who couldn't make the journey," I replied.

"Which is why so little of that knowledge remains," he said. "In many cases, the dreamers left behind entire empty cities. Nomadic tribes would discover these abandoned ancient cities and inhabit them. They would listen to the stories told by the ones left behind and try to mimic those activities in the hopes of discovering how such feats were accomplished. They began to write down what they heard because they were afraid of forgetting it. Their connection to the Unknown and direct knowledge wasn't powerful enough. This is where the wealth of written information begins to accumulate—*after the feat*. And because it was written down afterwards, the information is full of misleading exaggerations and distortions. It's been that way with all religions and cultures!"

"I always wondered why the sculptures of the various kings from places like Egypt all looked so unrelated," I said. "One looks distinctly African while the next looks strangely Asian." I paused, thinking. "But aren't there still bits of truth smattered throughout the legends and myths of those ancient cultures?"

"There are," he said. "But you will only discover those bits of truth if you are being led by direct knowledge. There was a man in our era that discovered some of those truths. He built a house out of solid rock without the aid of machines. Some of those coral blocks weighed many tons. He weighed around ninety pounds."

I knew that he was referring to an immigrant who had built Coral Castle in southern Florida.

"He built his small castle with a few million pounds of rock," I said, remembering some details. "The front door itself is a solid block. It's perfectly balanced on a pin, and needs only a slight push to rotate it. He said that the moon and the stars helped him to build his castle. People saw him laying his hands over the blocks before he moved them, but he would sense their presence and walk away. No one ever saw him move one of those blocks."

"He knew how the ancient pyramids were built," Court stated. "I don't think that he stopped because he sensed other peoples' presence, though. I think the force of their thoughts stopped him. Their disbelief interfered with his ability."

The sun was starting to penetrate the fog outside. A warm glow radiated into the room and we both put our feet up on the coffee table, directly in its path. Court's eyes glazed over and he went into a trance. He emerged a few minutes later.

"It's quite normal for us to accept the fact that animals hibernate through the winter," he said. "Did you know that there are some forms of awareness that hibernate for decades at a time, and don't wake up until certain conditions are just right?" He looked sideways at me. "Humans used to hibernate, too."

I looked at him, wondering what he was getting at. I knew that I had a tendency to sleep quite a bit, especially in the winter.

"People believe that ancient cultures were primitive and uncivilized simply because they didn't have the technology or modern conveniences that we have," he continued. "That is asinine. The primary focus of ancient civilizations was the world of the dreaming body, not the physical body. Just as animals hibernate, so did the ancients. As a matter of fact, they spent more time asleep than awake. For them, physical existence was rudimentary, much like sleeping is to us. They were awake just long enough to care for their physical bodies, much like a cat or a dog would do today."

"The main focus of their awareness was on the dream life," he said. "It contained meaning, culture, focus and purpose, sheer awareness, peerless lucidity, and endless possibilities. It was their civilization and it was very elaborate. It was the ultimate adventure. They were more aware of their dreaming bodies than their physical bodies. Their physical existence was secondary, but their physical bodies were immaculate and unfettered by limiting beliefs. Look at the sculptures that depict their physical grace and strength! While their physical bodies slept, their dreaming bodies lived. They lightly touched the earth and its resources and left no scars. In the dreaming world, all of the ancient cultures communicated, no matter what continent they lived on, no matter what their language. This is why their creation myths and other writings are so similar, even across continents. The difference is in their syntax."

"We have discovered their dreaming chambers in the Egyptian, Incan, and Mayan pyramids. They were all built with the same remarkable precision. The chambers for the men were all two hundred or more feet above sea level. No mummies or bones were ever found buried there, as some would like us to believe. These ancient cultures, along with the ancient Anasazis, Olmecs, Toltecs, Chinese, and Aztecs all mysteriously vanished off the face of the earth. Not only that, but the vast majority of these cultures existed within seven degrees north and seven degrees south of the Tropic of Cancer, the latitude at which the sun reaches its furthest position north of the equator. They all existed on power spots, or as they called them, holy or sacred places."

"Ancient Nubian and Kushite kings, too, left this world on dreaming adventures with their subjects," Court went on. "The recent scientific studies on their skeletons revealed that they were all in perfect health when they left. The ancient Greek orthodox monks built dreaming chambers in caves high up on sheer rock faces. Various Gnostic sects practiced dreaming at hidden locations until persecutors destroyed them and their writings. The catacombs, as well, were secret dreaming chambers. The aborigines believe that dreaming is part of the *present moment,* and can be re-entered at will. Plato's *Timaeus* states that our souls are the stars and that we return to those stars when we die."

"The ancient Egyptians called the dreaming body the *ka*. It contained the vital life force and was a duplicate of the physical body. It accompanied the physical body through life. At death, the ka went to the kingdom of the dead. Later Egyptians believed that the ka could not exist without the physical body, even in death, and so they created wood or stone replicas of the body in case the mummy was destroyed. The name of the dead person was also carved into the walls or replicas. Because of this belief, the enemies of a dead person would smash the mouth, poke out the eyes, and erase the name of the person on the replica so that the ka could not eat, see, or be spoken of. To speak of the dead was to make them live again. They believed that the dead could live forever if properly provided for."

"There are writings," I interjected, "that speak of the undead assimilating the energy of their organs and fluids in order to live in the next world. These writings say that death is only the beginning. The ancient Chinese plugged the cavities of their mummies so that the vital fluids and energy could not leave the body. Female mummies have been found in South America with cotton plugs in their vaginas."

"Those are the dreamers who chose the time of their death," Court replied. "For the ancients who lived primarily in the dream world, it was nothing to walk away from the physical world when they were ready. They had invested their energy in their dreaming bodies. They had no attachment to the physical. Their dreaming bodies consumed the energy of their blood and internal organs at the time of their physical deaths. The rest of their bodies–their muscles, tendons, ligaments, bones, and skin–served simply as housings for the energy of their vital energetic organs. Our internal organs are what assist us in dreaming. That's why the vital organs of the older mummies were never found. The heat produced by this process dries and dehydrates the body *from the inside*. That's how they became mummified. When entire kingdoms left this earth together, the energy generated by the event was so intense that it turned the nearby stone walls, buildings, and clay pots into black blobs of glass."

"Wasn't it the later dynasties that started the ritual of mummification?" I asked.

"Yes," he replied. "They were trying to mimic the mummification process of their ancestors by surgically removing the internal organs and by trying to dry the corpses from the outside with salts and oils."

"The Egyptians never wrote down how to mummify a human," I remembered. "The Greeks were the first to write it down." I paused, thinking. "I remember hearing about the Caucasian mummies found in the deserts of Xinjiang in ancient China. They were between two and four thousand years old. Caucasians were not thought to have traded with China that early. The mummies were found resting on mud bricks in various shallow underground chambers with thatched wooden roofs. They had ointments applied to their skin to prevent it from drying out in the desert air. Their mouths were tied shut, and there were scarves wrapped around their mouths and nostrils."

"The ancients took these precautions in order to keep from inhaling too much sand and suffocating while they were hibernating," Court said.

"That's right," I said excitedly. "One of the mummies was examined and it was determined that she had died from an accumulation of dust in her lungs. So she had died while dreaming?"

"In ancient Egypt," Court said, "the pharaoh and his female dreamers were watched over by attendants. Food was brought as an offering and left outside of the dreaming chambers, sometimes in rooms connected to the pyramids by secret underground shafts. The dreamers could be gone for weeks and months, and their physical bodies hibernated. Because of the vulnerability of their physical bodies in this state, the attendants guarded them closely. The attendants protected them from starvation and suffocation, or from attacks by their mortal enemies. That's why many of the ancient cultures had very well protected dreaming chambers within their kingdoms. Their cities, as well, were heavily guarded. The Egyptians called the pyramids *castles of eternity*. Their shape came from heaven, and they were designed to last forever. People who dreamed on the outskirts of cities or in remote locations, like the ones found in Xinjiang, were vulnerable to the elements, to their enemies, and to a sudden lack of food and water."

Court went on to say that the ancient dreaming chambers were built so as to completely remove outside light and noise–to provide perfect dreaming and hibernating conditions. The hieroglyphs and other writings were carved permanently into the walls so that the dreamer could view them if he or she needed assistance while dreaming. To write something down was also to cast a spell–it was magic. Hieroglyphs were not decorations–the ancients were too pragmatic for that. There was no art for art's sake. Their buildings, their writings, their wars, and their thoughts were all focused on the world of the dreaming body. That intention permeated their lives. To them, it was worth every effort.

He pointed out that Egyptian hieroglyphs contain depictions of the dreaming body hovering over the physical body, and the presence of flyers in the underworld. Temple hieroglyphs depict mysterious holes in the bellies of figures where the force of the will enters and exits. The white crown that was worn on the head of certain gods and pharaohs bears a striking resemblance to the appearance of the dreaming body as it rides above and guides the physical body. The crown even has a cobra's head emanating forth from the third eye energy center, the place where communication occurs between the dreaming body and the physical body.

He said that it is written in the hieroglyphs that the pharaoh ensured the continuation of the physical world each day. It was his responsibility to ensure that this physical dream could be reassembled, so that the world of the physical body could be tended to until his entire kingdom was ready to leave this earth.

"There is also a passage referring to a test in the underworld where the heart of the dead person is weighed on a balance opposite a feather," Court said. "The heart must be as light as the feather in order for the dreamer to be allowed to journey to the land of the setting sun, into the court of the god of resurrection. The heart is made light as a feather through living a path with heart. And for them, a path with heart was the world of the dreaming body. Those whose hearts were not as light as a feather were consumed by *The Eater*."

"If the ancients were so aware in dreaming, why did they have so many wars?" I asked.

"They had wars over power, just like we do," he replied. "The ancients were not perfect, by any means. They were just more skilled with their dreaming bodies. Power is just as intoxicating as sex, if not more so. Their wars were more focused on the acquisition of the pharaoh, king, or ruler because he was the consummate man of power–he led his subjects in dreaming and in their quest for power. When he and the other leaders were captured, the conquerors attempted to steal that power and knowledge by drinking their blood, eating them alive, or by piercing their energetic envelopes at the base energy center through anal intercourse. It's the base energy center that prevents the energy of the vital organs from leaking out. The conquerors then used that power for bizarre feats in dreaming."

Court stood up then and took his dishes to the kitchen. I followed, and we cleaned up. He suggested that we go for a walk. We walked out the front door and down the steps to the parking lot. The sun had burned through most of the clouds. There was a mixture of beautiful, white cumulus clouds dusted by what was left of the morning mist. A light breeze made it heavenly.

We walked in silence up the sidewalk along the hill and then I led him down a side street, past a small fence, and into the brush on the outskirts of the condominiums that I lived in. We followed a narrow trail and eventually wound up at a large cement storm drain. We climbed the steep side of the empty cement ditch, and perched ourselves above the red and black graffiti. The pavement was just starting to warm in the sun, and it radiated a pleasant heat. We sat comfortably. The air smelled clean and fresh.

"You mentioned earlier, Court, that the ancients communicated with each other through their dreaming bodies, regardless of where they lived or what their language was. Can I communicate with others in the same way?"

"You already do," he replied. "But you are not yet conscious of it like they were. Your dreaming body already decides whom you will meet, and how. It plans out sequences of events. It communicates with friends and family. People who are attached to you pursue you and sometimes weaken you."

"I've awakened on occasion feeling the heavy sadness of a family member's heart," I recalled. "I've felt that they were not experiencing joy or fulfillment, and that they were wondering if I knew something that they didn't. I've experienced the sudden presence of old, faraway friends, only to go to work the next day and meet a person from their entity. I immediately recognized the person as being someone from a particular friend's entity because I would *see* my old friend in their eyes. Sometimes this person was a charming elderly lady or an infant who could barely sit up. I knew that this person also recognized me, and I would experience a mild déjà vu. Sometimes I would recognize this person because of a gesture or a particular feature, or from the sound of their voice. I would feel an immediate kinship with this person, and we would be very comfortable with each other right from the start. One time I even went to a job interview and recognized all five people on the interviewing committee, even though I had never met any of them. Our conversations during that interview had already occurred. I knew that I would be advanced to the next level in the interviewing process, and I was."

"Your dreaming body, when you allow it to, advances you along your path," Court said. "You may work out problems that you've had with a particular person or entity in dreaming, and find that those problems have mysteriously vanished when you see that person again."

"Sometimes I feel them thinking about me during the day," I said. "I will suddenly see their face, almost like a ghost or apparition, or suddenly have a very strong memory of them."

Court chuckled. "When your thoughts are quiet, your dreaming body commands your life," he said. "That is *seeing*."

"One time, I was stocking a shelf at work. My thoughts were absent. I suddenly saw a couple that shopped there on occasion. Their image was superimposed on the containers of yogurt right in front of my face. I turned quickly to my right and saw the couple emerge from around the corner. I hadn't seen them for weeks. They hadn't made a sound."

Court stood up and walked to the top of the storm drain. I joined him there. We stared down into the dark, stagnant water on the other side. There were a few frogs croaking under the bushes at the edge of the water.

"How did we get here?" I asked.

"Who cares?" he replied. "You are here. I am here. Let's make the most of it."

We both looked at each other and smiled. I couldn't believe that I had almost never met this man. I laughed. We walked down the side of the drain and followed a path into the hills. We meandered along the path for the rest of the afternoon, and then eventually found ourselves in the park at the end of the condominium complex. The sun had just gone down behind the hill, and there was a luminescence settling over the park. We sat down in the grass at the edge of the hill. Twilight in southern California always created an untold yearning inside of me. I knew that I would never grow tired of it. Court recognized the faraway look in my eyes.

"Be sure to pace yourself as you journey through your adventures in awareness," he said quietly. "You will always have an intense desire to push forward, even at the expense of your physical well-being. Your internal organs constantly burn too hot. There is too much internal combustion. You need to learn to recognize when you're tired and turn off the influx of energy so that your body will last as long as you need it to. Otherwise, the energy will keep coming and coming."

He stared at me. "People who train their bodies for competition know that the trick to winning a race is not found in continual acceleration, but in *maintaining* their peak speed longer than anyone else. Spectators think that the leader is putting on speed during the last half of the race, but what they are really witnessing is the slowing of the other competitors as they burn themselves out prematurely. You need timing and endurance."

"I want to see through this dream," I said. "I get so impatient when I don't have enough energy to *see* completely the things that I know are right in front of me."

"We, as dreamers, are the last of the great adventurers," he said. "Back when the masses believed that the earth was flat, you and I would have been the ones who got into ships and sailed directly into the horizon. The explorers of that era were searching for the Unknown in the only way they knew possible. The world of dreams is our frontier."

"You and I, as men of power, have met in the struggle of life and death," he continued. "A battle is a struggle to live, not die. We have witnessed each other's battles. You have been a comfort to me during mine. I hope that I have been the same for you."

I looked at him, unable to express my profound affection for him. "How can I ever express to you in words what you already know inside?" I asked him. "The Unknown will tell you how much love I feel for you, just as it told me for you."

He smiled gently as the swirling blue-gray twilight rose up from the earth, and swallowed us both.

EPILOGUE

Court finished his last clove cigarette and we set out in the breeze of this pleasant, springtime evening to walk to the liquor store. The earth was bursting with the renewed vitality of life, and the sound of his flip-flop sandals echoed off of the nearby houses. I had been away in Oregon working on my book and hadn't seen Court in over two years. His body had become even stronger.

"The body replaces itself every seven years," he said to me as we finished crossing the street. He stopped by a small tree on a narrow patch of grass. It had just sprouted new leaves all over. I couldn't get over how much I had missed the sun and the energy of southern California.

He put his hand on my shoulder and looked into my eyes. "The cells of your entire body, especially your vital organs, die and are replaced on a continual basis. The elimination of your past and the altering of your perceptual energy changes the energetic makeup and intention of each new cell *as it is born*. As each organ re-grows and rebuilds itself over the years, it is literally born again with your new intention. The energetic becomes the physical."

He looked at the tree and smiled. "Your recapitulation is just about complete," he said. "Writing down and working through your experiences over the last two years has brought you even closer to realizing total freedom, the state in which your dreaming body awareness is freed from the rigid modes of syntax and the boundaries of perception. It has helped to solidify your purpose and intention, and has brought you stunning clarity. The cells that are being born inside of you now are bursting with the energy of unrestrained freedom. In just a few more years, the majority of your body will be filled with this new energy. Your physical body will manifest your dreaming body, and the two will work together. You will be free to move forward effortlessly into the Unknown. The slate has been wiped clean. You have taken back your life." He patted my shoulder profusely.

"Everything that has happened to you, including all of your blunders and mistakes, has made you what you are at this moment in time," he continued. "It is perfection, not because it's finished or complete, but because you have kept your eyes open. You have not been consumed by your own self-image. In the past, the Unknown has given you living examples of those who pursued their paths with unmistakable fervor. That passion has changed many lives, including your own. Now you can begin to do the same for others. The Unknown has manifested and come to life *through* you, as it will for any man or woman of power. It has filled you with affection and power, and now you overflow with possibilities. The Unknown leads you by the hand as an old friend. You are one–you are whole."

He kicked off his flip-flops and stood with his feet on the cool grass. He motioned to me to do the same. I watched him lightly grasp the grass with his toes. He looked up into the sky at the northern star as it became more visible in the dimming light.

"The energy from the universe has created your dreaming body, but the earth has conceived your physical form. These two aspects will never again exist in this configuration. It is a supreme challenge to make the most of it. Do you accept the challenge?"

"I do," I said.

"Impeccability is the act of embracing all of your energetic possibilities," he said. "We gratefully acknowledge this opportunity and accept it with joy." He put both hands on my face and stared deeply into me.

"This is only the beginning…"